■ The Hawaii State Constitution

The Oxford Commentaries on the State Constitutions of the United States
G. Alan Tarr, Series Editor

Professor G. Alan Tarr, Director of the Center on State Constitutional Studies at Rutgers University, serves as General Editor for this important new series which in its entirety will cover each of the 50 states. Each volume of The Oxford Commentaries on the State Constitutions of the United States contains a historical overview of the state's constitutional development, plus a section-by-section analysis of the state's current constitution. Other features included in the volumes are the text of the state's constitution, a bibliographic essay, table of cases, and index. This series provides essential reference tools for those investigating state constitutional development and constitutional law.

The Hawaii State Constitution

Anne Feder Lee

Foreword by John Waihee

THE OXFORD COMMENTARIES ON THE STATE CONSTITUTIONS OF THE UNITED STATES
G. Alan Tarr, Series Editor

OXFORD
UNIVERSITY PRESS

OXFORD
UNIVERSITY PRESS

Oxford University Press, Inc., publishes works that further Oxford University's objective of excellence in research, scholarship, and education.

Oxford New York
Auckland Cape Town Dar es Salaam Hong Kong Karachi Kuala Lumpur Madrid Melbourne Mexico City Nairobi New Delhi Shanghai Taipei Toronto

With offices in
Argentina Austria Brazil Chile Czech Republic France Greece Guatemala Hungary Italy Japan Poland Portugal Singapore South Korea Switzerland Thailand Turkey Ukraine Vietnam

Previously published in 1993 by Greenwood Press

Published by Oxford University Press, Inc.
198 Madison Avenue, New York, New York 10016

Library of Congress Cataloging-in-Publication Data

Lee, Anne Feder.
The Hawaii State Constitution / Anne Feder Lee ; foreword by John Waihee.
p. cm. — (Oxford commentaries on the state constitutions of the United States)
Includes bibliographical references and index.
ISBN 978-0-19-977905-5 (hardback)
1. Constitutions—Hawaii. 2. Constitutional law—Hawaii.
3. Constitutional history—Hawaii. I. Hawaii. Constitution (1950)
II. Title.
KFH401 1950.A6 L37 2011
342.96902—dc22 2011002409

Note to Readers
This publication is designed to provide accurate and authoritative information in regard to the subject matter covered. It is based upon sources believed to be accurate and reliable and is intended to be current as of the time it was written. It is sold with the understanding that the publisher is not engaged in rendering legal, accounting, or other professional services. If legal advice or other expert assistance is required, the services of a competent professional person should be sought. Also, to confirm that the information has not been affected or changed by recent developments, traditional legal research techniques should be used, including checking primary sources where appropriate.

(Based on the Declaration of Principles jointly adopted by a Committee of the American Bar Association and a Committee of Publishers and Associations.)

CONTENTS

■ SERIES FOREWORD

In 1776, following the declaration of independence from England, the former colonies began to draft their own constitutions. Their handiwork attracted widespread interest, and draft constitutions circulated up and down the Atlantic seaboard as constitution makers sought to benefit from the insights of their counterparts in other states. In Europe, the new constitutions found a ready audience seeking enlightenment from the American experiments in self-government. Even the delegates to the Constitutional Convention of 1787, despite their reservations about the course of political developments in the states during the decade after independence, found much that was useful in the newly adopted constitutions. And when James Madison, fulfilling a pledge given during the ratification debates, drafted the federal Bill of Rights, he found his model in the famous Declaration of Rights of the Virginia Constitution.

By the 1900s, however, few people would have looked to state constitutions for enlightenment on fundamental rights or important principles. Instead, a familiar litany of complaints was heard whenever state constitutions were mentioned. State constitutions were too long and too detailed, combining basic principles with policy prescriptions and prohibitions that had no place in the fundamental law of a state. By including such provisions, it was argued, state constitutions deprived state governments of the flexibility they needed to respond effectively to changing circumstances. This—among other factors—encouraged political reformers to look to the federal government, which was not plagued by such constitutional constraints, thereby shifting the locus of political initiative away from the states. Meanwhile, civil libertarians concluded that state bills of rights, as least as interpreted by state courts, did not adequately protect rights, and they looked to the federal courts and the federal Bill of Rights for redress. As power and responsibility shifted from the states to Washington, so too did the attention of scholars, the legal community, and the general public.

During the early 1970s, however, state constitutions were rediscovered. The immediate impetus for this rediscovery was former President Richard Nixon's appointment of Warren Burger to succeed Earl Warren as chief justice of the U.S. Supreme Court. To civil libertarians, this appointment seemed to signal a decisive shift in the Supreme Court's jurisprudence because Burger was expected to lead the Court away from the liberal activism that had characterized the Warren Court. They therefore sought ways to safeguard the gains they had achieved for defendants, racial minorities, and the poor from erosion by the Burger Court. In particular, they began to look to state bills of rights to secure the rights of defendants and to support other civil-liberties claims that they advanced in state courts.

This new judicial federalism, as it came to be called, quickly advanced beyond its initial concern to evade the Burger Court. Indeed, less than two decades after it originated, it has become a nationwide phenomenon, for when judges and scholars turned their attention to state constitutions, they discovered an unsuspected richness. They found not only provisions that paralleled the federal Bill of Rights but also constitutional guarantees—of the right to privacy and of gender equality, for example—that had no analogue in the U.S. Constitution. Careful examination of the text and history of state guarantees revealed important differences between even those provisions that most resembled federal guarantees and their federal counterparts. Looking beyond state declarations of rights, jurists and scholars discovered affirmative constitutional mandates to state governments to address such important policy concerns as education and housing. Taken all together, these discoveries underlined the importance for the legal community of developing a better understanding of state constitutions.

The renewed interest in state constitutions has not been limited to judges and lawyers. State constitutional reformers have renewed their efforts, with notable success. Since 1960, ten states have adopted new constitutions, and several others have undertaken major constitutional revisions. These changes have usually resulted in more streamlined constitutions and more effective state governments. Also, in recent years political activists on both the left and the right have pursued their goals through state constitutional amendments, often enacted through the initiative process, under which policy proposals can be placed directly on the ballot for voters to endorse or reject. Scholars have begun to rediscover how state constitutional history can illuminate changes in political thought and practice, providing a basis for theories about the dynamics of political change in America.

Anne Feder Lee's fine study of the Hawaii Constitution, part of The Oxford Commentaries on the State Constitutions of the United States series, reflects this renewed interest in state constitutions and contributes to our knowledge of them. Because the constitutional tradition of each state is distinctive, Lee's volume begins by tracing the history and development of Hawaii's constitutions. It then provides the full text of the state's current constitution, with each section accompanied by commentary that explains the provision and traces its origins and its interpretation by the courts and other governmental bodies. For readers with a particular interest in a specific aspect of Hawaii constitutionalism, this book offers a bibliography of the most important sources examining the constitutional history and constitutional law of the state. It also contains a table of cases cited and a subject index.

G. Alan Tarr

■ FOREWORD

Dr. Anne Lee's thorough work blends history and legal thought, giving all who will read this book a solid understanding of the major factors shaping Hawaii's constitution. For the first time, we have one volume that traces our constitutional history and analyzes, section by section, our constitution as it exists today.

Part I presents a very readable overview of the major historical events so important to our constitutional development, from the time of the Hawaiian kingdom, through the republic, the territory, the 1950 Constitutional Convention called as a prelude to statehood, and the conventions of 1968 and 1978. In Part II, Dr. Lee clearly explains the purpose of each section, giving insight into how the framers' intentions and judicial interpretations have shaped the document.

I have had the honor of serving the people of Hawaii as a delegate to the 1978 Constitutional Convention, as a member of the state house of representatives, as lieutenant governor, and as governor. Throughout, I have been keenly aware of the special role that the constitution plays in our body politic, not only by establishing the framework of government and the rights and responsibilities of all, but also by reflecting our extraordinary past, our unique blend of peoples, and the natural beauty of our island state.

Those of us who met in 1978 were dedicated to making certain that we would perpetuate—and enhance—these features through our constitution. We were of an activist mind, and we saw our role as establishing an agenda for the ensuing decade.

It should not trouble us that some constitutional issues remain unresolved or that they become the object of legal challenge or the subject of heated debate. The ultimate responsibility for determining when and if constitutional changes are needed rests with the people of Hawaii who will, I know, continue to enter into such deliberations in the spirit captured by the words of our Preamble: "with an understanding and compassionate heart".

John Waihee
Governor

■ ACKNOWLEDGMENTS

I am very much indebted to Norm Meller, professor emeritus of political science, University of Hawaii, for sharing his knowledge of Hawaii's political and constitutional history at frequent intervals during the course of my work; following a most thorough reading of the manuscript, he made many insightful comments. I am also very grateful to retired Associate Justice Edward Nakamura for reading the manuscript and making cogent suggestions for improvement. My good friend Pat Shutt was always available as a sounding board; I benefited from her recollections of the 1978 Constitutional Convention as director of the League of Women Voters of Hawaii Education Fund's Ka Po'e project for citizen education. Muriel Roberts and Susan Burke, Esq., also read an earlier draft and provided helpful suggestions. Mona Nakayama, researcher for the Hawaii Legislative Reference Bureau, cheerfully helped with many requests for detail.

Many others assisted me in various ways, and I want to express my appreciation to Susan Barr, Bill Bartlett, Billie Beamer, Russell Blair, Alan Burdick, Kirk Caldwell, Tony Chang, Lee Crowell, Mike Crazier, and Dan Davidson, friendly librarians at the Hawaii Kai library, and to Carol Fukunaga, Wytze Goiter, Anna Hoover, Bob Kamins, Mary Lou Kobayashi, Sumner La Croix, Jim Mak, Jim Manke, Barbara Marumoto, Neal Milner, Kiyoko Nitz, Ray Tabata, Dan W. Tuttle, Jon Van Dyke, Carl Varady, and Carol Whitesell.

I also want to thank my husband, Chung, and son, Geoffrey, for constant good humor in spite of my preoccupation with the Hawaii Constitution, as well as my mother, Maria K. Feder, for generously providing a grant to defray the costs of copying numerous materials. Throughout this project, I have been inspired by the memory of my father, Ernest Feder, and my grandfather, Hans Kelsen, who devoted a good portion of their lives to writing.

PART ONE

The History of the Hawaii Constitution

INTRODUCTION*

The Hawaiian Islands were originally inhabited by Polynesians who migrated from central Polynesia possibly as early as the fourth or fifth century A.D. Captain James Cook, arriving in 1778, was the first in what became a series of both Western and Eastern influences on the islands. Exposure to new diseases rapidly decreased the indigenous population, and the introduction of non-Hawaiian ideas and material goods dramatically eroded the traditional economic, social, and political life, eventually leading to the overthrow of Hawaiian rule.

Initially, Hawaii was a way station where Western merchant ships obtained food and supplies as they sailed the oceans. By the time the first American Protestant missionaries arrived in 1820, some Westerners had already settled in Hawaii on a permanent basis, and over time their numbers grew. Any study of Hawaii's constitutional history must include reference to the critical role played by the *haoles*, as the Western foreigners were called, in shaping island government and politics. Some became especially important as intimate advisors to and teachers of the Hawaiian royalty, and in these capacities they did much to

---

* Following the style of the Hawaii Constitution, diacritical marks are not indicated for Hawaiian words used in this work, except where they appear in quoted material or reference titles. Where to place the glottal stop and macron can be found in Hawaiian Dictionary; Hawaiian-English, English-Hawaiian by Mary Kawena Pukui and Samuel H. Elbert (Honolulu: University of Hawaii Press, 1986).

inculcate western concepts of government. Others were influential through threats of force, either on behalf of foreign governments or on behalf of the *haole* community.

Another major influx of outsiders, beginning in the mid-1800s, also played a role in the reshaping of the islands. Imported to work on the sugar plantations, thousands of foreign workers were brought to Hawaii, primarily from China, Japan, Korea, Portugal, the Philippines, and Puerto Rico. Many remained, contributing to the building of a community that is unique in its racial and ethnic composition. Individuals from these groups, particularly Japanese-Americans, also became prominent actors in Hawaii's politics, but not until well into the twentieth century.

Persons of Hawaiian ancestry have also contributed to the political and constitutional development in consequential ways. This is particularly true for the period of the Hawaiian monarchy and during the early years of the territory. Though for a long time thereafter their role was significantly diminished, the 1970s witnessed a resurgence of native Hawaiian interests. Today, this Hawaiian renaissance has become of critical importance in molding the law and politics of the islands.

Although Hawaii is this nation's youngest state, it has a long history of constitution making.[1] There were four constitutions during the constitutional monarchy, one for the republic of Hawaii, another "constitution" while Hawaii was a territory, and, finally, a statehood constitution. Once each of these seven constitutions was in place, perceived weaknesses stimulated revisions, resulting in a substitute or amended document. It should be noted that the constitution that was drafted and adopted in 1950 and that became effective when statehood was achieved in 1959 has never been replaced, only amended and revised. Since most of the amendments and revisions were the result of two constitutional conventions (in 1968 and 1978), it is common in Hawaii to refer to the different versions as the Statehood Constitution, the 1968 Constitution, and the 1978 Constitution.

CONSTITUTIONAL MONARCHY AND THE REPUBLIC OF HAWAII

Both King Kamehameha I, who united all the islands under his control in 1810, and his successor, Kamehameha II, ruled as absolute monarchs. The reign of Kamehameha III, 1825–1854, is distinguished as representing the birth of the constitutional monarchy. The first two constitutions, both adopted during his rule (in 1840 and 1852), included limitations on royal power to which he voluntarily acceded. Both were influenced generally by Western ideas and more specifically by the reaction of foreigners to the exercise of absolute rule.

[1] The major sources for this survey of the historical development are described in the Bibliographical Essay.

The first major step away from absolute rule was taken in 1839 when Kamehameha III promulgated the Declaration of Rights. Referred to as the Hawaiian Magna Charta, it "was a great and significant concession voluntarily granted by the king to his people."[2] Sounding very much like the American Declaration of Independence, it stated that "God has bestowed certain rights alike on all men, and all chiefs, and on all people of all lands" and that "in making laws for the nations, it is by no means proper to enact laws for the protection of the rulers only, without also providing protection for their subjects".[3]

Constitution of 1840

The Constitution of 1840, using an amended version of the Declaration of Rights as its preamble, formally inaugurated an era of constitutional monarchy. This first written constitution partially separated the legislative, executive, and judicial powers and established a process for constitutional amendment. In many respects, the Constitution of 1840 simply codified existing government structure and practice. For example, membership in the house of nobles continued to be based on heredity. However, the document was particularly noteworthy because it created a bicameral legislative branch by adding an elected house of representatives and brought into being a supreme court for adjudicating legal questions.

The Great *Mahele*

Another document was also promulgated under Kamehameha III, one that has had extraordinary consequences for Hawaii's political and constitutional development through the present day. Previously, all land was owned by the monarchy, and usage by others was only by sufferance. One of the Western ideas introduced into the islands was the concept of private ownership of land. The foreign pressure brought to bear against the traditional system resulted in the Great *Mahele*, or Great Division, proclaimed by the monarch in 1848. This royal action allowed private ownership of land in fee for the first time. (The Great *Mahele* is discussed in greater detail in Part II, under Article I, Section 20.)

Constitution of 1852

Hawaii's second constitution also became effective under Kamehameha III. But, while the first was written by the king and his chiefs, the second resulted from legislative action calling for a commission to review the earlier document.

---

[2] Ralph S. Kuykendall, *The Hawaiian Kingdom* (Honolulu: University of Hawaii Press, 1938), vol. 1, *1778–1854*, 160.

[3] The full text is given in Kuykendall, *The Hawaiian Kingdom*, vol. 1, *1778–1854*, 160.

The three commission members were appointed, respectively, by the king, the house of nobles, and the house of representatives, and the revisions they proposed resulted in an almost entirely new document. The legislature adopted the new constitution, after making some amendments, and on June 14, 1852, Kamehameha III appended his signature.

The Constitution of 1852 is significant because it expanded on the Declaration of Rights, granted universal (adult male) suffrage for the first time, and changed the house of nobles from a hereditary body to one where members were appointed, for life, by the king. It went further in institutionalizing a government of three branches by separating and defining the legislative executive, and judicial functions more along the lines of the American Constitution, thus placing more checks on the monarch.

Constitution of 1864

Although the next monarch, Kamehameha IV, was unhappy with the 1852 document because of its restrictions on royal power, he did take the oath to uphold it when he ascended the throne in 1854. Kamehameha V (1863—1872), however, refused to take the oath and set revision of that document as a major goal. He opposed universal suffrage, believing that there ought to be property qualifications for voters and members of the house of representatives. More fundamentally, he "thought 'the prerogatives of the Crown ought to be more carefully protected . . . and that the influence of the Crown ought to be seen pervading every function of government.' "[4]

Kamehameha V's first step was to call a convention to enact a new constitution. But not all went smoothly. Even before the convention convened on July 7, 1864, it became evident that its members—the king, the fifteen nobles, and twenty-six delegates elected by the voters—would not reach agreement on a number of issues, including voting qualifications. There was little disagreement over a literacy requirement for voting, but most delegates refused to agree to adding a property qualification, while the monarch and the nobles were adamant in its favor.

With the convention deadlocked, the king took matters into his own hands, dissolving it and announcing that he was abrogating the Constitution of 1852. During the following week, while no written constitution was in effect, the king and his close advisors drafted a new document. Hawaii's third constitution came into effect on August 20, 1864, the day Kamehameha V signed and took the oath to uphold it.

---

[4] Ralph S. Kuykendall, *Constitutions of the Hawaiian Kingdom*, Papers of the Hawaiian Historical Society, no. 21 (Honolulu: Hawaiian Historical Society, 1940), 31.

Not surprisingly, the document abolished universal suffrage and established literacy and property qualifications for voting. Most noteworthy was the attempt to restore royal power by, for example, stipulating that the monarch did not have to seek advice and counsel from the nobles and by making the cabinet directly subject to the king.

Constitution of 1887: The "Bayonet Constitution"

Kamehameha V's constitution remained in effect until 1887, despite his death in 1872. However, there was dissatisfaction with the 1864 constitution, and in 1874, shortly before the end of King Lunalilo's short reign, universal suffrage was restored. Conflicting views about Hawaii's relations with foreigners and widespread corruption and abuses of power eventually characterized the reign of Lunalilo's successor, Kalakaua, who ruled from 1874 to 1891.

The key event of the Kalakaua period was the Revolution of 1887. This bloodless revolt was led by a group known as the Hawaiian League, composed primarily of *haoles*, which was very worried about instability in the islands. On June 30, a huge mass meeting demanded concessions from the king. This show of popular force convinced Kalakaua, whose troops did not support him, that he had best agree with the demands, including demands for changes to the Constitution of 1864. The resulting revisions, proposed by members of the Hawaiian League, created a new document.

Referred to as the "Bayonet Constitution" of 1887, it significantly reduced royal powers by, for example, changing the house of nobles to an elected rather than an appointive body, allowing legislative override of a veto, and requiring legislative approval for removal of cabinet members.

Republic of Hawaii

Upon Kalakaua's death in 1891, his sister, Liliuokalani, succeeded him as queen. But she was not to rule for long. Wanting to restore the monarchy's powers, she asked the legislators to call a constitutional convention. When they refused, she attempted to promulgate her own new constitution. However, opposition quickly surfaced, and the queen hastily announced that she would not attempt any changes, other than by legal means.

But it was too late; a movement to bring the monarchy to an end had already been set in motion. Spearheading the overthrow were *haoles* who believed that the only way to bring stability to Hawaii was through annexation by the United States. They had first organized a secret group in 1892, called the Annexation Club, and in early January 1893, a Committee of Safety was formed, made up primarily of members of the Annexation Club. On January 17, the Committee of Safety took possession of a government office building, issued a proclamation abrogating the monarchy and establishing a provisional government, and obtained recognition by the American consul.

The Revolution of 1893 brought an end to the monarchy when the queen, under protest, abdicated. When rapid annexation by the United States was not forthcoming, the provisional government set up a constitutional convention which adopted a constitution for the republic of Hawaii on July 4, 1894. Put into force by decree, without popular vote, it remained in effect until 1900.

The constitution recognized the American pattern of separation of powers, though it limited presidential power by adding a cabinet and a council of state. Despite bringing the monarchy to an end, the government under the new constitution was essentially elitist. It clearly consolidated haole power by, for instance, establishing voting provisions so limiting that few of Hawaiian ancestry and no Orientals qualified.

■ THE ORGANIC ACT: HAWAII AS A TERRITORY

In 1898, Hawaii was formally annexed by the United States under the terms of the Joint Resolution of Annexation of July 7, 1898. The formal transfer of sovereignty from the republic to the United States took place on August 12. The joint resolution also authorized the president of the United States to appoint a commission to prepare and recommend to Congress legislation establishing a territory and its governance.

The five commission members presented their draft act and recommendations in December 1898. Congressional action was, however, delayed, and the Act to Provide a Government for the Territory of Hawaii, referred to as the Organic Act, did not pass until April 30, 1900. This "constitution" became effective when signed by President McKinley on June 14, 1900.

The Organic Act consisted of six chapters entitled General Provisions, The Legislature, The Executive, The Judiciary, United States Officers, and Miscellaneous. Its provisions for the three branches of government will look very familiar to those knowledgeable about U.S. federal and state constitutions. The act vested the legislative power in a bicameral body and spelled out the fundamental aspects of the legislative process. The executive power was vested in the governor who was responsible for the faithful execution of the laws; other than the secretary of the territory, all executive officers owed their appointments to the governor. Unlike the other U.S. territories, a territorial judiciary was established separate from the federal courts; the territorial judicial power was vested in one supreme court, circuit courts, and such inferior courts as the legislature might establish.

Though it created a structure similar to that of state governments, the Organic Act allowed the territorial citizens only limited self-government, a factor that led many in the islands to advocate statehood for Hawaii. While members of the territorial house of representatives and senate were popularly elected, the governor, secretary, territorial supreme court justices, and circuit court judges were appointed by the U.S. president with the advice and consent of the U.S. Senate. Ultimate power and control remained in the hands of Congress, for it could specifically legislate just for Hawaii, it could nullify legislation passed by the territorial legislature, and it alone could amend the Organic Act. The governor was given wide powers, enhanced by the fact that, as a presidential appointee, the governor was not dependent on local support. Although voters could elect a delegate to the U.S. Congress, that delegate had no vote on the floor of the House of Representatives.

From the point of view of many in the islands, the Organic Act was inadequate with respect to its treatment of non-Caucasians. The commission drafting the act had sought to require a property qualification for voters and office holders. Congress deleted this proposal, seeing it as deviating too far from American voting principles; instead, the act specified that citizens could vote if they were registered; male; twenty-one years of age or older; a resident of the territory for not less than one year; and able to speak, read, and write English or Hawaiian. The act also made all persons who were citizens of the republic as of August 12, 1898, citizens of the United States and of the territory. Native Hawaiians were thus included as citizens. Notwithstanding, had the property qualification remained in the document, many would have been barred from voting. Since other legislation made it impossible for the Oriental immigrants to Hawaii to become naturalized, though their children born in the territory were considered citizens, a large proportion of that population was excluded from the vote. (Among the amendments Congress made to the Organic Act over the years is that of 1930 which ended the disenfranchisement of women in the territory.)

THE 1950 CONSTITUTIONAL CONVENTION: HOPES FOR STATEHOOD

Not long after Hawaii became a territory, the territorial legislature adopted what was to become the first in a series of statehood petitions sent to Congress. Although bills were introduced in Congress on numerous occasions, no action occurred until 1947, when the House of Representatives, but not the Senate, passed a statehood act. Adoption by the House again took place in 1950 and 1953; in 1954, reversing roles, the Senate, but not the House, passed a joint Hawaii-Alaska statehood enabling act. Only after enabling legislation for Alaska surmounted the congressional hurdle, and not until 1959, did enabling legislation pass both chambers, finally bringing statehood to Hawaii.

During the long wait, considerable activity aimed at attaining statehood occurred within the islands, such as the 1940 plebiscite on the issue that received the approval of island voters by more than a two-to-one ratio. In 1947, the territorial legislature created a statehood commission that had the primary duty of lobbying Congress.

Although Congress had not passed enabling legislation, Hawaii held a constitutional convention in 1950. In so doing, Hawaii followed the example of the fifteen territories that drafted a constitution before gaining congressional approval of statehood; Alaska followed suit a few years later. The underlying motivation for adopting this course of action was to remove all congressional doubts about Hawaii's qualifications for statehood. With a completed constitution ready to implement, Congress would be convinced by its advance adoption that the people of Hawaii accepted American values and were ready to be a part of the Union. There was not only real frustration with congressional inaction, but also a strong desire to counteract congressional fears about the island's lack of similarity with the mainland because of its racial and ethnic mix and its supposed infiltration by Communists.

In 1949, the territorial legislature passed Act 334, calling for a constitutional convention to meet in 1950 and draw up a state constitution. Following its adoption by the voters of the territory, the document was to be forwarded to Congress. The legislation directed that sixty-three delegates be elected on a nonpartisan basis, at a primary and a general election, from a mix of single- and multi-delegate districts.

Two hundred forty-three candidates filed for the sixty-three positions, and spirited campaigning ensued. Even though the elections were nonpartisan, the two political parties identified the particular candidates they supported, making every effort to get them elected. The high level of interest among the voters is attested to by the fact that 73 percent of the registered voters cast ballots at the primary, while 79 percent did so at the general election.

The sixty-three delegates who gathered at the opening of the convention on April 4, 1950, embodied a broad cross section of Hawaii's population. As described by a delegate who was also a university professor, they included two pineapple company presidents, two union representatives, a circuit court judge, two former attorneys general, a member of the University of Hawaii Board of Regents, the superintendent of public schools, one physician, two dentists, the speaker and vice speaker of the territorial house of representatives, four members of the territorial senate, several schoolteachers, and several attorneys. Five of the delegates (two attorneys, two homemakers, and one legislator) were women.[5]

The delegates also reflected the multi-ethnic diversity in the islands as well as the relative strength of the various groups in the political arena. There were twenty-seven delegates (43 percent) of Caucasian ancestry, nineteen (30 percent)

[5] Harold S. Roberts, "Preface," in *Constitutional Convention, 1950 Proceedings* (Honolulu: State of Hawaii, 1960), vol. I, *Journal and Documents*, vii.

of Japanese ancestry, twelve (19 percent) of Hawaiian or part-Hawaiian ancestry, and five (8 percent) of Chinese ancestry.[6]

Republicans outnumbered Democrats, with 48 and 32 percent of the delegates identified with the two parties, respectively; the rest either were independents or had no known affiliation. That the Republicans constituted almost one-half of the convention reflects the domination that party had enjoyed in the islands up until then. But that strength was beginning to fade, and a hint of the political party transition yet to come may have been indicated by the combined 52 percent of Democratic and independent (or affiliation unknown) delegates.

The convention opened with stirring speeches pointing to the historic nature of the event. Also on that first day, all delegates signed a loyalty oath, a move deemed necessary because of the continuing and increasingly more accusatory congressional pronouncements about Communists in the islands and the undue influence they would exert over the writing of Hawaii's constitution. While at the moment this may have seemed a relatively harmless formality, it set the stage for subsequent convention actions which, at least as viewed from hindsight, cast a pall over the proceedings.

On the fifth day, delegate Richard M. Kageyama resigned, stating that he had cooperated with the House Un-American Activities Committee (HUAC) by testifying to his short membership in the Communist party. Kageyama declared that he had done so only to help expose Communist activity in the islands and that he was resigning in order not to embarrass the delegates or prejudice the cause of statehood.

Three days later, a resolution was offered to the convention establishing a special committee to investigate whether Frank G. Silva was qualified to retain his seat as a delegate because he had refused to testify under oath before the HUAC. Silva emotionally responded that he was not then, nor had he ever been, a member of the Communist party, but that he refused to testify as a matter of principle. Nonetheless, a committee was appointed, and during the following convention sessions there was considerable debate over the matter. When the delegates considered a resolution expelling Silva, fifty-three voted in favor and seven against. The governor by appointment filled the two positions left vacant.

With these matters of delegate qualifications resolved, the convention was finally ready to get to work, and for three and a half months the delegates met, debated, voted on, and finally reached agreement on a constitution. All but one delegate signed it on July 22, 1950 (see below).

At the time it was drafted, and in years since, the "hope chest" constitution—referred to as such because it was drafted prior to congressional action—received

---

[6] Norman Meller, *With an Understanding Heart: Constitution Making in Hawaii* (New York: National Municipal League, 1971), 42. Two of Meller's figures differ slightly from those given by Roberts who, in his "Preface" to the *1950 Proceedings*, vii, states that there were twenty delegates (32 percent) of Japanese ancestry and eleven (17 percent) of Hawaiian/part-Hawaiian descent.

high praise. Being "commendably short, some 14,000 words," it represented "the victory of those who held for sketching the structure of government, positing its powers in general language, and leaving out everything specific that was not essential".[7] Acclaimed as having an excellent structure and very acceptable choice of words and phrases, it stood as a "testimonial of careful work".[8]

The National Municipal League applauded it for setting " 'a new high standard in the writing of a modern state constitution by a convention' "[9] and for resisting " 'virtually all temptations and pressures to include the kind of restrictive and legislative details that have so encumbered most of the Constitutions of the older states.' "[10] As one convention watcher phrased it, "The Hawaiian Constitution will be commended for its clear and definite allocation of administrative authority, for its streamline organization, for its appointive judiciary, its declaration for civil service, . . . its adherence to short ballot principles and possibly most of all for its faith that the legislatures of the future will be capable of dealing with the problems of their day".[11] At the time of statehood, it was lauded as affording a "good structure for the governance of the fiftieth state";[12] almost twenty years after statehood, it was characterized as "incorporating many of the features favored by political scientists and constitutional experts".[13]

Although the constitution looked very much like many other state constitutions, and incorporated parts of the U.S. Constitution and the Organic Act, it was unusual—some called it innovative—in a number of respects. The document is set apart by specific provisions stating that there is to be no segregation in any state military organization, fixing the voting age at twenty while most states set it at twenty-one, and calling for periodic voter consideration of whether the constitution should be reviewed by a constitutional convention. It gave the governor exclusive authority to reapportion the lower chamber and the authority to appoint an administrative director for the executive branch. An unusual legislative provision was the inclusion of a mechanism for removing a bill from a committee so that the entire chamber could consider it. The constitution also limited the number of executive positions elected statewide to governor and lieutenant governor; established a single centralized school system for the state;

---

[7] Meller, *With an Understanding Heart,* 85.

[8] S. Gale Lowrie, "Hawaii Drafts a Constitution," *University of Cincinnati Law Review* 20 (1951): 236.

[9] As quoted in Meller, *With an Understanding Heart,* 5.

[10] As quoted in Roberts, "Preface," *1950 Proceedings,* x.

[11] Lowrie, "Hawaii Drafts," 237.

[12] Paul C. Bartholomew and Robert M. Kamins, "The Hawaiian Constitution: A Structure for Good Government," *American Bar Association Journal* 45 (1959): 1222.

[13] Richard H. Kosaki, "Constitutions and Constitutional Conventions of Hawaii," *The Hawaiian Journal of History* 12 (1978): 124.

and centralized responsibility for public health, public assistance, slum clearance, and low income housing and for conservation of the land.

Two other unusual components of the proposed constitution warrant brief mention here; they are discussed in greater detail under Article XII in Part II. Incorporated into the document were the provisions of the federal Hawaiian Homes Commission Act of 1920, which established a homesteading program for native Hawaiians in an attempt to offset the tremendous decline in their numbers and to ensure continuation of their culture, as well as a provision accepting a compact with the federal government to guarantee continuation of this trust obligation. Their inclusion was criticized, however, and one delegate refused to sign the document because of them.

In spite of these distinguishing features, the document drafted by the 1950 delegates "showed and was meant to demonstrate how thoroughly the people of the islands were imbued with American political and cultural traditions".[14] In short, it was neither intended to be, nor was it, path-breaking.

The "hope chest" constitution did, however, receive its share of criticism. The International Longshoreman Workers Union (ILWU), a powerful labor organization in the islands at the time, attacked the document as too conservative. It campaigned against ratification, based on opposition not to statehood, but to specific features in the document, such as using registered voters instead of population as the basis for reapportionment; granting the legislature too much power; appointing, instead of electing, judges; and requiring voters to speak, read, and write English or Hawaiian. Sensitivity to congressional concerns had led the delegates to include a loyalty oath provision without any substantial opposition. The ILWU also disapproved of this provision. In retrospect, one recent commentator views its inclusion as demonstrating how the constitution represented "some of the excesses associated with McCarthyism [and] compromised the rights of free speech and free association which the nation's Constitution and Bill of Rights were designed to guarantee".[15]

But the ILWU was alone in its organized efforts against ratification, and for the most part the constitution received strong support throughout the community. Voters who went to the polling booths on November 7, 1950, cast their ballots in a ratio of three to one in favor.

The people of Hawaii still had to wait almost ten years before the proposed constitution could become effective. Their final decision on statehood was not to take place until June 17, 1959. At the election on that day, voters actually faced three questions, each of which, according to the congressional enabling act, had to receive an affirmative vote if statehood were to be achieved. The first asked

---

[14] Meller, *With an Understanding Heart*, 84.

[15] Roger Bell, *Last Among Equals, Hawaiian Statehood and American Politics* (Honolulu: University of Hawaii Press, 1984), 181.

whether Hawaii should be admitted to the Union. The two other questions, both amending provisions in the constitution, were raised as additional conditions by Congress. One question asked whether the voters approved altering that part of the constitution defining the state's boundaries and thus removing Palmyra atoll from state jurisdiction, while the other asked whether they approved the addition of a section concerning the Hawaiian Homes Commission Act. (The enabling act also temporarily altered another provision in the constitution by reducing the number of representatives Hawaii would sent to Congress from two to one until the number was increased at the next House reapportionment occurring with the 1960 census.)

In response to these questions, the voters loudly and clearly reaffirmed their desire for statehood; those approving each of the three questions outnumbered those opposed by seventeen to one. Shortly thereafter, on August 21, 1959, Hawaii officially became the fiftieth state of the Union.

THE 1968 CONSTITUTIONAL CONVENTION

Because of a constitutional provision requiring the question to appear on the ballot at least once during each ten-year period, Hawaii's voters would have been asked to decide, within that period, whether or not to hold a constitutional convention. There is no way to know whether, under ordinary circumstances, they would have approved the calling of another convention. However, extraordinary events essentially forced the state to hold a convention in 1968.

The genesis of the 1968 convention is to be found in the U.S. Supreme Court's 1964 *Reynolds v. Sims* decision. In that case, the Court held that both chambers of a state legislature must be apportioned on the one person-one vote principle. Shortly after the case was decided, Hawaii's attorney general issued opinions, based on *Reynolds*, stating that both the state house and senate were unconstitutionally apportioned. In a somewhat circus atmosphere, resolution of the malapportionment issue was bounced among the legislative, executive, and judicial branches of government, leading one analyst to characterize the 1968 convention as the result of political ineptitude.[16]

When the issue made its way to the state supreme court, only the senate apportionment was ruled invalid (*Guntert v. Richardson*, 1964). However, the court declined to impose a solution, preferring to let the legislature do so. Although the governor attempted to aid the legislature by proposing a reapportionment plan to a special session, the legislature was unable to come to any agreement.

At the same time, the issue was taken before the U.S. District Court for the District of Hawaii, and in *Holt v. Richardson* (1965) (*Holt I*), it, too, found the

---

[16] Meller, *With an Understanding Heart*, 6.

senate apportionment unconstitutional. The district court directed the legislature to adopt an interim plan for the 1966 election and additionally ordered the legislature to place the question of calling a constitutional convention on the 1966 general election ballot so that a convention could propose a permanent districting plan. The court also indicated that a convention was needed to address a number of other reapportionment issues raised in *Holt I* and *Guntert*; for example, both the state and the federal courts had found the constitution seriously at fault because, while it provided a method for reapportioning the house of representatives, it was silent as to the senate. In its order, the district court made it clear that it would take on the redistricting chore if the legislature did not place the question on the ballot, if the voters did not approve of a convention, if the convention did not adopt a reapportionment plan, or if the voters rejected the convention-drawn plan.

Faced with this ultimatum, the legislature adopted an interim plan, which the district court found invalid (*Holt v. Richardson,* 1965 (*Holt II*)). However, in reversing the lower federal court's decision, the U.S. Supreme Court validated the interim plan in part because the Court expected a convention to meet, address the issues, and fashion a permanent plan (*Burns v. Richardson,* 1966).

Believing that the legislature could, and should, deal with the reapportionment problem, the governor and others in the state argued that a convention was unnecessary. But in November 1966, almost two-thirds of the voters indicated their approval of a convention. The enabling legislation adopted the following year, Act 222, both observed and broke with the precedents established by the 1950 convention.

As before, delegates would be elected on a nonpartisan basis, but at only one special election, rather than at a primary followed by a general election. For the 1968 convention there were to be eighty-two delegates, almost a one-third increase from the sixty-three at the earlier convention, and, as previously, they were to be elected from a mix of multi-delegate and single-delegate districts.

That there was over a 50 percent increase in the number of candidates who filed (1950: 240; 1968: 378) is more likely attributed to the increase in delegates to be elected than to high public interest. This conclusion is suggested by the fact that only 45 percent of the registered voters turned out to cast ballots for delegates on June 1, 1968, down considerably from the participation at the elections for 1950 delegates.

There were both some similarities and some differences in the characteristics of the delegates serving in the two conventions. The most striking difference was the dominance in the 1968 body of delegates with legislative experience. Of the forty-five incumbent legislators—almost 60 percent of the seventy-six-member state legislature—who filed as candidates, thirty-seven were elected. Another five ex-legislators joined their ranks, giving them a 51 percent majority. Since the major focus of the convention would be reapportionment, a topic having immediate pertinence for any incumbent legislator, it is not difficult to understand why so many of them wanted to participate. That the districting plan for electing delegates, established in the convention enabling legislation, would give an advantage to them was clearly not ignored by the incumbents. Forty-three single-delegate districts (up from eighteen in 1950) had been created by the 1968 enabling act, and over half of the incumbents (twenty-four) chose to run from these. Despite adverse opinion expressed publicly during the campaign about the large number of incumbent legislators seeking to be delegates, four-fifths succeeded in being elected.

Like the earlier convention, lawyers made up 30 percent of the delegates, and those having a business occupation constituted around 40 percent. Union organizers made up 3 percent in 1950 and 2 percent in 1968. The medical profession was more represented in 1950 (8 percent) than in 1968 (2 percent), while educators also lost relatively, constituting 11 percent in 1950 as compared with 7 percent in 1968. The share of delegates identified as full-time public officers remained unchanged (2 percent in each convention), as did the share of those identified as retired (2 percent each time). The 1968 convention, however, included one student and five civil service employees (6 percent). There were also more women serving in 1968: eight (10 percent), as compared with five (8 percent) in 1950. Although twelve who had served in 1950 were candidates for election in 1968, only seven won. Of interest is the fact that Richard Kageyama, who had resigned in the early days of the 1950 convention because of his testimony before the U.S. House Un-American Activities Committee, was a delegate to the 1968 convention.

Once again the delegate body bore witness to the multi-ethnic nature of Hawaii's population. However, the representation of different groups was mute testimony to the political changes that had occurred since the 1950 convention. Reflecting the power Japanese-Americans had come to enjoy in the political arena, the percentage of delegates of Japanese ancestry rose dramatically from 30 to 46 percent (thirty-eight delegates). The proportion of Caucasian delegates went down from 43 to 27 percent (twenty-two delegates). Hawaiians and part Hawaiians made up only 10 percent (eight delegates), as compared to 19 percent in 1950. The share of convention seats held by delegates of Chinese ancestry stayed about the same, 8 percent in 1950 and 9 percent (seven delegates) in 1968. Two ethnic groups not represented earlier were Filipinos, with four delegates (5 percent), and Koreans, with three delegates (4 percent).[17]

Also striking is the difference in the delegates' political party affiliation. The 1968 elections were again carried out on a nonpartisan basis, and though the political parties were less active than they had been earlier, it is possible to identify the political affiliation of most delegates. In 1950, Republicans clearly controlled the convention. In contrast, the number of Democrats in 1968 was

[17] Ibid., 42.

estimated to be 68 percent, compared with 28 percent Republicans (and 4 percent were independent or of unknown affiliation). This turnaround reflects the peaceful political revolution that had occurred in Hawaii, starting in the mid-1940s, resulting in a shift from a one-party Republican territory to a one-party Democratic state by the mid-1960s. The political scene today shows little sign of change.

Among all the issues before the convention, reapportionment was unquestionably the most prominent. The convention devoted considerable time to it and proposed major modifications to the constitution. Most important was the institutionalizing of a bipartisan commission to carry out future districting for both the house and the senate. This provision removed reapportionment from the hands of the governor, who, under the Statehood Constitution, had the power to redistrict the house. The amendments also incorporated provision for future senate apportionments, which, as previously noted, had not been included in the earlier document.

The convention retained the 1950 provision requiring that districts be apportioned among the basic island units (i.e., counties), but included a requirement for minimum representation for each unit in order to protect the neighbor islands from being overwhelmed by Oahu, where 80 percent of the state's population lived. For the same reason, it included a provision for "fractional votes" for legislators elected from neighbor islands. Eight criteria were specified to guide the commission, such as keeping district lines within a basic island unit and directing that districts be compact and contiguous. Although there was lengthy discussion about various population bases to use for redistricting, the final proposal continued with a registered voter base. The convention proposed a legislative redistricting map as well, to be written into the constitution and to remain in effect until the first commission met in 1973.

Delegates also addressed other parts of the document and proposed changes of substantive importance. In particular, staggered terms for senators were eliminated, the minimum qualifying age of legislators was reduced, a minimum time during which bills must be available to the legislators and the public for consideration before final passage was established, legislative salaries were increased, and a commission to set legislative salaries was created. A very significant alteration was the provision for annual sixty-day legislative sessions, ending the alternation of sixty-day sessions with thirty-day budget sessions as specified in the Statehood Constitution.

The convention proposed removing the requirement of the ability to read and write English or Hawaiian as a qualification for voting, reducing the voting age from twenty to eighteen, allowing the legislature to provide for a presidential primary, lengthening judicial terms, changing the state and county debt limits, requiring adoption of codes of ethics, reducing the minimum age for serving as governor, enabling collective bargaining for public employees, and slightly enhancing county home rule. Among the proposals concerning Article I, Bill of

Rights, the most noteworthy provisions added were those protecting against invasions of privacy and guaranteeing appointment of counsel for indigent defendants.

The 1968 convention completed its work on October 21, 1968, some three months after opening. In 1950, the convention had afforded voters the option of voting only "yes" or "no" on the entire document, but the 1968 delegates settled on a novel procedure. All amendments were incorporated into twenty-three proposals, and as to each, voters had three options. They could cast a single "yes" or "no" vote on all of them, or they could vote "yes-but," specifying only those proposals with which they did not agree. The last option resulted in counting every proposal not expressly "opposed" as an approval. On November 5, 1968, 32 percent of the voters selected "yes" for all proposals, 15 percent voted "no," and 52 percent opted for the "yes-but" category. The net effect was that the amendments contained in twenty-two of the proposals were ratified; the only one defeated at the polls called for the reduction of the voting age from twenty to eighteen.

A number of the delegates to the 1968 convention remained important figures in state politics: Nelson Doi, who had also been a delegate in 1950, was long active in elective politics, eventually serving as lieutenant governor; Nadao Yoshinaga was for many years a powerful figure in the state legislature; Frank Fasi became almost the perennial mayor of Honolulu; Patricia Saiki served in the state legislature and was elected twice to the U.S. House of Representatives; after a number of terms in the legislature, George Ariyoshi was elected lieutenant governor and then governor for three consecutive terms, becoming the first state governor of Japanese-American ancestry in the United States.

THE 1978 CONSTITUTIONAL CONVENTION

The 1978 convention, like its predecessor a decade earlier, was born amidst legal skirmishes, though its major product also ended up in court.

Because the question of whether or not to hold a constitutional convention had been on the ballot in 1966 and because the constitution required the lieutenant governor to place it on the ballot if the legislature had not done so during a ten-year period, questions arose as to the exact nature of the constitutional requirement. Some argued that the language mandated placing the question on the ballot no later than the 1976 general election, while others claimed that it could wait until 1978. Responding to a request by the lieutenant governor for an opinion, the attorney general concluded that if the legislature did not place the question on the 1976 ballot, the lieutenant governor was mandated to do so for the subsequent 1978 election.

This interpretation was then challenged in the state supreme court (*League of Women Voters v. Doi*, 1976). However, in the meantime, both troubled by the prospect of a court-imposed resolution and responding to public pressure, the legislature passed a measure placing the question on the 1976 ballot. The court consequently found the timetable issue moot, and its refusal to hand down any ruling left clarification of the issue for the future.

When voters cast their ballots on November 2, 1976, on the question of holding a convention, 74 percent approved, while 26 percent opposed. This implies not only a high level of general interest, but also the existence of constitutional issues requiring consideration. During the course of public discussion of possible topics for convention consideration, various community groups and the major newspapers supported calling a convention. However, unlike the 1950 convention which was held specifically to further statehood and the 1968 convention which was called to deal with confusion in the aftermath of reapportionment, the delegates convened in 1978 without any widespread agreement as to any salient issues demanding attention.

It has been suggested that the high voter approval for calling a convention was the result of "a desire to slap back at Hawaii's legislature" because of its controversial actions such as those involving legislative pensions and state salaries.[18] Also contributing was an "amorphous public dissatisfaction with government following Watergate".[19] Public interest groups supported a convention because it was "a healthy and democratic device to review basic government organization and procedures," while special interest groups supported it in order to have "yet another opportunity to write their platforms into the Constitution."[20]

In response to the many incumbent legislators serving in 1968, public and media consensus quickly developed that the convention ought to reflect grass-roots participation. But not until the delegates were well into their deliberations did it become clear what major constitutional issues would characterize their work.

In the enabling legislation, Act 17, the convention size was increased to 102 delegates, again elected on a nonpartisan basis at one special election. Unlike the earlier conventions, however, single-delegate districts were abandoned, and all districts elected two delegates each.

The voter turnout at the special election for delegates demonstrated relatively light public interest. Only 35 percent of the registered voters cast ballots, a considerably lower turnout than in delegate elections for the earlier conventions and the lowest of any election held in the state of Hawaii prior to that date. The large number of candidates who sought election (697) may be attributed to the emphasis on grass-roots participation as well as to smaller election districts.

The public and media disapproval of legislators running appeared to be an effective deterrent, for there were only two incumbents and two former

---

[18] Norman Meller, "The 1978 Con Con Appraised," *Honolulu Star-Bulletin*, 30 November 1978, A-19.

[19] Norman Meller and Richard S. Kosaki, "Hawaii's Constitutional Convention—1978," *National Civic Review* 69 (1980): 248.

[20] Kosaki, "Constitutions and Constitutional Conventions," 126.

legislators among the large field of candidates; all four won. This is not to suggest that all other "politicians" were dissuaded from participating. One incumbent Honolulu City Council member became a delegate, while a few others had previous elective or administrative experience at the state and local levels.

The 1978 convention brought many new faces to the political scene, and the delegates were also much younger than those of the prior conventions. For example, delegates between the ages of twenty and thirty made up only 9 percent in 1968, while in 1978 they comprised 32 percent. Thirty women (29 percent) were elected, a dramatic increase from previous conventions. In comparing occupations of those serving in 1968 and 1978, the latter body saw a decrease in lawyers, persons in business, and doctors, but an increase in educators, retirees, students, and civil service employees. Few delegates had previous convention experience: One had served in 1950, and five had been delegates in 1968.

Like the earlier conventions, that of 1978 reflected the ethnic diversity in the islands, and the ethnic makeup of the delegates is indicative of changes occurring on the political scene. A number of published works describe the ethnic composition for the 1950 and 1968 conventions. In contrast, there appears to be only one publication that even partially addresses the ethnic makeup of the 1978 convention.[21] By way of a cautionary note, it is always difficult in Hawaii, because of a high rate of intermarriage, to place individuals into neat ethnic or racial categories, and this problem is compounded as the out-marriage rate continues to grow. In order to develop information comparable to that available for the previous conventions, a delegate who served in 1978 kindly helped in analyzing the ethnic and racial composition of the convention: Japanese ancestry—forty (39 percent); Caucasian—twenty-eight (27 percent); Hawaiian/part-Hawaiian—nineteen (19 percent); Chinese—eight (8 percent); Filipino—two, Korean—two, and African-American—two (each 2 percent); and Samoan—one (1 percent).

In 1978, like 1968, those of Japanese ancestry made up the largest group of delegates, though there was a decrease in their percentage from 46 to 39 percent. These figures contrast with the 1950 convention when delegates of Japanese ancestry constituted the second largest grouping with 30 percent. The proportion of Caucasians among the 1978 delegates was the same as in 1968 (27 percent), considerably less than in 1950 when they made up the largest group at 43 percent.

At all three conventions, the third largest ethnic group was the Hawaiian/part-Hawaiian component (19, 10, and 19 percent, respectively). However, the 19 percent figure posited here for 1978 is slightly larger than that found in the partial analysis, published shortly after that convention, which placed the

[21] Meller and Kosaki, "Hawaii's Constitutional Convention," 251.

Hawaiians/part Hawaiians at 14 percent.[22] Whichever is correct, the fact that the 1978 convention included more Hawaiian/part-Hawaiian delegates than did the 1968 convention reflected a burgeoning movement in the 1970s, referred to as the Hawaiian renaissance. This movement was based on heightened awareness among persons of Hawaiian ancestry of the need to enhance their legal and political status. At the 1978 convention, the "Hawaiian component utilized its minority position skillfully, and realized material benefits for the island's indigenous peoples".[23] Their input had noteworthy constitutional consequences, forcing the state not only to acknowledge the significant contributions of persons of Hawaiian ancestry to island history, but also to redress major injustices, particularly with respect to land.

Although the proportion of Korean and Filipino delegates dropped slightly from 1968 to 1978 (from 4 to 2 percent and 5 to 2 percent, respectively), two new groups first attained representation in 1978: African-Americans, with two delegates (2 percent), and Samoans, with one delegate (1 percent).

The political parties played a minor role in the election for delegates, but the labor unions—closely aligned with the Democratic party—were much more involved than ever before and claimed a high success rate: At least half of their endorsed candidates won seats. The continued dominance of the Democratic party in state politics was clearly evident at the convention since 86 percent of the delegates can be identified as Democrats, with most of the remaining 14 percent identified as Republicans.

Not long after the convention convened on July 5, 1978, it became evident that a group of delegates "who loosely shared an ideological position, labeled 'palaka power,' aimed at resisting the introduction of change by newcomers to Hawaii."[24] (*Palaka* is the name of a particular check-patterned cotton cloth used during the plantation era for clothing worn by sugar and pineapple plantation workers.) This group, sometimes referred to as the Islands-oriented group, exerted considerable influence over the convention, especially in concert with the Hawaiian delegates.

The convention became divided between a majority group (whose core was the *palaka* power faction) and those referred to as the "independent" group. One of the most significant differences between them emerged over the issue of initiative, referendum, and recall, with the majority group opposed and the "independent" group in favor. Afterward, the convention president lamented this schism, claiming that it detracted from the body's work and produced many "unnecessary parliamentary wrangles".[25] This aspect also contributed to a fair

---

[22] Ibid.

[23] Ibid.

[24] Ibid., 252.

[25] William S. Paty, Jr., "Preface," in *Constitutional Convention, 1978 Proceedings* (Honolulu: State of Hawaii, 1980), vol. I, *Journal and Documents*, ix.

degree of negative press coverage, leading to the observation that the convention "probably received more criticism than praise".[26]

After two and half months, the convention completed its work. Considering it had opened without clear consensus on the parts of the constitution needing revision or amendment, most members of the public were surprised to find that the convention proposed a total of 116 changes. Every article was touched in some way, either stylistically or substantively. The most significant of the many stylistic changes involved substituting gender-neutral language throughout the entire document; all male references disappeared. From a substantive point of view, two new articles separated and expanded on subjects previously included in the document, thus increasing the number of articles to eighteen. Furthermore, by proposing nearly forty additional sections, the convention gave constitutional status to many new subjects.

All the proposed changes were grouped into thirty-four separate items for the ballot. As in 1968, the 1978 convention determined that voters would have three options: "yes" or "no" on all proposed changes or the "yes-but" alternative where the voter specified those items he or she opposed (with everything not "opposed" recorded as an affirmative vote).

Despite strong opposition to some of the amendments, all were approved when voting took place on November 7, 1978. Of those casting ballots on the proposals, 20 percent voted "yes" to all, and about the same number opposed all the proposals by voting "no". Even though almost 60 percent of the voters selected the third option, their negative votes on specific items were not sufficient to defeat any of them. An analysis of these election returns disclosed that no item owed its adoption to an expression of specific approval by the voters.[27] Given the large number of voters who had selected the "yes-but" option, under which every amendment not singled out with a specific "no" vote was credited with a "yes" vote, each received a total "yes" tally sufficient for ratification.

The Islands-oriented approach of the majority group in the convention resulted not only in a number of additions directed toward those of Hawaiian ancestry (the Hawaiian affairs package), but also in amendments addressing more general issues of life-style in Hawaii. The latter included new sections concerning conservation, marine and water resources, and the guarantee to each person of the right to a clean and healthful environment. Another cluster of changes reflected a strong desire for more openness in government and indicated a weakening of the political parties.

Three noteworthy changes to the bill of rights incorporated a right to privacy, the requirement of twelve-person juries in criminal trials, and the creation of an

---

[26] Meller, "The 1978 Con Con Appraised," A-19.

[27] Meller and Kosaki, "Hawaii's Constitutional Convention," 257.

independent counsel for grand juries. The right to privacy turned out to be particularly controversial, receiving a high number of "no" votes.

With respect to elections, the period between the primary and the general elections was expanded, and open primaries were reinstated. A "resign to run" provision was added, as were campaign finance and contribution controls, even though a significant number of voters opposed the adoption of these provisions.

The legislative process was altered by returning to staggered senate terms, requiring open committee meetings, and mandating a legislative recess. The governor and lieutenant governor were each limited to two consecutive four-year terms. A new method for selecting judges resulted in the introduction of a judicial selection commission; in addition, a new intermediate court of appeals was created.

Fiscal provisions came in for considerable modification: A tax review commission and a council on revenues were created, and tax rebates and an expenditure ceiling were specified. State-county relationships were readjusted by the addition of a requirement that the state share the costs of mandated local programs, and county home rule was enhanced by allowing local government to have power over real property taxation; this last provision also received much opposition at the polls.

Among the most controversial changes were those in the Hawaiian affairs package which received a substantial number of "no" votes. These amendments created an Office of Hawaiian Affairs, enhanced the Hawaiian Lands rehabilitation program, required the teaching of Hawaiian culture in the public schools, established Hawaiian as an official language, protected traditional and customary rights, and limited the use of adverse possession for acquiring title to land. In addition, constitutional status was granted to the state motto, written in Hawaiian, as well as to the edict of King Kamehameha called the "Law of the Splintered Paddle".

Shortly after the election ratifying the proposed amendments, legal challenges were heard by both the Hawaii Supreme Court and the U.S. district court. Two of the three questions before the state court, in *Kahalekai v. Doi* (1979), concerned the ballot format: Was it biased toward a "yes" by making it more difficult to vote "no," and should each proposed change have been presented as a separate ballot question? With respect to the first question, the court decided that the ballot language was not misleading. Just because it was mechanically easier to vote "yes," rather than to reject specific amendments, did not render the format defective. The court also ruled that it was not necessary to present each proposed change as a separate question because, "[u]nless otherwise provided in the Constitution, there is no limitation on the number of subjects that may be included in a proposed constitutional amendment".

The third question before the court centered on the informational materials prepared by the convention. In ruling on this issue, the court invalidated seven proposed changes because the informational materials did not contain the full text of those proposals. The fact that the convention failed to inform the public about the substantive content and effect of those amendments constituted a fatal defect, so the amendments were not validly ratified by the voters. The invalidated amendments covered a ride range of topics: deletion of a constitutional section on farm and home ownership, addition of definitions of "native Hawaiians" and "Hawaiians," and a number of matters relating to representation and reapportionment.

The issue before the U.S. district court also involved the ballot format, but the court declined to rule on it. Rather, in *Hart v. King* (1979), the court emphasized that the plaintiffs' failure to seek a pre-election remedy, when they knew what the ballot format was before the election was held, barred them from a post-election attempt to invalidate the results.

Although the ballot format was not found wanting per se in either court case, and the seven proposals invalidated in *Kahalekai* were relatively minor, the controversy engendered by those issues led the 1979 legislature to propose an amendment to Article XVII, Revision and Amendment. It encompassed two changes: requiring that when amendments proposed by a constitutional convention are placed on the ballot, they must be submitted in the form of questions embracing one subject, with designated spaces for voting "yes" or "no" for each; and adding language detailing a convention's responsibilities for public education. This amendment was ratified by the voters in 1980.

Like the preceding conventions, that of 1978 had a long-term impact not only because of the constitutional changes made, but also because of the considerable number of delegates who subsequently played influential roles in island politics. For example, eighteen delegates have since served in the legislature, and as late as 1992, thirteen delegates held legislative seats. In particular, delegate John Waihee must be singled out for mention. Although a political novice when elected, he was soon characterized as a "major architect of the convention's will".[28] He went on to serve in the state house of representatives, then as lieutenant governor, and currently is completing his second consecutive term as governor. Because the 1978 convention limited a governor to two consecutive terms, he is the first to feel the constraints of this change. Waihee is the first state governor of Hawaiian descent.

LEGISLATIVELY PROPOSED CONSTITUTIONAL CHANGES

Besides providing for periodic constitutional conventions, Hawaii's constitution allows the legislature to propose constitutional changes. All amendments, whether proposed by convention or by the legislature, must be ratified by the voters in

[28] Sandra S. Oshiro, "Young Turk Emerges at Con Con," *Honolulu Advertiser*, 20 September 1978, A-1.

order to become effective. That the legislature takes its role in proposing amendments seriously is evidenced by the considerable number of amendments introduced at each legislative session. Most, however, experience an early death, and only a few end up on the ballot.

Since statehood, forty legislatively proposed amendments have come before the voters; twenty-five passed, and fifteen failed. Some failed each time they were placed on the ballot, and several of those passing did so only after defeat at earlier elections.

It is not always apparent why particular amendments pass or fail. Unlike the coverage afforded in the mass media after each convention, the legislatively proposed amendments have had relatively little such attention, and that coverage most often occurs just shortly before election day. In a few instances, editorials and individual members of the public have endorsed or opposed proposals, but the legislators themselves have not taken an active role in promoting passage or defeat. It is not unfair to generalize that Hawaii's voters do not receive much information on which to base their votes. In some cases proposals have failed not because more negative votes were cast, but because the total number of affirmative votes cast was insufficient to satisfy the constitution's minimum requirement for ratification. This may be explained, at least partly, by the voters' lack of information.

Since 1980, the constitution has explicitly prescribed the responsibilities of a convention for wide dissemination of the full text of all proposals and for a program of voter education. As for legislatively proposed amendments, on the other hand, the constitution merely requires that they be published four times in a newspaper. Only recently has the legislature attempted to go beyond this.

Funds were appropriated for a 1990 pilot project, and a voter informational booklet was distributed in a few districts. No specific legislation has passed since for continuing this educational project.

In Part II, under the appropriate constitutional section, both successful and unsuccessful amendments are described.

■ VOTERS REJECT ANOTHER CONVENTION

In 1986, pursuant to the constitutional mandate, the question of whether to hold a constitutional convention was placed on the general election ballot. This time, however, editorials in both of the state's major newspapers opposed the holding of a convention. Only one news account dealt with the issue in any detail, and while no one was quoted in support, two 1978 delegates, one state representative, and one union leader were each quoted as opposed.[29] No issues needing

[29] Sterling Morita, "Voters Must Decide on a New Constitutional Convention," *Honolulu Star-Bulletin*, 22 October 1986, A-1.

convention attention surfaced, and there was no visible effort to encourage a "yes" vote. By a substantial margin, the voters expressed their disapproval of another periodic convention.

CONCLUSION

Starting as a relatively short, simple, and highly praised document, Hawaii's constitution has become longer and more detailed. The Statehood Constitution contained about 14,000 words, making it one of the shorter state constitutions. The current document stands at around 17,500 words, placing it midrange among state constitutions.[30]

In defense of this greater girth, many of the amendments have added to the rights of Hawaii's citizens and have contributed to making the constitution fairly progressive. With respect to its provisions relating to ethnic Hawaiians and their culture, it stands out as unique. Many of the amendments, particularly those authored by the 1978 convention, introduced significant new responsibilities to be undertaken by government. Yet the Hawaii Constitution still succeeds in avoiding much of the excessive detail found in some of the other state constitutions.

Neither the 1968 nor the 1978 constitution has received the public expressions of praise heaped on the document as drafted in 1950. While there is some important scholarly work on the conventions, little exists in terms of critical evaluation of the document and how it has changed. However, at least one longtime observer has commented that over time the constitution has been "cluttered up" by all the amendments.[31]

That Hawaii's constitution requires the voters to decide, on a periodic basis, whether there should be a convention, demonstrates its underlying premise—a constitution ought to be viewed not as a static document, but as one that benefits from ongoing review. Even so, ongoing review does not automatically lead to the conclusion that change is always necessary, as seen by the voter rejection in 1986 of a fourth convention.

Sometime before 2000, Hawaii's voters will once again have the opportunity to determine if major review by another con con—as they are popularly referred to in Hawaii—is in order. This in effect will constitute a decision on whether the current document satisfies the demands arising out of the transition from the twentieth to the twenty-first century.

---

[30] *The Book of the States, 1990–1991* (Lexington, Ky.: The Council of State Governments, 1990), 40. The exact word count presented there, as of 1990, is 17,453. Since this is the same figure found, as of 1987, in the 1988–1989 edition, the count does not appear to include amendments adopted in 1988 which added language to the constitution.

[31] This comment was made by Dan Turtle in an interview transcribed in *Perspectives on Hawaii's Statehood* (Honolulu: Social Science Oral History Project of the University of Hawaii at Manoa, 1986), 131.

PART TWO

The Hawaii Constitution and Commentary

Part II analyzes the text of the Hawaii Constitution, section by section, focusing on each provision's purpose, its date of adoption, its subsequent amendments, and its interpretation by the courts. Quite a number of the provisions in the constitution have been the subject of judicial review, and for some, particularly those in Article I, Bill of Rights, the case law is considerable. Where that is the situation, cases are cited that best explain the meaning and scope of the constitutional language, raise engaging points, or deviate from federal court decisions. The discussions following some of the sections do not include references to cases either because the provision has not undergone judicial scrutiny or because the cases are not of particular importance for the purposes of this work.

This commentary relies primarily on decisions handed down by the state's highest appellate court, the Hawaii Supreme Court. Where relevant, rulings by the Hawaii Intermediate Court of Appeals (in operation since 1980) and the federal courts, as well as opinions issued by the state's attorney general, are included.

As noted in Part I, the 1978 Constitutional Convention made many stylistic changes, such as modifying punctuation, substituting "as provided by law" for "in accordance with law" and, most importantly, "degendering" the language. As those changes had no impact on substance, specific references to them are omitted from the following commentary. That convention also revised the titles of some sections; such changes are referred to only if they are of substantive significance.

Because the 1978 convention also added two new articles and many new sections, the document underwent considerable internal renumbering. Except with respect to article designations, the text of this commentary ignores the numerical changes in subordinate provisions. Table 1 shows which articles and sections have been renumbered and when new articles and sections became part of the constitution.

TABLE 1 *Changes In Article/Section Numbers; Year Article/Section Added**

1978	1968	Statehood
Article I,	Bill of Rights	
I,1	I,1	I,1
I,2	I,2	I,2
I,3	Added 1972 as I,21	
I,4	I,3	I,3
I,5	I,4	I,4
I,6	Added 1978	
I,7	I,5	I,5
I,8	I,6	I,6
I,9	I,7	I,7
I,10	I,8	I,8
I,11	Added 1978	
I,12	I,9	I,9
I,13	I,10	I,10
I,14	I,11	I,11
I,15	I,13	I,13
I,16	I,14	I,14
I,17	I,15	I,15
I,18	I,16	I,16
I,19	I,17	I,17
I,20	I,18	I,18
I,21	I,19	I,19
I,22	I,20	I,20
Article II,	Suffrage and Elections	
II,1	II,1	II,1
II,2	II,2	II,2
II,3	II,3	II,3
II,4	II,4	II,4
II,5	Added 1978	
II,6	Added 1978	
II,7	Added 1978	
II,8	II,5	II,5
II,9	II,6	Added 1968
II,10	II,7	II,5

(Continued)

TABLE 1 *(Continued)*

1978	1968	Statehood
Article III,	The Legislature	
III,1	III,1	III,1
III,2	III,2	III,2
III,3	III,3	III,3
III,4	III,5	III,5
III,5	III,6	III,6
III,6	III,7	III,7
III,7	III,8	III,8
III,8	III,9	III,9
III,9	III,10	III,10
III,10	III,11	III,11
III,11	III,12	III,12
III,12	III,13	III,13
III,13	III,14	III,14
III,14	III,15	III,15
III,15	III,16	III,16
III,16	III,17	III,17
III,17	III,18	III,18
III,18	III,19	III,19
III,19	III,20	III,20
Article IV, Reapportionment: Added in 1978; part of the 10 sections were previously found in the article on The Legislature.		
Article V,	The Executive	
V,1	IV,1	IV,1
V,2	IV,2	IV,2
V,3	IV,3	IV,3
V,4	IV,4	IV,4
V,5	IV,5	IV,5
V,6	IV,6	IV,6
Article VI,	The Judiciary	
VI,1	V,1	V,1
VI,2	V,2	V,2
VI,3	V,3	V,3
VI,4	Added 1978	
VI,5	V,4	V,4
VI,6	V,5	V,5
VI,7	V,6	V,6

(Continued)

TABLE 1 *(Continued)*

1978	1968	Statehood
Article VII,	Taxation and Finance	
VII,1	VI,1	VI,1
VII,2	Added 1978	
VII,3	Added 1978	
VII,4	VI,2	VI,6
VII,5	VI,6	VI,7
VII,6	Added 1978	
VII,7	Added 1978	
VII,8	VI,4	VI,4
VII,9	VI,5	VI,5
VII,10	VI,7	VI,8
VII,11	Added 1978	
VII,12	VI,3	VI,3
VII,13	VI,3	VI,3
Article VIII,	Local Government	
VIII,1	VII,1	VII,1
VIII,2	VII,2	VII,2
VIII,3	VII,3	VII,3
VIII,4	VII,4	VII,4
VIII,5	Added 1978	
VIII,6	VII,5	VII,5
Article IX,	Public Health and Welfare	
IX,1	VIII,1	VIII,1
IX,2	VIII,2	VIII,2
IX,3	VIII,3	VIII,3
IX,4	Added 1978	
IX,5	VIII,4	VIII,4
IX,6	Added 1978	
IX,7	VIII,5	VIII,5
IX,8	Added 1978	
IX,9	Added 1978	
IX,10	Added 1978	
Article X,	Education	
X,1	IX,1	IX,1
X,2	IX,2	IX,2
X,3	IX,3	IX,3
X,4	Added 1978	
X,5	IX,4	IX,4
X,6	IX,5	IX,5

(Continued)

TABLE 1 *(Continued)*

1978	1968	Statehood
Article XI, Conservation, Control and Development of Resources		
XI,1	Added 1978	
XI,2	X,2	X,2
XI,3	Added 1978	
XI,4	Added 1978	
XI,5	X,4	X,4
XI,6	X,3	X,3
XI,7	Added 1978	
XI,8	Added 1978	
XI,9	Added 1978	
XI,10	X,5	X,5
XI,[11]	Added 1978	
Article XII,	Hawaiian Affairs	
XII,1	XI,1	XI,1
XII,2	XI,2	XI,2
XII,3	XI,3	Added 1959
XII,4	Added 1978	
XII,5	Added 1978	
XII,6	Added 1978	
XII,7	Added 1978	
Article XIII, Organization; Collective Barqaining		
XIII,1	XII,1	XII,1
XIII,2	XII,2	XII,2
Article XIV, Code of Ethics: Added in 1978: based on provision added in 1968 to the article on General an Miscellaneous Provisions		
Article XV, State Boundaries; Capital? Flag; Language and Motto		
XV,1	XIII,1	XIII,1
XV,2	XIII,2	XIII,2
XV,3	XIII,3	XIII,3
XV,4	Added 1978	
XV,5	Added 1978	
Article XVI, General and Miscellaneous Provisions		
XVI,1	XIV,1	XIV,1
XVI,2	XIV,2	XIV,2
XVI,3	XIV,3	XIV,3
XVI,4	XIV,4	XIV,4
XVI,5	XIV,6	XIV,5
XVI,6	XIV,7	XIV,6
XVI,7	XIV,8	XIV,7

(Continued)

TABLE 1 *(Continued)*

1978	1968	Statehood
XVI,8	XIV,9	XIV,8
XVI,9	XIV,10	XIV,9
XVI,10	XIV,11	XIV,10
XVI,11	XIV,12	XIV,11
XVI,12	Added 1978	
XVI,13	Added 1978	
XVI,14	XIV,13	XIV,12
XVI,15	XIV,14	XIV,13
XVI,16	XIV,15	XIV,14
Article XVII,	Revision and Amendment	
XVII,1	XV,1	XV,1
XVII,2	XV,2	XV,2
XVII,3	XV,3	XV,3
XVII,4	XV,4	XV,4
XVII,5	XV,5	Added 1968
Article XVIII,	Schedule	
XVIII,1	XVI,1	XVI,1
XVIII,2	Added 1978	
XVIII,3	XVI,7	XVI,17
XVIII,4	Added 1978	
XVIII,5	Added 1978	
XVIII,6	Added 1978	
XVIII,7	Added 1978	
XVIII,8	Added 1978	
XVIII,9	XVI,10	XVI,2
XVIII,10	XVI,11	XVI,3
XVIII,11	XVI,12	XVI,7

* Sections deleted in 1968 or 1978 are not included.

PREAMBLE

> We, the people of Hawaii, grateful for Divine Guidance, and mindful of our Hawaiian heritage and uniqueness as an island State, dedicate our efforts to fulfill the philosophy decreed by the Hawaii State motto, "Ua mau ke ea o ka aina i ka pono."
>
> We reserve the right to control our destiny, to nurture the integrity of our people and culture, and to preserve the quality of life that we desire.
>
> We reaffirm our belief in a government of the people, by the people and for the people, and with an understanding and compassionate heart toward all the peoples of the earth, do hereby ordain and establish this constitution for the State of Hawaii.

Although not specifically granting any rights or powers, the Preamble serves an important symbolic purpose, for it expresses a most basic assumption underlying the document. The relationship between the people and the government is clarified through the opening words, "We, the people," borrowed from the Preamble of the U.S. Constitution, and the phrase "We reaffirm our belief in a government of the people, by the people and for the people," employing the words immortalized in Lincoln's 1863 Gettysburg Address.

Prior to 1978, the Preamble consisted of only one paragraph:

> We, the people of the State of Hawaii, grateful for Divine Guidance, and mindful of our Hawaiian heritage, reaffirm our belief in a government of the people, by the people and for the people, and with an understanding heart toward all the peoples of the earth do hereby ordain and establish this constitution for the State of Hawaii.

While the 1978 delegates expressed their belief that the original Preamble was beautifully written, they also recognized that, when it was adopted in 1950, the primary focus was on attaining statehood. Now they intended to expand the Preamble to also address what they viewed as more current concerns of Hawaii's people. New themes incorporated included acknowledgment of the native Hawaiian heritage, Hawaii's uniqueness as an island state, the right of the residents to determine their own destiny, the importance of nurturing cultural integrity, and the need to preserve a high quality of life. By referring to the state motto, which translates as "The life of the land is perpetuated in righteousness," the delegates intended to pay homage to the beauty of Hawaii's land. (See Article XV, Section 5 for discussion of the motto.)

FEDERAL CONSTITUTION ADOPTED

> The Constitution of the United States of America is adopted on behalf of the people of the State of Hawaii.

This self-explanatory statement, originating in the Statehood Constitution follows the Preamble. The applicability of this sectionmaycome into question in the not-too-distant future as various groups in Hawaii work toward some form of sovereignty for ethnic Hawaiians.[1]

---

[1] For discussion about the Hawaiian sovereignty movement, see, for example, Haunani-Kay Trask, "Kūpa'a Aina: Native Hawaiian Nationalism in Hawaii," in *Politics and Public Policy in Hawaii*, ed. Zachary A. Smith and Richard C. Pratt (Albany: State University of New York Press, 1992); Melody Kapilialoha MacKenzie, ed., *Native Hawaiian Rights Handbook* (Honolulu: Native Hawaiian Legal Corp., 1991).

Article I

Bill of Rights

When Article I, Bill of Rights, was drafted by the 1950 convention, a number of its twenty sections included language almost identical to that found in the U.S. Constitution's Bill of Rights. Under the Organic Act, those living in the territory of Hawaii enjoyed most of the rights guaranteed by the federal Bill of Rights, and a major factor motivating Hawaii's framers to use essentially verbatim language was to ensure continuity of those rights, as interpreted by the federal courts, once statehood was achieved.

In the years since statehood, when considering the provisions in Article I, Hawaii's supreme court has often adopted the reasoning used, and the rules enunciated, by the U.S. Supreme Court. But it has not felt bound by them and has also established rules of law that are significantly different, as it explained in *State v. Miyasaki* (1980):

> We have not hesitated to "extend the protections of the Hawaii Bill of Rights beyond those of textually parallel provisions in the Federal Bill of Rights when logic and sound regard for the purposes of those protections have so warranted." We have recognized that "the Hawaii Supreme Court, as the highest court of a sovereign state is under the obligation to construe the state constitution, not in total disregard of federal interpretations of identical language, but with reference to the wisdom of adopting those interpretations for our state." In this regard, we have on occasion preferred a fair conception of the state constitution to judicial exegesis emanating

> from the [U.S.] Supreme Court, particularly where "unexpected" decisions from the Court "have forced a serious re-evaluation of . . . fundamentals." We are mindful, however, "that the fundamental principle in construing a constitutional provision is to give effect to the intention of the framers and the people adopting it."

A number of important modifications have been made to Article I since statehood, although most of the original language remains intact. Voters ratified amendments proposed by both the 1968 and the 1978 conventions. These include the 1978 convention's proposal deleting what had been Section 12, protecting the right to jury service regardless of gender, based on the understanding that the provision was redundant since, in 1972, the legislature proposed and the voters approved adding an equality of rights provision to the bill of rights (Section 3). The voters at the 1978 election also approved two new sections: Section 6, "Right to Privacy," and Section 11,"Grand Jury Counsel." Legislatively proposed modifications were subsequently ratified in 1982 (see Section 10) and 1988 (see Section 13).[2]

SECTION 1

> **Political Power.** All political power of this State is inherent in the people and the responsibility for the exercise thereof rests with the people. All government is founded on this authority.

Unchanged substantively since statehood, this section reiterates the basic philosophy expressed in the Preamble: All political power rests in the hands of the people, and the people grant government the authority to exercise those powers delegated to it. But the section is distinctive in also emphasizing that concurrent with this inherent political power is the responsibility for its exercise.

Although no court decisions have been based specifically on this section, it helps to lay the foundation for the state supreme court's observation that "the fundamental principle in construing a constitutional provision is to give effect to the intention of the framers and the people adopting it" (*State v. Miyasaki*, 1980).

SECTION 2

> **Rights of Individuals.** All persons are free by nature and are equal in their inherent and inalienable rights. Among these rights are the enjoyment of life, liberty and the pursuit of happiness, and the acquiring and possessing of property. These rights

---

[2] For discussion of cases decided under various Article I sections since 1983, see Jon M. Van Dyke, Marilyn M. L. Chung, and Teri Y. Kondo, "The Protection of Individual Rights Under Hawaii's Constitution," *University of Hawaii Law Review* 14 (1992): 311.

> cannot endure unless the people recognize their corresponding obligations and responsibilities.

Echoing the language found in the national Declaration of Independence, this section remains as it was originally written, and it elaborates on the basic concepts found in Section 1 and the Preamble. Like Section 1, it serves as a reminder that citizens have corresponding obligations and responsibilities if they are to enjoy the rights specified in the constitution.

Hawaii's supreme court has found that although the exact words are not used, the rights to freedom of movement and association are encompassed by the words "inalienable rights" and "for the enjoyment of life, liberty and the pursuit of happiness" (*State v. Kimball*, 1972; *State v. Shigematsu*, 1971). In *Shigematsu*, the court explained that these rights are "necessary foundations to our American way of life since their absence or denial characterizes confinement and imprisonment," and that they are as equally important to our way of life as are the rights or freedoms specifically enumerated in the constitution. When considering these rights, the court added, it will balance the state's police power to regulate for the protection of society and the people's rights of freedom of movement and association.

SECTION 3

> **Equality of Rights**. Equality of rights under the law shall not be denied or abridged by the State on account of sex. The legislature shall have the power to enforce, by appropriate legislation, the provisions of this section.

When Congress, in 1972, proposed an Equal Rights Amendment (ERA) for the U.S. Constitution, Hawaii was the first state to ratify it, with the state legislature voting favorably within the first hour after it had passed the U.S. Senate. Later that year, Hawaii voters approved (by an 87 percent affirmative vote) the legislature's proposal to add an equality of rights provision to the state constitution. Its first sentence is identical to the amendment proposed for the U.S. Constitution (which has not been ratified).

The Hawaii Supreme Court has had only two opportunities to decide cases on the basis of this section. At issue in *Holdman v. Olim* (1978) was a regulation requiring women to wear a bra when visiting an inmate at the state prison. The court declined to rest its decision squarely on this section, largely because it believed the "standard of review to be applied under an ERA has not been clearly formulated by judicial decision." Instead, the court opted to uphold the regulation under the equal protection clause in Section 5 and, using the test of strict scrutiny, found the regulation valid because there was a compelling state interest. The court explained that it was not prepared, even if a more stringent test were applied under Section 3, to prohibit exceptions based on physical characteristics unique to one sex. (See Section 5 below for discussion about the analysis used in equal protection cases.)

While only suggesting in *Holdman* that the state's equal rights provision allows exceptions based on physical characteristics unique to one sex, the court shortly thereafter specifically ruled that such exceptions were permitted.[3] *State v. Rivera* (1980) involved a challenge to the rape statute. Although amended in 1979 with gender-neutral language, the statute referred only to men raping women at the time of Rivera's conviction. The court found that the pre-amendment language did not violate either the equal protection clause or Section 3 and, with respect to the latter, held that a "classification based on a physical characteristic unique to one sex is not an impermissive under- or over-inclusive classification because the differentiation is based on the unique presence of a physical characteristic in one sex and not based on an averaging of a trait or characteristic which exists in both sexes."

The second sentence of Section 3 grants the legislature the "power to enforce, by appropriate legislation, the provisions of this section." Examples of legislative action taken pursuant to this provision include amendments to various criminal, employment, and housing laws and the 1985 directive [in Hawaii Revised Statutes (Haw. Rev. Stat.) § 23G-15] to the state revisor of statutes to "change any male or female gender term to a term which is neutral in gender when it is clear that the statute is not applicable only to members of one sex and without altering the sense, meaning, or effect of any act" in future volumes of the Hawaii Revised Statutes.

SECTION 4

Freedom of Religion, Speech, Press, Assembly and Petition. No law shall be enacted respecting an establishment of religion, or prohibiting the free exercise thereof, or abridging the freedom of speech or of the press or the right of the people peaceably to assemble and to petition the government for a redress of grievances.

The rights specified in this section, virtually unchanged since statehood, are often referred to as "first amendment rights" because they are identical to those found in the First Amendment to the U.S. Constitution.

Except for the rights to assemble and petition, all of the provisions in this section have been the subject of judicial review. In general, Hawaii's supreme court has interpreted those clauses by balancing the rights of individuals against the interest of the government in promoting the general welfare because the

[3] See Sherry Border and Beverly Wee, "Hawaii's Equal Rights Amendment: Its Impact on Athletic Opportunities and Competition for Women," *University of Hawaii Law Review* 2 (1979): 97.

rights guaranteed have not been viewed as absolute or, in other words, as totally free from governmental restrictions.[4]

The Establishment Clause

Like its counterpart in the U.S. Bill of Rights, the first part of this section is referred to as the establishment clause and is intended to ensure separation between church and state. But unlike the federal Constitution, Hawaii's constitution includes additional related provisions that result in a more solid wall of separation. Part of Section 4 in Article VII, Taxation and Finance, states the following: "No tax shall be levied or appropriation of public money or property made, nor shall the public credit be used, directly or indirectly, except for a public purpose. No grant shall be made in violation of Section 4 of Article I of this constitution." And Section 1 of Article X, Education, includes this injunction: "nor shall public funds be appropriated for the support or benefit of any sectarian or private educational institution."

In *Spears v. Honda* (1968), Hawaii's supreme court relied primarily on Section 1 of Article X to strike down the use of public funds for public and nonpublic student bus transportation. It found the child benefit theory, used by the U.S. Supreme Court in *Everson v. Board of Education of Ewing Township* (1947) to uphold such a program under the First Amendment, inapplicable because the 1950 convention specifically rejected that approach when it included not only an establishment clause, but the other provisions as well.

In a later case, *Koolau Baptist Church v. Department of Labor and Industrial Relations* (1986), the court held that a statute requiring employers to contribute to the state's unemployment compensation fund on behalf of employees, when applied to a church, was not a violation of the establishment clause since it did not foster excessive entanglement.

Pointing to the essentially identical establishment clauses found in the Hawaii and federal constitutions, the U.S. District Court for the District of Hawaii found there is "no case law which leads to the conclusion that the Hawaii courts interpret the Hawaii Constitution differently than the federal courts interpret the United States Constitution in the limited area of Establishment Clause jurisdiction" (*Cammack v. Waihee*, 1987). Concluding that the purpose of a state statute establishing Good Friday as a state holiday was clearly secular, the *Cammack* court upheld the statute as permissible under the First Amendment.

---

[4] Cases decided under this section, since 1983, are discussed in Jeffrey S. Portnoy, "The Lum Court and the First Amendment," *University of Hawaii Law Review* 14 (1992): 395.

The Free Exercise Clause

Where the Hawaii Supreme Court has confronted free exercise of religion clause challenges to state statutes, it has ruled against those arguing a violation of that right. In 1970, the court found that because there was no compulsion or coercion involved, a program for public school sex education classes did not violate the free exercise right for those who "honestly believe that exposure to certain subjects covered within those courses is sinful or that sex education must be accompanied by moral instruction" (*Medeiros v. Kiyosaki*). Since *Medeiros*, the court has been guided by the U.S. Supreme Court in determining whether there is a violation of the freedom of religion clause, and in *State ex rel. Minami v. Andrews* (1982), it held that requiring a license to operate a private school does not violate the right to freedom of religion. Relying on *Minami*, the Hawaii Intermediate Court of Appeals ruled that the state's proscription of marijuana did not violate the religious beliefs of those practicing Hindu Tantrism (*State v. Blake*, 1985).

When geothermal energy, a very controversial political issue in Hawaii, was challenged under the free exercise clause, the supreme court ruled in the state's favor. The decision in *Dedman v. Board of Land and Natural Resources* (1987) upheld the issuance of permits for geothermal energy developments on the island of Hawaii because that action did not unconstitutionally infringe on the free exercise of religion by Pele practitioners who argued that

> the goddess Pele migrated to the Northwestern Hawaiian Islands from Tahiti. She then moved down the island chain until she reached the island of Hawaii where she lives today. Areas in the island chain where she attempted to establish herself are considered sacred [and] [d]evelopment of geothermal resources in the area . . . will impinge on their right to freely exercise their religion.

Dedman has been criticized, however, on the grounds that it is based on traditional reasoning, which is inappropriate in nontraditional sacred-site claims made by native American Indians and native Hawaiians, and which may "improperly deny claimants the full first amendment protections that they deserve."[5]

The Right to Free Speech

Hawaii's supreme court takes the position that First Amendment protections are not absolute and there are situations where speech may justifiably be suppressed (*State v. Bloss*, 1981). The court has recognized that there is a distinction between speech and conduct and that certain conduct is not protected. It has stated that any other conclusion would mean there is a limitless variety of conduct that can be labeled speech just because the conduct was intended to express an idea,

[5] Note, "Dedman v. Board of Land and Natural Resources: Native Hawaiian Sacred Site Claims," *University of Hawaii Law Review* 10 (1988): 392.

a concept specifically rejected not only by the U.S. Supreme Court, but by Hawaii's high court as well (*Kleinjans v. Lombardi*, 1970).

The court has also distinguished commercial speech from other forms of speech. In *State v. Bloss* (1981), it explained that while commercial speech enjoys protection under the right to free speech, it is given lesser protection than are other forms of expression.[6] Nevertheless, an ordinance prohibiting distribution of handbills was an invalid regulation of commercial speech. One year later, this was reaffirmed in *State v. Hawkins* (1982). (See the related discussion under Article IX, Section 7.) Although the right to free speech is meant to limit the government, there are situations where that right will be protected even if it is exercised on private property. But distribution of leaflets and other expressions of anti-abortion views in the interior walkway of a hospital's main entrance is not such a situation because this private property is not traditionally associated with the right to free speech (*Estes v. Kapiolani Women's and Children's Medical Center*, 1990).[7]

Two recent free speech decisions, one by the U.S. district court and one by the U.S. Court of Appeals for the Ninth Circuit, are noteworthy because of their potential impact on politics in the state. An ordinance banning outdoor political signs is unconstitutional because the ordinance was "*not* content-neutral and there are less drastic means available for accomplishing the legislature's purposes" (*Runyon v. Fast*, 1981) (emphasis in original) (see also Article IX, Section 7). A state statute forbidding public disclosure of complaints made to the State Ethics Commission violates the right to free speech (*Roe v. Akamine*, 1991; see also Article XIV).

Following the U.S. Supreme Court's reasoning, Hawaii's high court has found that the right to free speech does not protect obscenity (*State v. Manzo*, 1977). However, the state is restricted from using any procedures it might want in enforcing pornography laws because of the important relationship between the right to free speech and the right to freedom from unreasonable searches and seizures found in Article I, Section 7. In two 1981 decisions, *State v. Bumanglag* and *State v. Furuyama*, the court found that it is the judiciary, not the police, that must determine what is legitimate or illegitimate speech. Consequently, prior to any seizure of allegedly obscene material the judiciary must concur that it is obscene; until then, the materials are assumed to be protected. In these decisions the court acknowledged that it deviated from the course followed by some

---

[6] See Recent Developments, "Handbilling in Waikiki: The Right of Commercial Speech in Hawaii—State v. Bloss," *University of Hawaii Law Review* 6 (1984): 693; Note, "Metromedia, Inc. v. City of San Diego: The Conflict Between Aesthetic Zoning and Commercial Speech Protection; Hawaii's Billboard Law Under Fire," *University of Hawaii Law Review* 5 (1983): 79.

[7] See Note, "Estes v. Kapiolani Women's and Children's Medical Center: State Action and the Balance Between Free Speech and Private Property Rights in Hawaii," *University of Hawaii Law Review* 13 (1991): 233.

federal courts because it found that the suppression of illegally seized materials is the only effective sanction against infringement of the right to free speech and the right to freedom from unreasonable searches and seizures.

Seven years later, in one of its most noteworthy decisions, the court again considered the relationship between this section and another, the right to privacy found in Article I, Section 6. While concluding that the pornography statute is not overbroad or vague (and thus reaffirming *Manzo*), the court held in *State v. Kam* (1988) that the right to privacy guarantees individuals a right to view pornography in the privacy of their own home. (See Section 6 for further discussion of this case.)

Freedom of the Press

Hawaii's high court has followed the U.S. Supreme Court's guidance when considering libel actions against a newspaper publisher for allegedly defamatory statements (*Tagawa v. Maui Publishing Co.*, 1968). In *Cahill v. Hawaiian Paradise Park Corp.* (1975), the court declined to deviate from that path when it held that Hawaii's freedom of the press clause does not grant more extensive privileges to the news media than those guaranteed under the First Amendment.

SECTION 5

Due Process and Equal Protection. No person shall be deprived of life, liberty or property without due process of law, nor be denied the equal protection of the laws, nor be denied the enjoyment of the person's civil rights or be discriminated against in the exercise thereof because of race, religion, sex or ancestry.

No substantive changes have been made to this section since its inclusion in the Statehood Constitution. The wording of the due process clause is identical to that found in the Fifth and Fourteenth Amendments to the U.S. Constitution, and the Hawaii equal protection clause has its counterpart in the Fourteenth Amendment.

However, this section also includes language not found in the U.S. Constitution. It specifically spells out that civil rights cannot be abridged and that discrimination based on race, religion, sex, or ancestry is illegal, making explicit what the equal protection clause implies. Section 5 embodies the "public policy of the State of Hawaii disfavoring racial discrimination "and, taken in conjunction with various statutes, shows that the" strength of this expressed public policy against racial discrimination is beyond question" (*Hyatt Corp. v. Honolulu Liquor Commission*, 1987).

Considered fundamental rights in our democratic system, due process and equal protection are neither easy to define nor easy to implement. The judicial rulings mentioned below highlight the fact that Hawaii's court, like other state and federal courts, has distinguished what is and what is not required by these two important constitutional provisions.

Due Process

At its core, due process both guarantees that procedures must be followed to assure fairness and justice in judicial or administrative proceedings (procedural due process) and protects against unreasonable governmental infringement on fundamental rights (substantive due process).

Although most of the rights and procedures guaranteed in the U.S. Bill of Rights have been made applicable to the states through the Fourteenth Amendment due process clause, the Hawaii Supreme Court has repeatedly stated that the state's due process protection "is not necessarily limited to that provided by the fourteenth amendment" because it "can find independent constitutional consideration of our rights under the Hawaii Constitution and is guided by the principle that" '[t]he touchstone of due process is protection of the individual against arbitrary action of government.'" (*State v. Bernades*, 1990).

Fairness requires that there be an absence of actual bias when cases are tried, and the legal system has always aimed at preventing even a possibility of unfairness (*State v. Brown*, 1989). Thus, due process is intended to guarantee procedures resulting in fair trials. For example, in one of its most significant decisions, *State v. Santiago* (1971), the court held that allowing the introduction of prior convictions in a criminal case, in order to prove the defendant's testimony is not credible, is a violation of due process (*Santiago* is further discussed under Section 10).

A more recent, and controversial, decision involved a fifteen-year-old rape victim. When she testified at the trial, a representative of a victim assistance program first sat next to her and later, while standing behind the witness chair, placed her hands on the victim's shoulders. The court, in *State v. Suka* (1989), concluded that because such actions were not necessary in order for the victim to continue testifying, they bolstered the victim's credibility and were thus prejudicial to the defendant, violating the due process right to a fair and impartial trial.[8] In a footnote, the court did, however, indicate that were a younger victim accompanied by a parent or other close relative, this would be less prejudicial because it would be interpreted as giving support, rather than lending credibility.

Numerous decisions have dealt with other procedural aspects of criminal trials. For example, if the prosecution suppresses evidence favorable to an

---

[8] See Recent Developments, "State v. Suka: Balancing the Need for Witness Accompaniment Against Its Prejudicial Effect," *University of Hawaii Law Review* 12 (1990): 461. See also Sue Ann Gregory, "Rape and Child Sexual Assault: Women's Perspectives Required to Dispel the Myths," *University of Hawaii Law Review* 14 (1992): 157.

accused where that evidence is material either to the guilt or to punishment, the due process right to a fair trial is violated, regardless of the good or bad faith of the prosecution (*State v. Moriwake,* 1990). Should the suppressed evidence not be material, no violation has taken place (*State v. Kaiu,* 1984). Nor does a violation occur when evidence is destroyed if there is no showing of bad faith on the part of the prosecution and the evidence was not favorable to the defense (*State v. Matafeo,* 1990).

Due process includes a right to confront witnesses (*State v. Calbero,* 1989), although there is no right per se to examine witnesses at a pre-trial suppression hearing (*State v. Mitake,* 1981). Once a defendant gives the government the names of alibi witnesses, there is a reciprocal right to obtain the names of those witnesses the government intends to call for rebutting or discrediting the alibi witnesses (*State v. Davis,* 1981).

As a final example of procedural due process in criminal cases, mention must be made of *State v. Faafiti* (1973). In that case, the court held that, while a judge must appoint an interpreter when a defendant cannot understand and speak English, the judge has the discretion whether or not to do so if a defendant has some knowledge of English and is reasonably able to converse in it. In one of those rare flashes of subtle humor incorporated into a judicial decision, the court asked, "[H]ow many of us even though educated in the United States are *completely* familiar with the English language?" (emphasis in original) and appended a footnote to add: "This fact is substantiated in decisions of this court and other supreme courts which show obvious grammatical errors."

Quasi-judicial hearings do not require observance of all the procedural due process rights that must be adhered to in a court of law (*Sandy Beach Defense Fund v. City Council of City and County of Honolulu,* 1989). But administrative convenience or even necessity cannot take precedence over the basics of due process (*Yamada v. Natural Disaster Claims Commission,* 1973), such as adequate notice, an opportunity to be heard, and decision making that is not based on unreasonable, arbitrary, capricious, or discriminatory considerations (*Silver v. Queen's Hospital,* 1981). To determine what specific procedures are required, the court will balance the private interest that will be affected; the risk of an erroneous deprivation of such interest through the procedures actually used and the probable value, if any, of additional or alternative procedural safeguards; and the governmental interest, including the burden that additional procedural safeguards entail (*Medeiros v. Hawaii County Planning Commission,* 1990).

With respect to substantive due process, the court has held that while the right to work is ensured by due process (*Maeda v. Amemiya,* 1979), requiring the retirement of all public employees at age seventy is not a violation. Even though such a law affects an individual's freedom to work, it has a fair and substantial relationship to an important governmental interest (*Daoang v. Department of Education,* 1981). (The statute requiring retirement at seventy was subsequently repealed in 1984.) Over the years, the court has invalidated statutes on due process grounds because the right requires legislative enactments to provide fair warning of proscribed conduct and clear guidelines to prevent arbitrary application and enforcement (see, e.g., *State v. Albano*, 1984). However, in some instances, statutory provisions have withstood challenges based on vagueness (see, e.g., *State v. Kameenui*, 1988).

Equal Protection

The essence of equal protection is that all persons similarly situated will be treated alike (*Mahiai v. Suwa*, 1987). It does not mean that all discrimination and classifications are impermissible. In its 1989 *Sandy Beach Defense Fund* decision, the court explained that "equal protection does not mandate that all laws apply with universality to all persons [for] the State 'cannot function without classifying its citizens for various purposes and treating some differently from others.'" But the court also made it clear that when the legislature does create classifications, it may not do so arbitrarily or in a capricious manner and that the classifications must be reasonably related to the purpose of the legislation.

Following the guidance of the U.S. Supreme Court, the court will evaluate a statute challenged under equal protection by using either the strict scrutiny test or the rational basis test (*Sandy Beach Defense Fund*). Previously, in *Nagle v. Board of Education* (1981), the difference between these two standards was clearly described:

> Under the strict scrutiny standard, the State carries a heavy burden in arguing for the validity of a statute. . . . A court will carefully examine a statute to determine whether it furthers compelling state interests and is narrowly drawn to avoid unnecessary abridgement of constitutional rights. . . . As a standard for judicial review, the strict scrutiny test is applicable where equal protection challenges involve "suspect" classifications or fundamental rights. Where "suspect" classifications or fundamental rights are not at issue, this court has traditionally employed the rational basis test. . . . Under that test, the court essentially asks whether a statute rationally furthers a legitimate state interest. . . . In making this inquiry, a court will not look for empirical data in support of the statute. It will only seek to determine whether any reasonable justification can be conceived to uphold the legislative enactment.

Where it has used the rational basis test, the court has, in some cases, found no violation of equal protection (see, e.g., *Sandy Beach Defense Fund*), while in other instances, it has found a violation because no rational reason existed for the classification (see, e.g., *Shibuya v. Architects Hawaii Ltd.*, 1982).

A claim that the "right to work" is a fundamental right and that laws impinging on it ought to be examined under the strict scrutiny test has not found favor with the court; where economic interests are concerned, it will utilize the rational basis test (*Maeda v. Amemiya*, 1979). The court has also rejected arguments that age is a suspect category. Although the statute at issue was repealed in 1984, the court earlier upheld the requirements that public employees retire at age seventy (*Daoang v. Department of Education*, 1981) and that public school teachers retire at age sixty-five (*Nagle v. Board of Education*, 1981) as having a rational basis.

In addition, the court has declined to find that poverty is a suspect classification which requires use of the more stringent strict scrutiny standards, rather than the rational basis standard. Use of the less rigorous test led the court in *Nachtwey v. Doi* (1978) to conclude that equal protection was not violated by requiring indigent political candidates to obtain a prescribed percentage of voter signatures in order to have their names placed on the ballot because there is a rational basis supporting such a requirement. However, in *Joshua v. MTL* (1982), the court found that there was no rational basis for a no-fault insurance law's discriminatory effect on indigents.

In both *State v. Rivera* (1980) and *Holdman v. Olim* (1978), litigants argued that sex-based classifications were inherently suspect and required use of the strict scrutiny test because Section 5 specifically lists sex along with race, religion, and ancestry and because the constitution also includes an equality of rights provision (Section 3). The court did not agree. In *Rivera*, the court stated that to "withstand judicial scrutiny under the equal protection clause, a sex-based distinction 'must serve important governmental objectives and must be substantially related to achievement of those objectives.'" As it had explained in the earlier *Holdman* decision, this is a standard "in between" the rational basis and the strict scrutiny tests. (See also the discussion under Section 3, "Equality of Rights.")

Equal protection may be denied when a law, neutral on its face, is administered in such a way as to unjustly discriminate between persons in similar circumstances. Proof of such an allegation requires that the plaintiff satisfy a two-part test, showing (1) that the law has not been enforced against others similarly situated and (2) that the enforcement was purposefully based on an unjustifiable standard such as race, religion, or other arbitrary classification (*Mahiai v. Suwa*, 1987).

In two recent cases, the Hawaii Supreme Court considered the use of peremptory challenges to potential jurors and in both instances found violations of equal protection. The rule of law adopted in *State v. Batson* (1990) is that "whenever the prosecution so exercises its peremptory challenges as to exclude entirely from the jury all persons who are of the same ethnical minority as the defendant, and that exclusion is challenged by the defense, there will be an inference that the exclusion was racially motivated, and the prosecutor must, to the satisfaction of the court, explain his or her challenges on a non-ethnical basis."

A few months later, this rule was expanded to include gender, religion, and ancestry in addition to race. In *State v. Levinson* (1990), the defense attorney excluded female jurors (the defendant was accused of murdering his wife). Excluding women jurors solely because of their gender denied them equal protection, the court held, because the constitution guarantees the right to serve on a jury as a privilege of citizenship.[9] This right cannot be taken away because of race, religion, sex, or ancestry, and when there is a prima facie case that peremptory challenges by the defense discriminate against potential jurors on one of these prohibited bases, the trial judge must require an explanation that demonstrates that the challenge is not discriminatory.

In 1991, Hawaii's statutory provisions delineating illegal employment practices were amended to include "sexual orientation" (Haw. Rev. Stat. § 378-1 and § 378-2). As of the following year, only seven states had passed such legislation.[10] When challenged in the U.S. District Court for the District of Hawaii, the case was dismissed for lack of ripeness (*Voluntary Association of Religious Leaders, Churches, and Organizations v. Waihee*, 1992). However, a challenge to the law's scope, possibly based on equal protection grounds, may come before the state courts in the not-too-distant future.

SECTION 6

> **Right to Privacy**. The right of the people to privacy is recognized and shall not be infringed without the showing of a compelling state interest. The legislature shall take affirmative steps to implement this right.

The history of this section is closely tied in to what is now Section 7, "Searches, Seizures and Invasion of Privacy." Section 6 was added in 1978 with the intention of reducing confusion about the scope of new phrases added ten years earlier to the provision on searches and seizures.[11] As the 1978 Convention's Committee Report explained:

> In 1968 the Constitution was amended to include the prohibition against unreasonable invasions of privacy, but its inclusion within a section patterned after the Fourth Amendment right against unreasonable searches and seizures and the debate during the 1968 constitutional convention have engendered some confusion as to the extent and scope of the right. Although it appears clear that the proponents of the concept saw the right as broader than one limited to protection against invasions of privacy in criminal cases, the convention devoted most of the debate to the relationship between the proposed amendment and concern over wiretapping. This has led the Hawaii supreme court to state that the privacy right emanated from a concern over extensive use of electronic surveillance, thus limiting the right to privacy by implying that it did not encompass the concept of a right to personal autonomy. . . . Thus it may be

---

[9] See Recent Developments, "State v. Levinson: Limitations on a Criminal Defendant's Use of Peremptory Challenges," *University of Hawaii Law Review* 13 (1991): 279.

[10] "Gay Job Bias is Outlawed in California," *Honolulu Star-Bulletin*, 26 September 1992, A-1.

[11] See Note, "The Tort of Invasion of Privacy in Hawaii," *University of Hawaii Law Review* 1 (1979): 127.

> unclear whether the present privacy provision [in Section 7] extends beyond the criminal area.[12]

The 1978 convention, therefore, decided to leave the section on "Searches, Seizure and Invasion of Privacy" untouched, with the understanding that it was limited to criminal cases, but to add a new section relating to privacy in the informational and personal autonomy sense. Aware that the right of privacy has various meanings, the convention's standing committee believed it necessary to be explicit about the intended scope and nature of the new provision, and its report goes into considerable detail regarding such areas as the common law right of privacy or tort privacy, the issue of informational privacy, the right to be left alone, and the right to control highly personal and intimate affairs.

After the convention, acting as a committee of the whole, adopted the proposed new section, its report explained that the two privacy provisions were not to be construed as identical in intent. The language in Section 7, prohibiting unreasonable searches and seizures and invasion of privacy, was not to be viewed as granting fundamental rights, but rather as protecting against unreasonable searches and seizures in light of the U.S. Supreme Court's use of a reasonable expectation of privacy concept. With respect to the proposed new section, the Committee of the Whole Report stated:

> By amending the Constitution to include a separate and distinct privacy right, it is the intent of your Committee to insure that privacy is treated as a fundamental right for purposes of constitutional analysis. Privacy as used in this sense concerns the possible abuses in the use of highly personal intimate information in the hands of government or private parties but is not intended to deter the government from the legitimate compilation and dissemination of data. More importantly, this privacy concept encompasses the notion that in certain highly personal and intimate matters, the individual should be afforded freedom of choice absent a compelling state interest. This right is similar to the privacy right discussed [by the U.S. Supreme Court] in cases such as *Griswold v. Connecticut, . . . Eisenstadt v. Baird, . . .* [and] *Roe v. Wade, ...* It is a right that, though unstated in the federal Constitution, emanates from the penumbra of several guarantees of the Bill of Rights. . . . By inserting clear and specific language regarding this right into the Constitution, your Committee intends to alleviate any possible confusion over the source of the right and the existence of it.[13]

The 1978 delegates also made it clear that they did not intend to create an absolute right to privacy that could never be infringed on. However, by including

---

[12] *Constitutional Convention, 1978 Proceedings* (Honolulu: State of Hawaii, 1980), vol. I, *Journal and Documents* (hereinafter cited as *1978 Proceedings I*), Standing Committee Report no. 69, 674.

[13] *1978 Proceedings I*, Committee of the Whole Report no. 15, 1024.

language requiring a showing of a compelling state interest, the provision places a heavy burden on the government when it justifies any challenged restriction.

In light of concerns that the current U.S. Supreme Court will reject the idea that a right to privacy, with respect to reproductive rights, is guaranteed under the U.S. Constitution, some in Hawaii argue that Section 6 will protect the right to abortion within the state. This argument is based on the convention's specific reference to the *Roe v. Wade* (1973) decision in defining the section's scope, thus indicating the framers' intent to protect a woman's right to choose. When Hawaii repealed its anti-abortion law in 1970 (three years before the *Roe* decision), it was one of the first states to do so.[14] Although there is a vocal lobbying effort within Hawaii for limiting or prohibiting abortion, the legislature has so far declined to reverse its earlier action.

The Hawaii Supreme Court's decisions in *Medeiros v. Kiyosaki* (1970) and *State v. Renfro* (1975) were based on the approach taken by the U.S. Supreme Court—that is, a constitutional penumbra protected privacy from governmental intrusion. That principle, as applied in *Medeiros*, did not support a claim that the right of privacy was violated by the showing of sex education films in public schools and, as applied in *Renfro*, did not support a claim that privacy was infringed on when the legislature proscribed the possession of marijuana for private use.

In *Medeiros*, the court recognized that Hawaii's citizens were afforded a specific right of privacy because of the 1968 amendment to Section 7 which added the right to be secure against invasions of privacy to the already existing "search and seizure" section. However, in 1973, those new words were narrowly interpreted as intended only to protect against extensive governmental use of electronic surveillance techniques (*State v. Roy*), and it was this limiting view that provided the fuel for the 1978 convention action which resulted in a new privacy section.

Not long after the separate right to privacy was added to the constitution, the Hawaii Supreme Court reviewed the convention proceedings and made a point of distinguishing Sections 6 and 7. In *State v. Lester* (1982), the court explained that Section 6 relates to privacy in the informational and personal autonomy sense and is concerned with possible abuses of highly personal and intimate information by government or private parties. On the other hand, Section 7 is limited to criminal cases and relates to the reasonable expectation of privacy, where privacy is considered not a fundamental right, but rather a prohibition against unreasonable searches and seizures. A few years later, in *State v. Okubo* (1982), the intermediate court of appeals repeated this distinction; when the supreme court affirmed *Okubo*, in 1984, it did so without discussing the distinction (see Section 7 for further discussion).[15]

---

[14] For a study of the history of the repeal, see Patricia G. Steinhoff and Milton Diamond, *Abortion Politics, The Hawaii Experience* (Honolulu: University Press of Hawaii, 1977).

[15] See Recent Developments, "Electronic Eavesdropping: Which Conversations Are Protected from Interception?—State v. Okubo and State v. Lee," *University of Hawaii Law Review 1* (1985): 227.

The court has also declared it is not bound by U.S. Supreme Court precedents since Section 6 affords a much greater scope to privacy rights than does the U.S. Constitution. As "the ultimate judicial tribunal with final, unreviewable authority to interpret and enforce the Hawaii Constitution, [it is] free to give broader privacy protection than that given by the federal constitution" (*State v. Kam*, 1988).

Recently the court characterized its holdings, under Section 6, as protecting at least two different kinds of interests. The first is "the individual's interest in avoiding disclosure of personal matters," while the second concerns "freely making certain kinds of important personal decisions" (*McCloskey v. Honolulu Police Department*, 1990).

With respect to the interest in avoiding disclosure of personal matters, *Nakano v. Matayoshi* (1985) raised the issue of whether financial disclosure by public employees, as mandated by county codes of ethics enacted pursuant to Article XIV of the state constitution, violates the right to privacy. In its decision, the court found that, based on the intentions expressed by the 1978 convention, the people of Hawaii have a legitimate expectation of privacy where their personal financial affairs are concerned. However, an employee of the state or one of its political subdivisions cannot reasonably expect privacy in financial affairs to the same degree as expected by other citizens because the same convention that added the new privacy section also proposed constitutional language subjecting public employees to an ethics code.

While recognizing that the right to privacy protects the ability to make certain kinds of important decisions regarding personal autonomy, the court, in *State v. Mueller* (1983), refused to hold that a decision to engage in sex for hire in the privacy of one's own home is a fundamental right deserving protection. In its most recent privacy decision, the court, following a majority of the states and the U.S. Supreme Court, ruled that no reasonable expectation of privacy exists in personal bank records (*State v. Klattenhoff*, 1990).

However, the previous year, in *State v. Rothman* (1989), the court refused to follow the U.S. Supreme Court's ruling that installing pen registers—a device that allows identification of outgoing and incoming telephone numbers—was not a search requiring a warrant under the Fourth Amendment.[16] The court noted that even if it were willing to adopt such an approach under Hawaii's search and seizure provision, it could not do so because Section 6 expressly establishes a right of privacy. Under the right, persons using telephones in Hawaii "have a reasonable expectation of privacy, with respect to the telephone numbers they call on their private lines, and with respect to the telephone numbers of calls made to them on their private lines."

---

[16] See Note, "State v. Rothman: Expanding the Individual's Right to Privacy Under the Hawaii Constitution," *University of Hawaii Law Review* 13 (1991): 619.

Decisions in two cases have rested on the court's consideration of a "compelling state interest" as balanced against a claim of right to privacy. In its pathbreaking *State v. Kam* (1988) decision, the court reviewed the 1978 convention proceedings and found that it clearly intended that a compelling state interest must exist before the government can intrude into certain highly personal and intimate affairs of life.[17] The question posed in *Kam* was, "[W]hat should take precedence: [the] State's police power to regulate obscene material versus an individual's fundamental privacy right to have pornography at home?"

The court found it obvious "that an adult person cannot read or view pornographic material in the privacy of his or her own home if the government prosecutes the sellers of the pornography." And, since "a person has the right to view pornographic items at home, there necessarily follows a correlative right to purchase such materials for this personal use, or the underlying privacy right becomes meaningless." Because Section 6 incorporates the privacy right to read or view pornographic material in one's home, that right can only be infringed on if the state shows a compelling state interest; the state was unable to satisfy the court that there was such a compelling interest.

Significantly, the court added a footnote carefully limiting its holding. It was not reaching any conclusion as to the state's compelling interest in certain types of obscenity cases such as banning child pornography, selling pornography to minors, and showing pornography to a captive audience and regulating pornography by zoning areas for adult businesses.

In contrast to *Kam* is the decision in *McCloskey v. Honolulu Police Department* (1990), where drug testing by the police department was upheld as serving three compelling interests: ensuring that the police officers perform their duties safely, protecting the public's safety, and preserving the integrity of the department and its ability to perform its job effectively. Although the appellant did not rely on the U.S. Constitution, the court felt it important to note that the U.S. Supreme Court "has expressly held that drug screening tests at the work place do not per se violate the fourth amendment to the federal constitution."

Section 6 mandates that the legislature take affirmative steps to implement the right to privacy. An example of legislative action in this regard can be found in the Uniform Information Practices Act (Haw. Rev. Stat. ch. 92F), where it provides that all government records are open to public inspection, but specifies exceptions such as when disclosure of governmental records would constitute a clearly unwarranted invasion of personal privacy (Haw. Rev. Stat. ch. 92F-13).

---

[17] See Note, "State v. Kam: The Constitutional Status of Obscenity in Hawaii," *University of Hawaii Law Review* 11 (1989): 253; for a discussion of a case two years earlier involving the same litigants where the Hawaii Supreme Court ruled that in a prosecution for promotion of pornography the jury must be specifically instructed to find that a contemporary community standard exists and the materials violated it, see Recent Developments, "Criminal Law—State v. Kam: Do Community Standards on Pornography Exist?" *University of Hawaii Law Review* 9 (1987): 727.

The statute also provides that disclosure shall not constitute a clearly unwarranted invasion of personal privacy if the public interest in disclosure outweighs the privacy interests of the individual and enumerates examples of information where the individual has a significant privacy interest (i.e., information relating to one's medical, psychiatric, or psychological history) (Haw. Rev. Stat. ch. 92F-14).

SECTION 7

> **Searches, Seizures and Invasion of Privacy.** The right of the people to be secure in their persons, houses, papers and effects against unreasonable searches, seizures and invasions of privacy shall not be violated; and no warrants shall issue but upon probable cause, supported by oath or affirmation, and particularly describing the place to be searched and the persons or things to be seized or the communications sought to be intercepted.

When adopted at statehood, this section mirrored the Fourth Amendment to the U.S. Constitution. Amendments in 1968 added two phrases: "and invasions of privacy" and "or the communications sought to be intercepted."

After the 1968 changes, as discussed above under Section 6, confusion existed as to whether the framers intended to add a broad or limited privacy right. Although Justice Bernard H. Levinson argued in a concurring opinion that the 1968 convention intended the new words to go beyond protecting against extensive governmental use of electronic surveillance techniques, the rest of the justices did not agree (*State v. Roy*, 1973). This led the 1978 convention to propose a new section specifically guaranteeing a right to privacy and to clarify their understanding that Section 7 would thus be limited to criminal cases. As also noted following Section 6, both the supreme court and the intermediate court of appeals have since recognized this distinction (*State v. Okubo*, 1982; *State v. Lester*, 1982).

The fundamental purpose behind the right to freedom from unreasonable searches and seizures is protecting individuals and their personal belongings from being searched or seized without a valid reason. It is intended to prohibit the government from what the Hawaii high court once described as a "veritable Easter egg hunt" to see if any incriminating evidence is there to be found (*State v. Joyner*, 1983).

Because this right only prohibits "unreasonable" searches and seizures, much of the case law, in Hawaii and elsewhere, focuses on determining what a reasonable search or seizure is where no warrant is necessary and where a warrant is required.

Fundamental to the court's approach is the principle that a search conducted without a warrant is initially presumed to be unreasonable (*State v. Perham*, 1991). While the court has recognized some exceptions (*State v. Wiley*, 1988), it has nevertheless emphasized that the government must show both that the facts of the case justify a warrantless police search and that the search was no broader than necessary in order to demonstrate why it departed from the warrant requirement in the first place (*State v. Perham*, 1991).

Where there is probable cause for an arrest, a search incidental to that arrest is reasonable, but such a search is limited in scope to what is reasonably necessary to discover the results or instruments of the crime for which the defendant is arrested, to protect police from attack, or to prevent an escape (*State v. Enos*, 1986). Warrantless searches have also been limited in scope to the person arrested and the area under that person's immediate control (*State v. Ritte*, 1985).

A warrantless search may be justified if the police have probable cause for the search (*State v. Wiley*, 1988); for example, where objects are in plain view (*State v. Barnett*, 1985). Exigent (urgent) circumstances may support a warrantless search (*State v. Wiley*, 1988); for example, when the police are in hot pursuit (*State v. Elderts*, 1980). Exigent circumstances are not present, however, when an individual has already been arrested and his or her belongings are under the control of law enforcement officers; in such situations, a warrant must be obtained before searching those items (*State v. Wiley*, 1988).

An important cluster of search and seizure cases revolves around the concept of a reasonable expectation of privacy. Where there is such an expectation, a warrantless search is deemed unreasonable and therefore invalid; when there is no such expectation, a warrantless search is permissible. To determine whether a reasonable expectation of privacy exists, the court uses the following test: (1) individuals must demonstrate an actual subjective expectation of privacy, and (2) that expectation must be one society recognizes as objectively reasonable (*State v. Biggar*, 1986). The court has also taken the nature of the place, the precautions taken to ensure privacy, and the position of the viewing government officer into account in deciding whether there is a reasonable expectation of privacy (*State v. Barnett*, 1985).

Hawaii decisions indicate that a reasonable expectation of privacy exists, for example, in personal telephone calls (*State v. Rothman*, 1989) (see also Section 6); in a toilet stall, particularly where the door to the stall was closed (*State v. Biggar*, 1986);[18] where officers came upon the defendant who was outside her home in the nude, a fence bounded the land from the only direction from which public access was possible, and the marijuana plants were not visible from the road or air (*State v. Barnett*, 1985); in closed trash bags (*State v. Tanaka*, 1985); in luggage (*State v. Rosoborough*, 1980); where there were thick and tall grasses preventing the police from seeing the marijuana except by climbing the fence (*State v. Render*, 1978); in a locked shed, even if it was possible to look inside (*State v. Hook*, 1978); where drapes and venetian blinds covering a window were closed

[18] See Recent Developments, "Search and Seizure—State v. Biggar: A Reasonable Expectation of Privacy in a Public Restroom," *University of Hawaii Law Review* 9 (1987): 753.

(*State v. Kaaneena,* 1978); and where there was a fence of lapped construction, making observation through it almost impossible (*State v. Boynton,* 1978). An individual's expectation of privacy is, however, diminished with respect to automobiles (*State v. Wong,* 1985) and to lost property (*State v. Ching,* 1984).

Courts have determined there is no expectation of privacy, for example, in personal bank records (*State v. Klattenhoff,* 1990); in a backyard where, even though there was a fence and the marijuana plants could not be seen from the road, the defendants had not built the fence or made any repairs to it or attempted to provide any other screen from the neighbor's yard (*State v. Jensen,* 1988); when conversations were recorded and one participant in the conversation consented to the recordings (*State v. Lee,* 1984); in a knapsack that the police officer had properly seized (*State v. Ortiz,* 1984); in the airspace surrounding luggage (*State v. Snitkin,* 1984); and when individuals knowingly display objects to the public, even in their own home or office (*State v. Kapoi,* 1981). Although in some instances there may be a reasonable expectation of privacy in the airspace overhead, this is not true for observation carried out by police helicopter from a reasonable height without aerial harassment or prolonged aerial surveillance (*State v. Stachler,* 1977).[19]

State v. Kaluna (1974) is often referred to when the court explains that Section 7 can guarantee greater protection than does the Fourth Amendment of the U.S. Constitution. Recently reaffirming *Kaluna,* the court explained, in *State v. Perham* (1991),

> We note that the Fourth Amendment to the United States Constitution does not require police to use less intrusive means to safeguard an arrestee's property. . . . However, in *Kaluna* we held that our state constitution provision protecting individuals from unreasonable searches and seizures provides greater protections from inventory searches than the Fourth Amendment. *Kaluna* held that less intrusive means of accomplishing the State's purpose must be used if feasible.

Perham, like *Kaluna,* involved a pre-incarceration search. The court made it clear that while police are justified in requiring individuals to empty their pockets in order to prevent dangerous items and contraband from being taken into jail, this cannot justify searching an item once it is surrendered because, as *Kaluna* held, the less intrusive method of meeting the state's purpose must be used where possible. In a strong rebuke, the court emphasized that "despite the fact that *Kaluna* has never been overruled in its 16-year history," there was no indication the police were using less intrusive procedures.

In *State v. Enos* (1986), the court ruled that in an arrest for drunken driving it is reasonable for officers to conduct a pat-down for weapons since they have the

---

[19] See Recent Developments, "Search and Seizure: A Reduced Reasonable Expectation of Privacy—State v. Ching; State v. Snitkin; State v. Ortiz," *University of Hawaii Law Review* 7 (1985): 557.

right to protect themselves.[20] However, where there is no justification, the police cannot search further. The court explicitly acknowledged that the U.S. Supreme Court had found such further search and seizure permissible under the Fourth Amendment; nevertheless, a warrantless search and seizure, beyond a pat-down for weapons, is a violation of the Hawaii Constitution.

In *State v. Kim* (1985), Hawaii's supreme court pointed out that while the U.S. Supreme Court found police have the power to order a driver out of a car when stopped only for a traffic violation, Hawaii's constitution, in contrast, requires officers to have, at a minimum, some reasonable basis of "specific articulable facts" to believe a crime has been committed before ordering the driver out of the car.

One of the court's most significant decisions is that of *State v. Tanaka* (1985).[21] Notwithstanding federal appellate court holdings that, under the Fourth Amendment, society is not prepared to recognize expectations of privacy in garbage, Hawaii's Section 7 "recognizes an expectation of privacy beyond the parallel provisions in the Federal Bill of Rights." As the court explained:

> People reasonably believe that police will not indiscriminately rummage through their trash bags to discover their personal effects. Business records, bills, correspondence, magazines, tax records, and other telltale refuse can reveal much about a person's activities, associations, and beliefs. If we were to hold otherwise, police could search everyone's trash bags on their property without any reason and thereby learn of their activities, associations, and beliefs. It is exactly this type of overboard governmental intrusion that article 1, [section] 7 of the Hawaii constitution was intended to prevent.

Recently, in *State v. Quino* (1992), the court continued to broaden the coverage of the state constitution beyond that protected by the U.S. Constitution and once again parted ways with the nation's High Court. *Quino* involved a police drug interdiction program, used at the Honolulu airport, called "walk and talk." It did "not employ any type of 'drug courier profile' or require the officers to have a reasonable suspicion that a person may be in possession of illegal drugs, or may be engaged in criminal activity." Rather, "members of the detail [were] trained to engage in 'consensual encounters' whereby airline passengers [were] approached and, in a 'conversational manner,' requested to consent to a search of their luggage or person." The court found that in such "staged police-citizen" encounters, the police controlled the interaction although no physical force was used and that a reasonable person would not believe it possible to ignore the officer's

[20] See Recent Developments, "Search and Seizure—State v. Enos: Reaffirming the Narrow Interpretation of the 'Incident to Lawful Arrest' Exception," *University of Hawaii Law Review* 9 (1987): 761.

[21] See Recent Developments, "State v. Tanaka: How Reasonable Is an Expectation of Privacy in Trash?" *University of Hawaii Law Review* 8 (1986): 643.

questions and walk away. Concluding that the program violated the Section 7 right against unreasonable seizures, the court declared:

> We cannot allow the police to randomly "encounter" individuals without any objective basis for suspecting them of misconduct and then place them in a coercive environment in order to develop reasonable suspicion to justify their detention. This investigative technique is based on the proposition that an otherwise innocent person, who comes under policy scrutiny for no good reason, is not innocent unless he or she convinces the police that he or she is. Such a procedure is anathema to our constitutional freedoms.

SECTION 8

Rights of Citizens. No citizen shall be disfranchised, or deprived of any of the rights or privileges secured to other citizens, unless by the law of the land.

This section has been carried over verbatim since the Statehood Constitution. When the 1950 framers used the phrase "law of the land," they believed that it meant the same as "due process of law." That is, the government could not act arbitrarily in depriving one of rights and privileges. Thus, the section overlaps with the due process clause found in Section 5. However, the primary focus here is on voting, for there is specific reference to protecting "citizens" from being disenfranchised unless by the law of the land (i.e., due process).

The one significant decision by the Hawaii Supreme Court centering on this section came in *Mink v. Pua* (1985). At issue was whether a provision in the Honolulu City Charter violated Section 8 by disqualifying councilmembers who lose their positions at a recall election from running in a special election to fill the vacancies in the unexpired terms created by their being recalled. The court held the disqualification neither disenfranchised nor deprived the recalled councilmembers of any rights or privileges secured to other citizens except by the law of the land. "State and local governments have obvious and legitimate interests in provisions limiting an office holder's right to reelection or reappointment," the court stated. To illustrate, it referred to Article V, Section 1, limiting the governor to two consecutive terms, and made it clear that its decision was based on the assumption that those who take office know and accept such requirements and are therefore subject to them.

SECTION 9

Enlistment; Segregation. No citizen shall be denied enlistment in any military organization of this State nor be segregated therein because of race, religious principles or ancestry.

Substantively, this section remains the same as it was in the Statehood Constitution. The 1950 delegates wanted to make certain their "hope chest" constitution would present a strong statement against discrimination, and this section clearly reflects distaste for the U.S. military's unequal treatment of Americans of Japanese ancestry, living in Hawaii, during World War II.

Although the due process and equal protection provisions included specific words prohibiting the denial of rights and discrimination based on race, religion, sex, or ancestry, this section prohibiting discrimination in any state military organization, as well as other provisions, was included in the constitution because the framers wanted to be explicit in delineating the impermissible. The constitution also has a provision, found in the article dealing with education (now Article X), stating that there shall be no discrimination in public educational institutions because of race, religion, sex, or ancestry. In addition, another provision prohibited disqualification from jury service on the basis of sex (this was former Section 12 of the bill of rights that was subsequently deleted; the reasons and wording can be found in the commentary following Section 12 below).

SECTION 10

Indictment; Preliminary Hearing; Double Jeopardy; Self-Incrimination. No person shall be held to answer for a capital or otherwise infamous crime, unless on a presentment or indictment of a grand jury or upon a finding of probable cause after a preliminary hearing held as provided by law, except in cases arising in the armed forces when in actual service in time of war or public danger; nor shall any person be subject for the same offense to be twice put in jeopardy; nor shall any person be compelled in any criminal case to be a witness against oneself.

Like some of the other rights guaranteed in Article I, those in this section, and their counterparts in the Fifth Amendment of the federal Bill of Rights, are designed to check the misuse of the judiciary for persecution, rather than proper prosecution. To this end, limits are placed on the government's ability to charge individuals with a crime, to try individuals repeatedly in the hope of eventually getting a conviction, and to base a case on information forced from the accused. Only one substantive change has been made to this section since its original adoption.

Grand Jury and Preliminary Hearing

Prior to 1982, this section mirrored the Fifth Amendment of the U.S. Constitution in requiring that an individual be formally charged with a capital or otherwise infamous crime—that is, a felony—only by a grand jury. The grand jury, long a part of Anglo-American judicial tradition, protects citizens from hasty, malicious, and oppressive persecution and plays the all-important role of standing between the accuser and the accused (*State v. Pacific Concrete & Rock Co.*, 1977). Made up of citizens selected in the same random manner as are petit jurors for a trial, the grand jury determines whether there is probable cause to issue a formal charge against an individual. Depending on whether the grand jury itself or the prosecutor initiates the case, the formal charge handed down is referred to as a presentment or as an indictment, respectively. Grand juries can, of course, refuse to find probable cause; in such a case, a "no true bill" is issued.

States are not limited to the grand jury process because the Fifth Amendment right to a grand jury has never been made applicable to the states via the Fourteenth Amendment. In 1982, Hawaii's voters approved a legislatively proposed amendment adding the words "or upon a finding of probable cause after a preliminary hearing held as provided by law." In making this change, Hawaii joined about half the states in allowing an alternative process for bringing criminal charges, which provides for a preliminary hearing before a judge alone to determine whether probable cause exists to proceed. The formal charge is then called an information.

Where Section 10 exempts cases arising in the armed forces when in actual service in time of war or public danger, it follows the language found in the Fifth Amendment. However, in the Hawaii Constitution, this exception now includes both the grand jury and the preliminary hearing procedures. Although this section refers to capital crimes, Hawaii has not used capital punishment since it was abolished by the territorial legislature in 1957.

When considering cases, a grand jury must not be burdened by external influences, for its independence must be safeguarded (*State v. Pacific Concrete & Rock Co.*, 1977). But the grand jury hearing is not intended to be a minitrial, and it is not required to consider any and all evidence tending to exculpate the defendant; however, if the evidence clearly establishes self-defense, the prosecutor must explain its significance (*State v. Bell*, 1978).[22] Similarly, if the evidence shows that the defendant committed only a lesser offense, this must be explained (*State v. O 'Daniel*, 1980). Hearsay may be used by the grand jury as long as it is not deliberately used to improve the case for an indictment (*State v. Miyazaki*, 1982).

Double Jeopardy

The right against double jeopardy is intended to prohibit multiple prosecutions and thus guard against oppression by the government (*State v. Lemalu*, 1991). It protects against a second prosecution for the same offense when there is an

[22] See David Bettencourt and Duff Zwald, "The Prosecutor's Duty to Disclose Exculpatory Evidence to the Grand Jury: Did the Hawaii Supreme Court Retreat from Fundamental Fairness?" *University of Hawaii Law Review* 2 (1979): 145.

acquittal determined by a jury verdict or by the court's direction, either after the prosecution has completed its case or after all evidence is presented (*State v. Dow*, 1991).

A question that often arises in double jeopardy cases is, When does jeopardy attach (i.e., at what point in the proceedings is the individual placed in "danger" such that the right cannot be infringed)? Jeopardy attaches when a court, trying a case without a jury, begins to hear evidence or, in a jury trial, when the jury is impaneled and sworn in (*State v. Martin*, 1980). Once jeopardy has attached, if the prosecution wishes to terminate a case with a nolle prosequi entered with the consent of the defendant, subsequent prosecution for the same offense is not necessarily forbidden; however, if the nolle prosequi is entered over defense objections, not only must the prosecution be terminated, but also a subsequent trial for the same offense cannot occur (*State v. Murray*, 1988). Where the prosecution is granted a nolle prosequi without notice to the defendant and without a hearing, in order to substitute a new indictment on charges that would result in a more severe sentence, a new trial under that indictment constitutes double jeopardy (*State v. Estrada*, 1990).

The question of double jeopardy comes into play when a judge rules that there has been a mistrial, thus bringing a trial to a halt. According to *State v. Hoke* (1987), double jeopardy rights are considered properly waived when a defendant successfully moves for a mistrial, but re-prosecution cannot take place when the defense motion is a necessary response to judicial or prosecutorial misconduct intended to deny the right to a fair trial. In so ruling, the *Hoke* court reaffirmed its 1977 *State v. Pulawa* decision and declined to adopt "a more liberal test that would expand the instances wherein a reprosecution will be barred."

Although holding that double jeopardy does not require the dismissal of an indictment after two trials, both resulting in hung juries, the court, in *State v. Moriwake* (1982), added a footnote expressing disbelief in the idea that "an infinite number of retrials, whatever the reason, are consistent with double jeopardy principles." Acknowledging that there may be a breaking point, the court left the issue open for future determination.

Self-Incrimination

Often misunderstood, the privilege against self-incrimination is intended to protect individuals from being forced to testify against themselves in criminal cases by placing the burden of establishing a case on the state and thus preventing arbitrary use of power against individuals (*State v. Narvaez*, 1986). Determining the dimensions of this protection has spawned considerable case law; there is space here for highlighting only a few noteworthy decisions.

Following the U.S. Supreme Court's landmark ruling in *Miranda v. Arizona* (1966), the Hawaii Supreme Court in *State v. Santiago* (1971) declared that before any statements made by the accused during a custodial interrogation can be used at the trial, the state must show that certain safeguards were followed prior to the interrogation: that is, the accused must be warned that he or she has the right to remain silent, that anything said can be used against the individual, that he or she has a right to the presence of an attorney, and that an attorney will be appointed if the accused is unable to afford one.

Santiago was the first instance when the court considered the scope of the *Miranda* requirements, and it explicitly declined to follow the U.S. Supreme Court with respect to the extent *Miranda* applies when the credibility of a defendant, taking the witness stand, is under attack. If "the rationale underlying *Miranda* is sufficient to warrant the exclusion of prior statements from the prosecutor's case in chief," the court explained, "then that same rationale precludes use of those statements for impeachment." Unlike the U.S. Supreme Court, Hawaii's court held that unless the *Miranda* warnings are given, statements made by the accused cannot be used to impeach that person's credibility during rebuttal or cross-examination.

Santiago is also important because the court found the *Miranda* protections "have an independent source in the Hawaii Constitution's privilege against self-incrimination." This was reaffirmed thirteen years later when the court stated that it was "constrained to seek primary guidance from precepts enunciated in the seminal decision [*Santiago*], which have been incorporated into . . . our constitution, and our own cases rather than from later federal decisions" (*State v. Russo*, 1984).

In another notable decision, the court, in *State v. Miyasaki* (1980), upheld a challenge to a statutory provision allowing "use" and "derivative use" immunity (as contrasted with "transactional" immunity) for compelling testimony from a witness. The court ruled that use and derivative use immunity do not afford protection "coextensive" with the self-incrimination clause in Section 10. In so ruling, the court explained, the protection of Hawaii's self-incrimination clause is extended beyond that guaranteed by the U.S. Constitution since the U.S. Supreme Court has found this type of immunity sufficient for protecting the Fifth Amendment right against self-incrimination as made applicable to the states via the Fourteenth Amendment.

Three recent decisions illustrate additional aspects of the self-incrimination protection. In considering whether a statement made while in custody was offered freely and voluntarily, the court will examine the totality of circumstances (*State v. Villaza*, 1991). After being arrested, Villaza waived his *Miranda* rights. All his clothing except for his undershorts was taken away, and during the subsequent hour and forty-six minutes of questioning, his only other covering was a blanket. The court found that the denial of clothing could be, under certain circumstances, humiliating or used as a psychologically coercive tactic and condemned such police practices. Even so, it found that *Villaza* did not involve "outrageous factors," and, under the totality of circumstances, the confession was given freely and voluntarily.

Where a trial judge ordered the defendant to commence his defense before hearing all of the state's evidence against him, there is a violation of the right against self-incrimination. The defendant was entitled to have the state present its entire case against him before providing any evidence in his defense or deciding whether or not to take the witness stand (*State v. Grindles*, 1989). In *State v. Morris* (1991), the court ruled that requiring testing for drugs as part of probation does not violate the right against self-incrimination.

SECTION 11

Grand Jury Counsel. Whenever a grand jury is impaneled, there shall be an independent counsel appointed as provided by law to advise the members of the grand jury regarding matters brought before it. Independent counsel shall be selected from among those persons licensed to practice law by the supreme court of the State and shall not be a public employee. The term and compensation for independent counsel shall be as provided by law.

Throughout its long history, the grand jury has been often criticized, particularly in terms of being a mere rubber stamp or puppet of the prosecutor, in contrast to playing the independent role critics believe was intended. In the late 1960s and early 1970s considerable criticism was voiced, and allegations of prosecutorial misuse of grand juries for political purposes, especially at the federal level, received widespread coverage.[23]

Added in 1978, this section was intended to overcome a conflict present in the traditional role played by the prosecutor in grand jury proceedings. As a 1978 convention standing committee pointed out, while the prosecutor serves as the legal advisor to the grand jury, "there seems to be a conflict between presenting evidence to a grand jury in the hope they will return an indictment and being their legal advisor."[24] The committee also explained that under the new section, the independent counsel's role would be to advise the grand jury, but not any witnesses or the prosecutor. Although some delegates presented lively debate in opposition, they were unsuccessful in their attempt to deflect the adoption of this new section.

The framers specifically phrased the section so as to exclude public employees from serving as the grand jury counsel in order to avoid the incongruous possibility of a prosecutor or an attorney general being appointed. They intended that only private practitioners would be appointed so as to guarantee true independence. Legislation subsequently passed to implement this section provides

[23] For a review of the criticisms and relevant literature, see Anne Feder Lee, "The Grand Jury in Ohio: An Empirical Study," *University of Dayton Law Review* 4 (1979): 325.

[24] 1975 *Proceedings 1*, Standing Committee Report no. 69, 673.

for appointment, and removal, by the chief justice of the state supreme court; the term of office is one year, and a grand jury counsel cannot be reappointed to serve consecutive terms; compensation is on a per-diem basis (Haw. Rev. Stat. §§ 612–51, 612–53, 612–55).

Following ratification of the provision in November 1978, the 1979 legislature passed implementation legislation, but it was vetoed by the governor.[25] Finally, in June 1980, implementation legislation was signed into law. Since there was an interim period during which Section 11 was in effect, but grand juries did not have independent counsel, a series of cases reached the Hawaii Supreme Court in 1981 and 1982 challenging indictments handed down during that period.

Starting with *State v. Rodrigues* (1981), the court consistently upheld indictments brought during the interim. It ruled that the provision was not "self-executing" and therefore did not require the appointment of independent counsel. Where the phrase "as provided by law" is found in the constitution, it is "construed as a direction to the legislature to enact implementing legislation," and in this situation the legislature clearly intended to implement the provision.

Another question, brought up initially in *Rodrigues,* focused on whether Section 11 supplemented the due process rights of those accused of crime. Citing *Rodrigues* as controlling, the court subsequently concluded that the independent counsel's role is to advise the grand jury, not to serve as an advocate on behalf of an accused; even though Section 11 is of indirect benefit, it does not create a substantive right for the accused (*State v. Hehr,* 1981). In addition, the constitutional provision does not require that the independent counsel be physically present during the grand jury proceedings (*State v. Kahlbaun,* 1981).

SECTION 12

Bail; Excessive Punishment. Excessive bail shall not be required, nor excessive fines imposed, nor cruel or unusual punishment inflicted. The court may dispense with bail if reasonably satisfied that the defendant or witness will appear when directed, except for a defendant charged with an offense punishable by life imprisonment.

The first sentence, prohibiting excessive bail and cruel or unusual punishment, has been carried over verbatim since the Statehood Constitution, and, until 1968, the section consisted of that sentence only. At that time the second sentence was added.

Bail

Following the exact language of the Eighth Amendment in the national Bill of Rights, this section only prohibits the imposition of excessive bail; it does not

[25] See Bettencourt and Zwald, "The Prosecutor's Duty," 145.

establish bail as a right. However, Hawaii has long granted bail as a right for those offenses and circumstances defined by statute as "bailable" (Haw. Rev. Stat. §§ 804–3, 804–4). The second sentence, unique to Hawaii's constitution, was added in 1968 to remove any doubts as to the discretion courts have in granting bail.

In 1982, the court handed down its most significant decision to date regarding bail. In *Huihui v. Shimoda*, the court held unconstitutional a statutory provision denying bail to those charged with a serious crime for which the proof is evident and the presumption great where the accused is already free on bail on another felony charge. Following a review of the history behind Section 12 and a lengthy discussion of the conflict among the federal courts regarding bail, the court concluded:

> It therefore defies logic to interpret that constitutional provision as prohibiting bail set so unreasonably high as to be unobtainable and not reflective of legitimate concerns on one hand, while on the other as permitting the outright denial of bail absent reasonable grounds, since both actions, under the circumstances, amount to the same thing. Accordingly, we hold that article I, section 12 of the Hawaii Constitution, prohibiting excessive bail, also protects persons accused of crimes from the unreasonable or arbitrary denial of bail.

The statutory provisions at issue in *Huihui* were thus invalid both because they conflicted with the fundamental notion that an accused is presumed innocent until proven guilty and because they unreasonably presumed a defendant was dangerous simply because of being previously charged with a serious crime and then again with a felony. Since the statute removed the judge's discretionary power, it also violated the second sentence of Section 12 which was specifically included to clarify that discretion. The language does not mean a judge is prohibited from denying bail in a particular case, the court added, because having discretion means being able to release the defendant with or without bail.

The next year, in *State v. Handa* (1983), the court concluded that the judicial discretion provided for in Section 12 was intended to apply only to the preconviction stage and not to the appeals stage because at the latter point the presumption of innocence is no longer present and the right to freedom is significantly qualified.

Cruel and Unusual Punishment

The standard for determining if a punishment violates the prohibition against cruel and unusual punishment used by Hawaii's supreme court is "whether in the light of developing concepts of decency and fairness, the prescribed punishment is so disproportionate to the conduct proscribed and is of such duration as to shock the conscience of reasonable persons or to outrage the moral sense of the community" (*State v. Kumukau*, 1990). Under this standard, a life sentence imposed on an individual who is a multiple offender is not cruel and unusual punishment (*State v. Iaukea*, 1975), nor is a statutory provision requiring a minimum five-year period of incarceration without possibility of parole for repeat offenders (*State v. Freitas*, 1979). While a statute permitting consecutive mandatory minimum terms of imprisonment is not unconstitutional on its face, judicial discretion was abused when the maximum minimum term for each conviction to be served consecutively resulted in a prison term of 136 years before being eligible for parole (*State v. Kumukau*, 1990).

Note: Section 12 in the Statehood and 1968 constitutions dealt with jury service and read: "No person shall be disqualified to serve as a juror because of sex." Because the equality of rights provision (now Section 3) was adopted in 1972, the 1978 convention believed the jury provision was no longer necessary, and its proposal to delete the section was approved by the voters.

SECTION 13

Trial by Jury, Civil Cases. In suits at common law where the value in controversy shall exceed five thousand dollars, the right of trial by jury shall be preserved. The legislature may provide for a verdict by not less than three-fourths of the members of the jury.

Patterned after the Seventh Amendment to the U.S. Constitution, this section guarantees a right to jury trials in civil cases where the amount in controversy exceeds the minimum amount set by the constitution. While the minimum amount in the Seventh Amendment remains at $20 for federal suits, the $100 minimum originally set in the Statehood Constitution has been increased twice. The 1978 Convention raised the figure to $1,000; in 1988, voters approved a legislatively proposed amendment increasing it to $5,000.

Another difference between this section and the Seventh Amendment is that Hawaii's constitution expressly grants the legislature power to provide for verdicts that are not unanimous, although such a law may not permit verdicts by less than three-fourth of the jurors. Presently Hawaii statute (Haw. Rev. Stat. § 635-20) permits verdicts by five-sixths of the jurors.

As the Seventh Amendment has not been made applicable to the states via the Fourteenth Amendment, questions about the right guaranteed in Section 13 will be settled by an interpretation of the state's constitution, statutes, and rules of civil procedure (*Harada v. Burns*, 1968). Over the years, distinctions have been made between those civil actions that do or do not require a jury trial. For example, the Hawaii Intermediate Court of Appeals held that since a paternity action is not a suit at common law, there is no constitutional right to a trial by jury (*Doe v. Roe*, 1985). In a recent case involving some issues that were by right triable by jury, and others that were not, and where the defendant did not object to a jury trial of the latter, the Hawaii Supreme Court ruled that all claims at issue should be tried by the jury (*Kimball v. Lincoln*, 1991).

SECTION 14

Rights of Accused. In all criminal prosecutions, the accused shall enjoy the right to a speedy and public trial by an impartial jury of the district wherein the crime shall have been committed, which district shall have been previously ascertained by law, or of such other district to which the prosecution may be removed with the consent of the accused; to be informed of the nature and cause of the accusation; to be confronted with the witnesses against the accused; to have compulsory process for obtaining witnesses in the accused's favor; and to have the assistance of counsel for the accused's defense. Juries, where the crime charged is serious, shall consist of twelve persons. The State shall provide counsel for an indigent defendant charged with an offense punishable by imprisonment.

When this section was included in the Statehood Constitution, it consisted of only one sentence that was almost identical to the Sixth Amendment to the U.S. Constitution. That sentence remains substantively the same. The second and third sentences (adopted in 1978 and 1968, respectively) were added in response to U.S. Supreme Court decisions.

The provision granting indigent defendants the right to appointed counsel was added in 1968, in order to conform to the U.S. Supreme Court's landmark decision in *Gideon v. Wainwright* (1963). Because the right was seen as applying only in felony, but not misdemeanor, cases, the new sentence stated: "The State shall provide counsel for an indigent defendant charged with an offense punishable by imprisonment *for more than sixty days"* (emphasis added). The 1978 convention deleted the words "for more than sixty days" in order to incorporate the U.S. Supreme Court's expansion of that right in 1972 to all cases where imprisonment was a possibility.

In contrast, the provision requiring twelve-person juries, when the crime charged is serious, represents the specific attempt by the 1978 convention to counteract U.S. Supreme Court holdings that criminal cases can be tried by juries of less than twelve. The delegate introducing this amendment from the convention floor argued that twelve-person juries needed to be preserved in the state's constitution as they had been used in Hawaii since the monarchy and had become an integral part of the state's judicial system.

Trial by Jury

The Hawaii Supreme Court has held that individuals charged with a "petty" offense are not constitutionally entitled to a jury trial (*State v. Shak*, 1970), and even though the right is very important in our system of justice, it is not absolute (*State v. Kaspruzycki*, 1982). *Kaspruzycki* is particularly significant because the court declined to use the opportunity to adopt the six-month-prison-term dividing line, used by the U.S. Supreme Court, to distinguish serious from petty offenses.

A few years later this became an important factor in *State v. O'Brien* (1985) when the supreme court upheld a decision by the intermediate court of appeals that driving under the influence (DUI) cases were serious, thus entitling defendants to jury trials.[26] Referring to its departure from the U.S. Supreme Court's guideline, the court stated that while the possible prison term for a DUI conviction does not exceed six months, the punishments established by statute clearly demonstrate that the people of Hawaii view such cases as serious ones. It opened the door to future departures by adding:

> In recognizing that punishments other than imprisonment exceeding six months can require the constitutional guarantees of a jury trial, we act on our belief that our interpretation of the mandate of the constitution must accord with the changing circumstances of modern times and the exigencies of life in a society dependent on technology such as the automobile.

Recently, the supreme court was called upon to consider the situation where a trial judge made statements leading a defendant to believe a demand for a jury trial would result in a more severe sentence. It determined that constitutional rights were thereby denied (*State v. Mata,*1990).[27]

Speedy Trial

The guarantee of a speedy trial "is an important safeguard to prevent undue and oppressive incarceration prior to trial, to minimize anxiety and concern incident to public accusation and to limit the potential impairment of the ability of an accused to defend himself" (*State v. Almeida,* 1973).

In 1972, Hawaii's high court followed the lead of the U.S. Supreme Court in ruling that the right to a speedy trial arises only when an individual becomes an "accused," but does not arise just because there is a decision to prosecute (*State v. Bryson*). The following year, in *State v. Almeida* (1973), the court explained further that this means the point when a formal indictment or information is returned or the individual's liberty is restrained by arrest, whichever comes first.

Because the court believed it unwise to set a specific and arbitrary time period within which an accused must be brought to trial, it adopted the test put forth by the U.S. Supreme Court for determining when the speedy trial provision is violated (*State v. Almeida,* 1973). That test calls for balancing the following four factors: length of delay, reason for delay, defendant's assertion of the right, and prejudice to the defendant resulting from delay. However, the test will come into

[26] See Note, "State v. O'Brien: Right to Jury Trial for Driving Under the Influence of Intoxicating Liquor," *University of Hawaii Law Review* 8 (1986): 209.

[27] See Note, "State v. Mata: Disqualification of a Trial Judge," *University of Hawaii Law Review* 13 (1991): 641.

play only if the delay is initially found to be "presumptively prejudicial." Where a delay is caused by the defense filing numerous pre-trial motions and where the defendant asserts the right to a speedy trial without showing that prejudice resulted from the delay, there is no violation (*State v. Nihipali*, 1981). A three-month delay is not presumptively prejudicial and does not warrant further consideration (*State v. O Daniel*, 1980).

Public Trial

Because openness serves to protect the court's integrity, the public cannot be excluded as long as there is no disorderly conduct or overt act intended to influence or possibly influencing the jury (*State v. Hashimoto*, 1963). Although reaffirming its commitment to open judicial proceedings, in 1978 the court held that upon a defense request those parts of a preliminary hearing concerning admissibility of evidence at trial may be closed to the public (*Gannett Pacific Corp. v. Richardson*).

Impartial Jury

Inherent in the right to an impartial jury is the requirement that the jury be free from outside influences. Examples of decisions where the Hawaii Supreme Court has found violations include the following: when a dictionary was discovered in the jury room following deliberations (*State v. Williamson*, 1991), when comments made by a juror indicate that the person looks negatively upon a defendant who does not take the witness stand (*State v. Sugiyama*, 1990), and when jurors were possibly exposed to news accounts prejudicial to the defendant (*State v. Keliiholokai*, 1977).

Confrontation and Compulsory Process

The purpose of the confrontation clause is to ensure the accused's right to cross-examine any and all witnesses against the person in order to provide the opportunity to challenge witness credibility and truthfulness (*State v. Narvaez*, 1986).[28] Where a defendant is not allowed reasonable cross-examination of a complaining witness, the right to confrontation is denied (*State v. Calbero*, 1989). While the right to confrontation is a fundamental one, it is not absolute and can be waived (*State v. Oyama*, 1981).

An exception to the right of confrontation may be permitted if a witness is unavailable, and under such a situation the former testimony is admissible at trial (*State v. Lincoln*, 1990). However, it is insufficient to show only that the

---

[28] See Recent Developments, "Criminal Procedure—State v. Narvaez: A Rejection of Vicarious Standing Under the Exclusionary Rule," *University of Hawaii Law Review* 9 (1987): 743.

witness is not in Hawaii; the state must establish a good faith attempt to locate and secure the witness's presence (*State v. Bates*, 1989).

The right to compulsory process means that defendants have the power to compel witnesses for their own defense to attend and be heard. Although this right is of fundamental importance in allowing a meaningful defense and a fair trial, it is not absolute; it is limited to defense witnesses who will give relevant and beneficial testimony (*State v. Savitz*, 1984; *State v. Mitake*, 1981).

Assistance of Counsel

This provision encompasses more than just being represented by an attorney. For example, in the 1986 case *State v. Smith*, the state supreme court found that this provision was violated when the defendant's lawyer had rendered ineffective assistance. In reaching this holding, the court reviewed a number of earlier decisions establishing that the right to the assistance of counsel can be satisfied only if the assistance is effective. While this does not necessitate errorless assistance, it must be within the range of competence demanded of lawyers in criminal cases.

Significantly, *Smith* reaffirmed the test adopted earlier in *State v. Antone* (1980): To meet the burden, the defendant must show there were specific errors or omissions that demonstrate the defense counsel's lack of skill, judgment, or diligence and these errors or omissions resulted in either the withdrawal or the substantial impairment of a potentially meritorious defense. In continuing to rely on *Antone*, the *Smith* court refused to follow a more limiting standard established by the U.S. Supreme Court which, as the court pointed out, has been "criticized as being unduly difficult for a defendant to meet."[29]

An interesting component of this provision became clear in *State v. Reis* (1983), decided by the Hawaii Intermediate Court of Appeals.[30] In *Reis*, the defense attorney had a longstanding and ongoing professional association with one prosecution witness, and another adverse witness was a stockholder and corporate officer in a business the attorney's firm advised. According to the court, this caused a conflict of interest that violated the right to effective assistance of counsel.

SECTION 15

Habeas Corpus and Suspension of Laws. The privilege of the writ of habeas corpus shall not be suspended unless, when in cases of rebellion or invasion, the public safety may require it.

---

[29] See Note, "State v. Smith: The Standard of Effectiveness of Counsel in Hawaii Following Strickland v. Washington," *University of Hawaii Law Review* 9 (1987): 371.

[30] See Recent Developments, "Attorney Conflict of Interest in Criminal Defense Cases: State v. Reis," *University of Hawaii Law Review* 6 (1984): 707.

> The power of suspending the privilege of the writ of habeas corpus, and the laws or the execution thereof, shall never be exercised except by the legislature, or by authority derived from it to be exercised in such particular cases only as the legislature shall expressly prescribe.

No substantive changes have been made to this section since it was adopted in the Statehood Constitution. The language of the first sentence is identical to that found in Section 9 of Article I of the U.S. Constitution which sets forth limits on legislative power. Because the Hawaii provision appears in the bill of rights, rather than in the legislative article, the 1950 framers added the second sentence to make explicit the fact that the power to suspend rests only with the legislature, not with the executive, even though the last phrase allows the legislature to delegate the power.

Habeas corpus is Latin for "you have the body," and a writ of habeas corpus is a legal order requiring that an imprisoned individual be brought before a judge to determine if that person is being held unlawfully. If the judge concludes that the detention is unlawful, the individual must be released. The privilege of the writ may be suspended only in very extraordinary circumstances, underscoring its importance in Anglo-American judicial history. It is often referred to as the most fundamental privilege in protecting individual liberty against the exercise of unjust or oppressive governmental power.

SECTION 16

> **Supremacy of Civil Power.** The military shall be held in strict subordination to the civil power.

No changes have been made to the language of this section. Its purpose is to make certain that military power remains subordinate to civil power.

SECTION 17

> **Right to Bear Arms.** A well regulated militia being necessary to the security of a free state, the right of the people to keep and bear arms shall not be infringed.

There have been no substantive changes to this section. It uses language identical to the U.S. Constitution's Second Amendment, which has not been made applicable to the states.

When included by the 1950 convention, delegates explained that they did not intend the provision to keep the legislature from enacting reasonable restrictions. Although the 1968 convention proposed no changes, there was a strong feeling that the section's scope needed to be made more explicit, and the delegates stressed that it was intended to refer only to the right to bear arms as a member of a state militia. The 1978 convention did not debate the issue.

Controversy continues to surround this section. In the 1992 legislative session, for example, questions arose as to whether the legislature has the power to restrict possession of semiautomatic handguns (assault pistols) without a specific constitutional amendment to that effect. However, legal opinions presented to the legislature indicated that such an amendment was not needed, and the legislation was enacted.

SECTION 18

Quartering of Soldiers. No soldier or member of the militia shall, in time of peace, be quartered in any house, without the consent of the owner or occupant, nor in time of war, except in a manner provided by law.

Adopted in the Statehood Constitution, this section is almost identical with the Third Amendment of the U.S. Constitution, which does not apply to the states via the Fourteenth Amendment.

SECTION 19

Imprisonment for Debt. There shall be no imprisonment for debt.

This section originated in the Statehood Constitution, and its language remains intact. The framers explained they intended the provision to apply as a protection for those who have debts arising out of contract obligations, not for those who do not pay fines or penalties imposed upon conviction by a court of law.

SECTION 20

Eminent Domain. Private property shall not be taken or damaged for public use without just compensation.

When included in the Statehood Constitution, this section used language similar to that in the Fifth Amendment of the U.S. Constitution. However, in 1968, the words "or damaged" were added.[31] This section has the effect of declaring that the state's power to take public property for a public use "is limited only to the extent that the purpose of the taking is rationally related to the public

---

[31] See Ian L. Mattoch, "The Amended Just Compensation Provision of the Hawaii Constitution: A New Basis for Indemnification of the Condemnee," *Hawaii Bar Journal* 6 (1969): 55.

objective sought, and just compensation must be paid for the property" (*City and County of Honolulu v. Trotter, Inc.*, 1988).

Litigation based on this section, and its counterpart in the Fifth Amendment, has been of great significance to the politics, economy, and constitutional development of Hawaii. Most noteworthy is a parallel sequence of cases simultaneously moving through the state and the federal courts and focusing on Hawaii's Land Reform Act of 1967 and the question of what constitutes "public use."

The concept of private landownership is one of the many Western ideas early introduced by foreigners coming to the islands for missionary and trade purposes. Pressure exerted by these *malahini* (newcomers) led Kamehameha III, in 1848, to sign the Great *Mahele* or Great Division. It divided the land among the monarch, the Hawaiian government, and the *Alii* (the chiefs) and established a process by which indigenous commoners could receive title to land they occupied.

In 1850, foreigners were also given the right to acquire land. While many native Hawaiians were slow in formalizing their claims, foreigners acted quickly. In addition, and with unfortunate consequences, many native Hawaiians disposed of their land to foreigners, not appreciating the consequences to their life-style from being separated from the land. Sugar plantations, which were just beginning to become viable enterprises, obtained huge holdings, and other areas were acquired by a few wealthy individuals. But not all the big landowners were foreigners; some of the *Alii* also possessed large tracts in various parts of the islands. When the will of a Hawaiian princess left the royal lands she inherited in trust, the Bishop Estate became the largest private landowner (see also Article VI).

By the late 1800s, this pattern of large private landholdings was well established, resulting in a system of landownership very different from that found throughout the United States. This concentration of land control in governmental and a few private owners continues to exist today. While the holdings of the six largest nongovernmental owners have decreased somewhat, particularly within recent years, as of 1991 they owned 22.5 percent of the land in the islands. Of that portion, the Bishop Estate alone controls over one-third (or 8 percent of the state's total land).

Particularly since the end of World War II, the demand for residential properties has steadily increased, due primarily to growing in-migration and the demands of labor unions for better working conditions, including greater availability of private residences. Juxtaposed against this, the land available for residential development was limited. Not only did a few landowners control usage of substantial portions, but also 12 percent of the total land area of the state is characterized by steep volcanic slopes and other inhospitable features, making it unsuitable for housing. In addition, the 1961 statewide land-use plan, which zoned the state into urban, rural, agricultural, and conservation areas, also impacted negatively on availability.[32]

Although leaseholds were used for residential and commercial purposes during the monarchy, the territorial legislature considered ways to encourage, or force, landowners to make more of their lands available for residential purposes. In response, more substantial portions of privately owned lands were leased for residential developments, not only to raise income, but also to offset possible legislative action. Thus, many in Hawaii owned their homes, but leased the land under them, and although more homes became available this way, many in the state remained dissatisfied because of a strong belief that this was contrary to an important element of the American heritage.

Enacted in 1967, the Land Reform Act, through use of the state's power of eminent domain to condemn the leasehold lands, allowed leaseholders under specified conditions to purchase the land on which houses were built. Although amended in other respects since them, this fundamental aspect of the act remains.[33]

In 1979, the Bishop Estate filed a lawsuit in federal court challenging the act on the grounds that it violated the Fifth Amendment of the U.S. Constitution because the land was not being taken for public use and was just being transferred from one private owner to another. In response, the state and the homeowners argued that by converting land to fee simple, a public purpose was being realized.

The U.S. district court found the act only partly constitutional, while the Ninth Circuit ruled it all in violation of the Fifth Amendment (*Midkiff v. Tom,* 1979, 1983). However, when the case reached the U.S. Supreme Court in 1984, the entire act was upheld (*Hawaii Housing Authority v. Midkiff*).[34] Writing for a unanimous Court (with Justice Thurgood Marshall not taking part), Justice Sandra Day O'Connor stated that

> The people of Hawaii have attempted, much as the settlers of the original 13 Colonies did, to reduce the perceived social and economic evils of a land oligopoly traceable to their monarchs. The land oligopoly has, according to the Hawaii Legislature, created artificial deterrents to the normal function of the State's residential land market and

---

[32] See David L. Callies, "Dealing with Scarcity: Land Use and Planning," in Smith and Pratt, eds., *Politics,* 131. See also David L. Callies, "Land Use: Herein of Vested Rights, Plans, and the Relationship of Planning and Controls," *University of Hawaii Law Review* 1 (1979): 167.

[33] See James P. Conahan, "Hawaii's Land Reform Act: Is It Constitutional?" *Hawaii Bar Journal* 6 (1969): 31.

[34] See Note, "Midkiff v. Tom: The Constitutionality of Hawaii's Land Reform Act," *University of Hawaii Law Review* 6 (1984): 561; although written prior to the U.S. Supreme Court's ruling, that decision is covered in the "Addendum" at 601. See also Thomas J. Coyne, "Hawaii Housing Authority v. Midkiff: A Final Requiem for the Public Use Limitation on Eminent Domain?" *Notre Dame Law Review* 60 (1985): 388.

> forced thousands of individual homeowners to lease, rather than buy, the land underneath their homes. Regulating oligopoly and the evils associated with it is a classic example of a State's police powers.

The Court agreed that the "use" was a public one because The mere fact that property taken outright by eminent domain is transferred in the first instance to private beneficiaries does not condemn that taking as having only a private purpose. The Court long ago rejected any literal requirement that condemned property be put into use for the general public. "It is not essential that the entire community, nor even a considerable portion, . . . directly enjoy or participate in any improvement [for it] to constitute a public use." As the unique way titles were held in Hawaii skewed the land market, exercise of the power of eminent domain was justified. The Act advances its purposes without the State's taking actual possession of the land. In such cases, government does not itself have to use property to legitimate the taking; it is only the taking's purpose, and not its mechanics, that must pass scrutiny under the Public Use Clause.

Meanwhile, the same issue was being litigated in the state courts against the challenge that it violated the state constitution. One year after the U.S. Supreme Court's decision, the Hawaii Supreme Court ruled that under Section 20, the act was constitutional (*Hawaii Housing Authority v. Lyman*, 1985).

The unique relationship between land and politics in Hawaii led to developments that may have important consequences far beyond the state boundaries. One commentator on land use in Hawaii suggests that, because *Midkiff v was* an "unusually broad decision," it could have an impact throughout the rest of the country by sanctioning "legislative interference with large landholdings of any sort, since there is nothing in its language that restricts its application to residential conversions in Hawaii."[35]

Leasehold conversion remains a live issue in Hawaii. The 1967 act dealt only with single-family homes. However, Hawaii has a very significant number of residents owning condominiums. Many are built on leasehold land, so these condominium owners are paying rent for their respective portions of that land. In the past few years, the state legislature has debated the enactment of bills allowing condominium owners to acquire the fee simple title to their land. However, the issue is complex because ownership of the underlying land is not concentrated in a few, and it is safe to predict that it will face a challenge in the courts should legislation pass.

---

[35] David L. Callies, *Regulating Paradise, Land Use Controls in Hawaii* (Honolulu: University of Hawaii Press, 1984), 67.

SECTION 21

Limitations of Special Privileges. The power of the State to act in the general welfare shall never be impaired by the making of any irrevocable grant of special privileges or immunities.

This section remains substantively the same as adopted in the Statehood Constitution. It requires that actions taken by the state benefit all the people since irrevocable grants of special privileges or immunities cannot be made. However, privileges or immunities that are revocable, such as tax exemptions, are not prohibited.

SECTION 22

Construction. The enumeration of rights and privileges shall not be construed to impair or deny others retained by the people.

Unchanged since statehood, and stated in words like those in the Ninth Amendment to the U.S. Constitution, this section is referred to as the savings clause; it seeks to guard against an unintended interpretation. Just because certain rights and privileges are listed in the constitution should not be taken to mean that the people of the state cannot enjoy other unlisted rights.

Article II

Suffrage and Elections

Of the various suffrage and election proposals considered by Hawaii's constitutional conventions, most noteworthy is the rejected right of initiative—a process permitting citizens by petition to place proposed state laws on the ballot so the voters can adopt or reject them. Brought up at all three conventions, the initiative failed each time (as did the related referendum and recall processes). Except for voting on proposed constitutional amendments, a type of referendum, statewide voters in Hawaii are not able to vote on ballot issues.

Proponents of the right of the citizens to enact state laws directly through use of the initiative continue their efforts, actively lobbying for a legislatively proposed constitutional amendment that would permit its use. They contend that it would be ratified once placed before the voters. While twenty-one states presently permit an initiative process for adopting state laws, the remaining twenty-nine, including Hawaii, do not.

Through their charters, each of Hawaii's four counties allows use of the initiative for county ordinances. There are limitations, however, reflecting the counties' limited home rule powers: For example, that process cannot be used for rezoning land because to do so violates state laws governing land use and zoning decisions (*Kaiser Hawaii Kai Development Co. v. City and County of Honolulu*, 1989).[36]

---

[36] See Callies, "Dealing with Scarcity"; Note, "Kaiser Hawaii Kai Development Company v. City and County of Honolulu: Zoning by Initiative in Hawaii," *University of Hawaii Law Review* 12 (1990): 181.

SECTION 1

Qualifications. Every citizen of the United States who shall have attained the age of eighteen years, have been a resident of this State not less than one year next preceding the election and be a voter registered as provided by law, shall be qualified to vote in any state or local election.

Since statehood, two major modifications have been made to this section: A literacy requirement was deleted (1968), and the voting age was lowered from twenty to eighteen (1972). In both instances, change did not come easily, for Hawaii's voters have been cautious in altering voter qualifications.

From the time of Hawaii's constitutional monarchy (1840–1893), during the short-lived Republic (1893–1900), and while Hawaii was a territory (1900–1959), voters were required to meet various literacy requirements. The Statehood Constitution continued the practice, specifying that "No person shall be qualified to vote unless he is also able, except for physical disability, to speak, read and write the English or Hawaiian language." When a constitutional amendment to repeal the requirement was proposed by the legislature and placed on the 1964 ballot, it failed. The more then century-long disenfranchisement of illiterate citizens ended when the 1968 convention's proposal to remove the literacy requirement was ratified by the voters.

A voting age requirement of twenty, first established in 1850, continued until 1900 when the Organic Act set the age at twenty-one. Although the 1950 convention delegates rejected the idea of lowering the age to eighteen, they did return to the pre-territorial voting age of twenty.

Attempts to extend the franchise to eighteen-year-olds continued. The 1967 legislature proposed such an amendment, but because of a procedural flaw, it did not appear on the ballot. When the 1968 convention included it in the proposed constitution, it had the dubious distinction of being the only amendment put forth that the voters refused to ratify. Two years later it was again on the ballot, as a result of a legislative proposal, and again the voters did not approve.

In early 1971, Hawaii's legislature became one of the first to vote in favor of the Twenty-Sixth Amendment to the U.S. Constitution, extending suffrage rights to eighteen-year-olds. Shortly after this amendment was successfully ratified, the legislature once more proposed changing the voting age qualification in the state constitution, to make it conform with the U.S. Constitution, and the voters finally gave their approval at the 1972 election.

For the related issue of the referendum at the county level, see David L. Callies, Donna H. Kalama, and Mahilani E. Kellet, "The Lum Court, Land Use, and the Environment: A Survey of Hawaii Case Law 1983–1991," *University of Hawaii Law Review* 14 (1992): 119; Comment, "Development Agreement Legislation in Hawaii: An Answer to the Vested Rights Uncertainty," *University of Hawaii Law Review* 7 (1985): 173; Benjamin A. Kudo, "Nukolii: Private Development Rights and the Public Interest," *The Urban Lawyer* 16 (1984): 279.

The voting age qualification again came before the voters when the 1988 ballot contained a proposal lowering the age slightly below eighteen, in order to allow all those turning eighteen during the election year to vote, even if the birthday was after the election date. The voters' failure to ratify this amendment demonstrated their wariness of tinkering with voter qualifications.

Residency requirements were not new to the islands when a one-year period was included in the Statehood Constitution. Although this requirement remains, it has little effect, due to the U.S. Supreme Court's ruling in *Dunn v. Blumstein* (1972) that a one-year residency requirement is unconstitutional. In 1988, a proposed amendment to remove the one-year requirement, thus bringing the constitution into conformity with federal guidelines (and the actual practice of enforcing a cutoff date thirty days prior to an election), appeared on the general election ballot. The voters failed to ratify the deletion, but the original language still cannot be implemented, and the practice of establishing residence thirty days prior to an election remains.

A unique aspect of the Hawaii Constitution raises an intriguing legal question regarding voter qualifications. Concern with the status of the ethnic Hawaiian population led the 1978 convention to establish, through Article XII, an Office of Hawaiian Affairs (OHA) with a board of trustees elected "by qualified voters who are Hawaiians." In 1980, two state senators requested an opinion by the attorney general as to whether limiting OHA voting to persons of Hawaiian ancestry violates this section. The attorney general concluded that it did not (Op. Att'y Gen. 80–8, 1980), and the courts have not ruled on the question.

SECTION 2

Disqualification. No person who is non compos mentis shall be qualified to vote. No person convicted of a felony shall be qualified to vote except upon the person's final discharge or earlier as provided by law.

Hawaii's constitution has always disqualified the insane from voting. With respect to those convicted of a felony, a change was made to this section in 1968 when the convention substituted "except upon the person's final discharge or earlier as provided by law" for the original "unless pardoned and restored to his civil rights," with the intention of expanding the ways in which the right could be restored after a felony conviction.

SECTION 3

Residence. No person shall be deemed to have gained or lost residence simply because of the person's presence or absence while employed in the service of the United States, or while engaged in navigation or while a student at any institution of learning.

Hawaii's strategic location has assured it of a permanent military presence in the islands. This section, having its origins in the Organic Act, clarifies that resident status is not obtained by virtue of being stationed in the state, nor is residency lost when Hawaii residents leave the state while in the military service, while a sailor, or while a student. It has not been changed substantively since the Statehood Constitution.

SECTION 4

Registration; Voting. The legislature shall provide for the registration of voters and for absentee voting and shall prescribe the method of voting at all elections. Secrecy of voting shall be preserved; provided that no person shall be required to declare a party preference or nonpartisanship as a condition of voting in any primary or special primary election. Secrecy of voting and choice of political party affiliation or nonpartisanship shall be preserved.

According to this section, the legislature determines the methods to be used for voter registration and voting, but whatever the voting methods, ballot secrecy must be guaranteed.

The only major change that has been made occurred when the 1978 convention incorporated the current language mandating open primaries. In so doing, the legislature was deprived of the power it had previously enjoyed to determine whether primaries would be open or closed. Previously, Hawaii's voters had experienced both types. Before statehood and through 1963, primary elections were open. Coinciding with the solidification of Democratic party control in the state, in 1963, the statute was changed to require closed primaries. The 1968 convention declined to mandate open primaries through the constitution.

Given this background, it is not surprising that a fierce battle over the issue took place at the 1978 convention. A thirty-member subject committee discussed, but finally rejected, proposals requiring open primaries. However, the convention while in committee of the whole, after lengthy and contentious debate, voted to include the mandate for open primaries—on a very close vote of fifty-one to forty-eight. This amendment has been pointed to as demonstrating a weakening in organized party control in the state.[37]

An important case arising in Hawaii related to voting was recently decided by the U.S. Supreme Court. Although about half the states limit write-in voting in some fashion, Hawaii is one of four states that actually prohibit it. *Burdick v. Takushi* (1992) arose out of a 1986 challenge to this prohibition. Although some state courts have found such prohibitions invalid and the federal courts have considered state laws limiting, but not banning, write-in voting, *Burdick*

---

[37] Norman Meller and Richard H. Kosaki, "Hawaii's Constitutional Convention—1978," *National Civic Review* 69 (1980): 253.

became one of two cases (the other was from Indiana) where for the first time a ban was at issue before federal courts.[38]

In the course of the litigation, the Hawaii Supreme Court was presented with certified questions regarding the prohibition and concluded that under both Hawaii's constitution and its election laws, state officials may not permit, count, or publish write-in votes and that there was no right to write-in voting (*Burdick v. Takushi*, 1989). Disagreeing with this response, the U.S. District Court for the District of Hawaii found the prohibition unconstitutional (*Burdick v. Takushi*, 1990).

Upon appeal, the U.S. Court of Appeals for the Ninth Circuit reversed, holding that while the prohibition may limit political speech, it does not violate the right to free speech, for it "serves legitimate state interests and is part of a comprehensive election scheme that provides [voters] with adequate opportunities and alternatives to exercise [their] rights of expression and association" (*Burdick v. Takushi*, 1991). In a six-to-three decision, the U.S. Supreme Court agreed, emphasizing that the state's election laws make it extremely easy to get on the ballot and that "any burden imposed by Hawaii's write-in vote prohibition is a very limited one" (*Burdick v. Takushi*, 1992).

Both prior to and after the Supreme Court's ruling, syndicated *Washington Post* columnist David Broder criticized Hawaii's ban on write-in votes, thus giving national coverage to the issue.[39] Interestingly enough, the state's chief election officer, the lieutenant governor, immediately responded to the Court's decision by calling for legislation allowing write-in voting, to be exercised within certain limits, stating that he believed the state's legislators are receptive to giving voters more choices.[40]

SECTION 5

Campaign Fund, Spending Limit. The legislature shall establish a campaign fund to be used for partial public financing of campaigns for public offices of the State and its political subdivisions, as provided by law. The legislature shall provide a limit on the campaign spending of candidates.

See the commentary following Section 6.

---

[38] See Recent Developments, "First Amendment—Voters' Speech Rights—Federal District Courts Mandate Availability of Write-In Voting—Paul v. Indiana; Burdick v. Takushi," *Harvard Law Review* 104 (1990): 657.

[39] David S. Broder, "The Court Rides Roughshod," *The Washington Post*, 22–28 June 1992, National weekly edition, 4; David Broder, "Hawaii's Bogus Write-In Law," *Honolulu Advertiser*, 14 April 1991, D–2.

[40] Kevin Dayton, "Cayetano to Again Press for Write-In Balloting," *Honolulu Advertiser*, 9 June 1992, A–1; Gregg K. Kakesako and Richard Borreca, "Allow Write-In, Cayetano Says," *Honolulu Star Bulletin*, 8 June 1992, A–6.

SECTION 6

> **Campaign Contributions Limits.** Limitations on campaign contributions to any political candidate, or authorized political campaign organization for such candidate, for any elective office within the State shall be provided by law.

Added in 1978, Sections 5 and 6 are so closely related in subject matter that they can be discussed together. Both sections were extremely controversial, and almost a quarter of the 1978 delegates rose to speak on them during debate. Those in support emphasized, in emotional tones, the need to minimize the role of money in campaigns and expressed their amazement at the sums spent by candidates in the state. Those against exhibited slightly less emotion, but it is clear their feelings ran equally deep. They opposed leaving details to the legislature and believed the provisions unfairly protected incumbents in addition to abridging freedom of speech.

The first sentence of Section 5 directs the legislature to set up a campaign fund so that state and local candidates can receive partial public funding. The second sentence directs the legislature to set a limit on candidate campaign expenditures. Section 6 requires the legislature to establish limits on campaign contributions made to candidates and political campaign organizations.

In debating these provisions, both opponents and supporters referred to the U.S. Supreme Court's 1976 *Buckley v. Valeo* holding that, while the rights to free speech and association are not violated by campaign contribution limits, they are violated by limits on campaign spending. Delegates opposing Section 5 argued that the *Buckley* ruling made it invalid. Supporters argued that *Buckley* allowed spending limits for those receiving public financing, even though they acknowledged that it presented a constitutional hurdle regarding limiting expenditures for candidates not receiving public funds.

The standing committee report and comments made during debate left no question of the supporters' intent that the legislature implement the section by limiting spending for all candidates (i.e., for those who do and do not receive public funds). While recognizing that "litigation will be necessary to determine the validity of any limits on spending by those who do not receive public financing," they viewed litigation as "welcome because the public interest served by campaign spending limits is so essential."[41] Despite these hopes, no legislation has ever passed limiting spending by candidates not receiving public funds, and the issue has not been tested through litigation.

A fund for partial public funding has been established along with spending limits for those who use it. In practice, few candidates elect to subject themselves to such limits as the amount they would receive from public funds is paltry.

---

[41] *1975 Proceedings I*, Standing Committee Report no. 72, 680.

The legislature has carried out the mandate of Section 6, and the contribution limit is currently set at $2,000 per candidate, per election.

A Campaign Spending Commission administers these and related statutory provisions (Haw. Rev. Stat. § 11–191 *et seq.*). The commission has received criticism, particularly with respect to its enforcement role over campaign contributions. One long-time observer criticizes the commission's interpretation that contribution limits apply for each election without regard for term of office. With elections held every two years, this "undermines the intent of the constitutional provision and the implementation legislation because it means that those enjoying four-year terms, rather than two-year terms, may raise funds (though subject to the limits) even for those elections in which they are not candidates."[42]

SECTION 7

Resignation from Public Office. Any elected public officer shall resign from that office before being eligible as a candidate for another public office, if the term of the office sought begins before the end of the term of the office held.

This "resign to run" section, added by the 1978 convention, also provoked considerable debate. Opponents questioned its legality, clarity, and fairness. Supporters won the day with arguments stressing that by running for another office, elected officials signal they no longer want to fulfill the responsibilities of the office currently held. Despite the high plane on which the debate was carried out, convention observers note that it was in fact specifically aimed at the mayor of Honolulu, Frank Fasi, whose aspiration to the office of governor was well known.[43] Today, it is commonly referred to as the "Fasi law."

Left uncertain in the language is whether it applies only to elected state and county officials who run for other state/county offices or whether it includes those who are candidates for federal offices. Noting that the provision is ambiguous, the Hawaii Supreme Court found that the framers did not indicate a clear intent to include candidates for federal office within its scope. In its absence, a state senator was not forced to resign in order to run for the U.S. House of Representatives (*Cobb v. State*, 1986).

In 1990, the provision was challenged in the federal courts by Frank Fasi, once again mayor of Honolulu and still interested in being governor. However, the U.S. district court held that the "resign to run" requirement did not violate

---

[42] Interview with Ian Lind, editor and publisher of *Hawaii Monitor, A Newsletter About Money and Politics*, 1 June 1992.

[43] Recent Developments, "Fasi v. Cayetano: Challenging Hawaii's 'Resign-to-Run' Amendment," *University of Hawaii Law Review* 13 (1991): 339–40; Meller and Kosaki, "Hawaii's Constitutional Convention," 254.

the First and Fourteenth Amendment rights of elected officials desiring to hold other state and county elective offices (*Fasi v. Cayetano*).[44]

Although the issue has not been ruled on specifically, the attorney general, referring to the 1978 convention record, opined that Section 7 was not intended to apply to any elected official whose term expired at an election where they were a candidate for a different office (Op. Att'y Gen. 86-17, 1986). In *Fasi*, the federal court indicated its approval of this interpretation and also stated that it is reasonable to exempt federal officials and those seeking federal office from the provision's scope.

SECTION 8

General, Special and Primary Elections. General elections shall be held on the first Tuesday after the first Monday in November in all even-numbered years. Special and primary elections may be held as provided by law; provided that in no case shall any primary election precede a general election by less than forty-five days.

Since the Statehood Constitution, two parts of this section have remained intact: (1) General elections are held on the first Tuesday after the first Monday in November in all even-numbered years, and (2) special elections may be held as provided by law. The original section, titled "Elections," also included a provision stating that "[cjontested elections shall be determined by a court of competent jurisdiction in such manner as shall be provided by law." In 1968, the title was changed to "General and Special Elections" since the provision regarding contested elections was removed to a separate section (Section 10).

The current language (including another new title) was adopted in 1978 to incorporate primary elections as well as to establish a minimum number of days between primary and general elections. This latter issue produced lively debate, with the convention rejecting a sixty-day minimum (approximately double that established by statute at the time) in favor of a forty-five-day minimum. By specifying a minimum, the constitution in effect both limited the discretion of the legislature and forced it to expand the existing period between elections. Although the addition of this provision may have demonstrated the weakened position of organized party control in the state, subsequent legislative action did not constitute much of a change.[45] When the legislature amended the statute, it set the primary day as close to the required forty-five-day minimum as the calendar permits. Thus, Hawaii holds its primary elections later than almost all other states. A complaint raised at the 1978 convention can still be heard: The very

---

[44] For a discussion of the case prior to the federal court's ruling, see Recent Developments, "Fasi v. Cayetano," 327. See also Van Dyke, Chung, and Kondo, "The Protection of Individual Rights," 367.

[45] Meller and Kosaki, "Hawaii's Constitutional Convention," 253.

short time between the primary and the general elections gives an advantage to incumbents.

The phrase "Special . . . elections may be held as provided by law" has the effect of requiring specific statutory authorization. Without it, the chief election officer (the lieutenant governor) cannot call for and hold a special election (*State v. Gill*, 1970).

SECTION 9

Presidential Preference Primary. A presidential preference primary may be held as provided by law.

The 1968 convention added this provision. Until late in the session, it appeared the delegates would approve a provision mandating presidential primaries, but at the last minute they left it to the legislature to decide. The language was not changed substantively by the 1978 convention. Because enabling legislation has never succeeded in passing both chambers, Hawaii, among the minority of states not using presidential primaries, relies on party caucuses.

SECTION 10

Contested Elections. Contested elections shall be determined by a court of competent jurisdiction in such manner as shall be provided by law.

Originally a portion of what is now Section 8, this provision became a separate section in 1968; no substantive changes have been made. Although Article III, Section 12 provides that "[e]ach house shall be the judge of the elections, returns and qualifications of its own members," this section is controlling because it requires the courts to "be the forum and the final arbiter" when there is a contested election (*Akizaki v. Fong*, 1969).

Article III

The Legislature

Since statehood, a number of significant changes have been made to this article. While some of the amendments altered such details as the legislative starting date and the minimum age for legislators, others had wider impact in terms of the legislature's relationship with the public and the executive branch and its ability to oversee the implementation of enacted policies.

Adding mandates for open legislative committee meetings, a bill introduction cutoff date, a required legislative recess, and an extension of the time bills must be available in final form before passage constitutes part of an attempt to increase the body's public accountability. While the Statehood Constitution allowed session extensions and the convening of special sessions only upon gubernatorial action, subsequent amendments adjusted the balance between the legislative and the executive branches by granting similar power to the legislature itself. The change from regular sessions alternating with shorter budget sessions to annual regular sessions enhanced the body's oversight function.

Prior to 1978, reapportionment provisions were also set forth in this article, but the convention of that year separated them and created a new Article IV.

SECTION 1

Legislative Power. The legislative power of the State shall be vested in a legislature, which shall consist of two houses, a senate and a house of representatives. Such power shall extend to all rightful subjects of legislation not inconsistent with this constitution or the Constitution of the United States.

This section, vesting legislative power in a bicameral legislature made up of a house of representatives and a senate, has remained unchanged since the Statehood Constitution. All three constitutional conventions included vocal proponents of unicameralism, though each time they made up a small minority able to launch no more than a "mock battle."[46]

Legislative power means, according to the Hawaii Supreme Court, the power to enact laws and declare what the law shall be (*Sherman v. Sawyer*, 1980). This power includes the authority to enact statutes to modify or change the common law as it has been established by judicial decision (*Bissen v. Fujii*, 1970), the broad power to define words for a particular legislative purpose (*State v. Kantner*, 1972), and the power to establish the subject matter jurisdiction of the state courts (*Sherman v. Sawyer*, 1980).

SECTION 2

Composition of Senate. The senate shall be composed of twenty-five members, who shall be elected by the qualified voters of the respective senatorial districts. Until the next reapportionment the senatorial districts and the number of senators to be elected from each shall be set forth in the Schedule.

A senate consisting of twenty-five members originated in the document drafted by the 1950 convention. At that time there were fifteen members of the territorial senate, a number established by the Organic Act of 1900. But in 1956, following the lead of the 1950 convention, Congress amended the act by increasing the size of the senate to twenty-five. When the constitution became effective with statehood in 1959, the senate size remained constant.

In addition to setting the number of senators, this section of the Statehood Constitution included specific descriptions of the districts from which they would be elected. However, it did not provide for future senate redistricting and was therefore defective because there was no other way to reapportion that chamber except by constitutional amendment (*Holt v. Richardson*, 1965 [*Holt I*]; *Guntert v. Richardson*, 1964). (See the discussions of the 1968 convention in Part I and the commentary following Article IV.)

In response, the 1968 convention provided for future senate and house redistricting by amending other sections (see Article IV); placing the district descriptions in the Schedule (Article XVIII); and adding the sentence specifying that until the next reapportionment, those districts would be effective. To make this

[46] Norman Meller, *With an Understanding Heart: Constitution Making in Hawaii*. (New York: National Municipal League, 1971), 102.

section consistent with reapportionment provisions in Article IV, the 1978 convention proposed the following substitute sentence: "The senatorial districts and the number of senators to be elected from each shall be as set forth in the reapportionment plan as established by the reapportionment commission." Since this amendment was ruled not validly ratified by the voters in *Kahalekai v. Doi* (1979), the 1968 wording remains, directing the reader to the Schedule. There, one now finds a note that the descriptions of senate districts are omitted as obsolete.

From territorial time until 1982, almost all Hawaii state senators were elected from multi-member districts. In 1966, in a case coming from Hawaii, the U.S. Supreme Court upheld the use of such districting (*Burns v. Richardson*, 1966). This practice ended with the imposition of a court-ordered redistricting plan, following the U.S. district court's invalidation of the state's 1981 reapportionment plan (*Travis v. King*, 1982). Since then, all of the state senators have been elected from single-member districts. (See Article IV.)

SECTION 3

Composition of House of Representatives. The house of representatives shall be composed of fifty-one members, who shall be elected by the qualified voters of the respective representative districts. Until the next reapportionment, the representative districts and the number of representatives to be elected from each shall be as set forth in the Schedule.

Under the Organic Act of 1900, the territorial house was comprised of twenty-five members. As it did with respect to the size of the territorial senate, Congress amended the act in 1956 and increased the house to fifty-one members, conforming to the number in the document drafted by the 1950 convention.

As with Section 2 above, the 1978 convention proposed changing the last sentence of this section to make it consistent with Article IV 's reapportionment provisions. However, this amendment was also ruled not validly ratified by the voters (*Kahalekai v. Doi*, 1979).

The Organic Act, the Statehood Constitution, and the 1968 Constitution included precise descriptions of the house districts. They are now deleted from the Schedule as obsolete. Since the beginning of the territory, most of the state representatives, like state senators, were elected from multi-member districts. This was upheld by the U.S. Supreme Court in the 1966 *Burns v. Richardson* case challenging Hawaii's districting plan. When the U.S. district court found the state's 1981 plan unconstitutional, a court-ordered redistricting map, using single-member districts for representatives, went into effect (*Travis v. King*, 1982). Ever since then, all members of the state house have represented single-member districts. (See Article IV.)

SECTION 4

Election of Members; Term. Each member of the legislature shall be elected at an election. If more than one candidate has been nominated for election to a seat in the legislature, the member occupying that seat shall be elected at a general election. If a candidate nominated for a seat at a primary election is unopposed for that seat at the general election, the candidate shall be deemed elected at the primary election. The term of office of a member of the house of representatives shall be two years and the term of office of a member of the senate shall be four years. The term of a member of the legislature shall begin on the day of the general election at which elected or if elected at a primary election, on the day of the general election immediately following the primary election at which elected. For a member of the house of representatives, the term shall end on the day of the general election immediately following the day the member's term commences. For a member of the senate, the term shall end on the day of the second general election immediately following the day the member's term commences.

Since 1959, only one change was made to this section, and it was of major importance. In 1988, voters ratified an amendment deleting the word "general" from the first sentence and inserting the third sentence which reads, "If a candidate nominated for a seat at a primary election is unopposed for that seat at the general election, the candidate shall be deemed elected at the primary election." The name of any candidate who wins a party primary and is not opposed during the general election no longer appears on the general election ballot since the individual has already "won" the election. The reason advanced for this amendment was to cut down on ballot printing costs for the general election by omitting names of unopposed candidates. It is not clear how this provision can be implemented should legislation allowing write-in voting be enacted (see the discussion under Article II, Section 4).

Under this section, representatives serve two-year terms and senators four-year terms. Since it states that legislative terms begin and end on the general election day, candidates must be qualified to serve at the time of their election because the language implicitly requires that legislators be available for service at all times during their elected terms, in regular sessions and in special sessions (*Hayes v. Gill*, 1970). This practice contrasts with that for U.S. senators and representatives who have to be qualified only on the date they actually take their seat.

SECTION 5

Vacancies. Any vacancy in the legislature shall be filled for the unexpired term in such manner as may be provided by law, or, if no provision be made by law, by appointment by the governor for the unexpired term.

As a territory, Hawaii was required by the Organic Act to fill midterm vacancies in the territorial legislature by special elections. But, when the 1950 convention presented its final product to the voters, it included the language, still found today, stipulating that unless there is legislation providing otherwise, the governor fills vacancies by appointment.

There is no clear evidence showing why the 1950 delegates decided not to follow the practice established under the Organic Act. The records of the convention indicate only one delegate questioning it. Upon statehood, the legislature passed a law requiring special elections for filling vacancies, but in 1963 it was repealed and replaced with procedures for gubernatorial appointment. Little evidence exists to illuminate why this change occurred except for the bill's purpose clause which implies that eliminating the costs of special elections was a factor. Apparently legislators were satisfied that the potential abuse of appointment power was tempered by including a requirement that any appointee be of the same political party as the person vacating the seat.

The statutes cover three situations: house vacancies, senate vacancies occurring during the last two years of the four-year term, and senate vacancies occurring within the first two years (Haw. Rev. Stat. §§ 17-3, 17-4). The governor appoints replacements in the first two instances and in the third makes a temporary appointment, which is followed by a special election held concurrently with the next general election in order to fill the final two years of the senate term.

An unusual situation arose when an unopposed senate candidate was murdered just prior to the 1970 general election, leaving the seat vacant. It then became clear that the law did not cover vacancies caused by the absence of a candidate. The attorney general by opinion (Op. Att'y Gen. 70-26, 1970) determined that the vacancy was to be filled by the governor following the provisions of this section in Article III. Taking an opposing position, the lieutenant governor issued a proclamation calling for a special election to fill the vacancy under Article II, Section 8.

In ruling on the issue, the Hawaii Supreme Court held that a special election could not be called because Article II, Section 8 requires specific legislative authorization for special elections. While legislation existed for filling vacancies in other elective offices, none existed to cover this particular situation (*State v. Gill*, 1970). As a result, the governor had the power to appoint a senator for the full term.

The issue then made its way into the U.S. District Court for the District of Hawaii which acknowledged that filling a legislative vacancy by appointment is a well-recognized practice in American law, within the state's legitimate power to regulate elections. Nevertheless, the court continued, when a vacancy occurs in the candidacy for the office of state senator and the governor is empowered to appoint a state senator for a full four-year term, this creates an irrational classification contrary to the equal protection clause of the U.S. Constitution (*Patterson v. Burns*, 1971). Declining to order a special election, the court left resolution up to the legislature, which quickly authorized a special election to fill the empty seat and subsequently passed legislation covering such situations.

While scant consideration was paid to the issue of filling midterm vacancies during the 1968 and 1978 conventions, it suddenly received considerable attention in the late 1980s. In 1987 and 1988, an unusual number of vacancies occurred due to death, retirement, appointment to administrative positions, and appointment of incumbent representatives to fill vacant senate seats. As a result, the governor was able to appoint ten of the total seventy-six legislators (13 percent). Citizens expressed outrage at being represented by those whom they did not elect, questioning whether the governor's appointive powers should be circumscribed and criticizing the absence of any time limit for making an appointment. Attempts to enact legislation changing the process were unsuccessful in 1988, 1990, and 1991, but the issue would not die, for, in October 1991, a representative resigned, giving the governor the opportunity to make his eleventh legislative appointment. In 1992, legislation was enacted requiring that such appointments be made within sixty days, thus placing some limits on the governor.

SECTION 6

Qualifications of Members. No person shall be eligible to serve as a member of the senate unless the person shall have been a resident of the State for not less than three years, have attained the age of majority and be a qualified voter of the senatorial district from which the person seeks to be elected. No person shall be eligible to serve as a member of the house of representatives unless the person shall have been a resident of the State for not less than three years, have attained the age of majority and be a qualified voter of the representative district from which the person seeks to be elected.

The Organic Act and Statehood Constitution set the minimum age of thirty for senators and twenty-five for representatives, following the requirements for members of Congress. When the constitution was changed in 1968 by substitution of "age of majority" for the specific ages, the minimum age for both senators and representatives was in fact lowered to twenty since that was then the legal age of majority. It is now eighteen.

The 1968 convention considered whether to eliminate or reduce the three-year residency requirement found in the Statehood Constitution, but decided in favor of retention. Two years later, when this qualification for service in the legislature was challenged, the Hawaii Supreme Court found that it was neither devoid of rational basis nor invidiously discriminatory (*Hayes v. Gill*, 1970). A proposal to reduce the residency requirement to one year was essentially ignored by the 1978 Constitutional Convention.

The court noted in *Hayes* that, although there is ambiguity in this section because it does not state the date as of which the qualifications must be met, the proper date to be read into it is the date of the general election since Article III specifies that terms of office begin and end at the time of election.

SECTION 7

Privileges of Members. No member of the legislature shall be held to answer before any other tribunal for any statement made or action taken in the exercise of the member's legislative functions; and members of the legislature shall, in all cases except felony or breach of the peace, be privileged from arrest during their attendance at the sessions of their respective houses, and in going to and returning from the same.

The substance of this section, covering two types of privileges, remains unchanged since the Statehood Constitution. It first faced legal challenge in 1974 when the state supreme court was asked to decide whether statements made by a senator in his senate office during an interview by a newspaper reporter, in which he elaborated on a speech made before the senate, were an exercise of legislative function and thus absolutely privileged. The court answered affirmatively (*Abercrombie v. McClung*).[47]

Reviewing the proceedings of the 1950 convention, the court pointed to comments and votes demonstrating that delegates wanted the provision to have broad coverage and that since the delegates did not include any restrictions on the time and place of a legislator's exercise of legislative function, they meant for the courts to make a final determination as to the scope of legislative immunity. The conclusion in *Abercrombie* was that the "clarifying statement by the legislator, though not made in a forum of the legislature, not only fulfills his duty to keep the public informed, but serves the public interest."

Not quite ten years later, the issue was before the court again. In its ruling in *Mehau v. Gannett Pacific Corp.* (1983), the court distinguished the case from *Abercrombie*. It found a claim of legislative privilege unjustified under the following circumstances: The statements occurred after the adjournment of the legislative session; the statements related to the subject matter of resolutions, which, unlike bills, do not remain viable beyond the session in which they are introduced; and the statements were made by a legislator to a group of citizens in a district other than his or her own.

A 1987 opinion by the attorney general gives insight into areas that might be excluded from the second clause granting privilege from arrest (Op. Att'y Gen. 87-5, 1987). In the attorney general's view, a traffic violation is not covered because it is a breach of the peace; a parking ticket does not qualify as an arrest and is therefore not included within the privilege; the scope of the immunity

---

[47] See Comment, "Defamation: A Study in Hawaii Law," *University of Hawaii Law Review* 1 (1979): 88–89.

granted is narrow because the clause grants a privilege only where there is an actual physical detention of a legislator en route to, during, or returning from a legislative session; and the privilege cannot be invoked for any criminal offenses, no matter how minor the violation. The Hawaii courts have not yet been presented with these issues.

SECTION 8

Disqualifications of Members. No member of the legislature shall hold any other public office under the State, nor shall the member, during the term for which the member is elected or appointed, be elected or appointed to any public office or employment which shall have been created, or the emoluments whereof shall have been increased, by legislative act during such term. The term "public offices," for the purposes of this section, shall not include notaries public, reserve police officers or officers of emergency organizations for civilian defense or disaster relief. The legislature may prescribe further disqualifications.

No substantive changes have been made to this section. It prohibits a legislator from being appointed to, or running for, an office before the current legislative term expires if, during that term, the office was created or the salary increased. (See Article III, Section 4 for the definition of the beginning and ending of terms.) However, when the legislature passes legislation providing for special elections to fill vacancies, a new office is not created; and the legislature's passing a law that applies to all public employees generally does not disqualify a member who took part in the enactment from seeking another public office because the benefit contemplated in such legislation is too remote and contingent to be a disqualification (*Bulgo v. Enomoto*, 1967). While this section allows the legislature to prescribe further disqualifications, it has not done so.

SECTION 9

Salary; Allowances; Commission on Legislative Salary. The members of the legislature shall receive allowances reasonably related to expenses as provided by law, and a salary prescribed by the commission on legislative salaries pursuant to this section which shall be payable in installments and at such times as provided by law.

There shall be a commission on legislative salary, which shall be appointed by the governor on or before November 30, 1978, and every eight years thereafter. Not later than the fortieth legislative day of the 1979 regular legislative session and every eight years thereafter, the commission shall submit to the legislature and the governor recommendations for a salary for members of the legislature, and then dissolve. The recommended salary submitted shall become effective as provided in the recommendation unless the legislature disapproves the recommendation by adoption of a concurrent resolution prior to adjournment sine die of the legislative session in which the recommendation is submitted or the governor disapproves the recommendation by a message of disapproval transmitted to the legislature prior to such adjournment. Any change in salary which becomes effective shall not apply to the legislature to which the recommendation for the change in salary was submitted.

Frequent change characterizes this section. The Statehood Constitution placed the power to set legislative salaries in the legislature's hands, limited by the stipulation that "any increase or decrease in the amount thereof shall not apply to the legislature which enacted the same."

The concept of a commission on legislative salary evolved over time, first appearing in the 1968 Constitution. The commission, appointed by the governor every four years, submitted its recommended salary plan to the legislature. However, the work of the commission was purely advisory, and the legislature retained the final word.

Expressing the belief that legislators are reluctant to set their own salaries because taxpayers often negatively respond to legislative pay increases, the 1978 convention acted to relieve legislators of this burden. It made a number of significant modifications to the commission provisions. The commission is now appointed by the governor and meets every eight years. It submits its recommendations to both the governor and the legislature. Either may disapprove the recommendation, but the recommended salary will become law if neither disapproves. This allows the legislature to remove itself from the process if it so chooses.

Two changes have been made since: In 1984, voters approved using "salary" instead of "salary plan" and adding "which shall be payable in installments and at such times as provided by law" to the first sentence. The latter change was based on the belief by some legislators that it was disadvantageous, from a tax point of view, to receive their salary only during the sixty days the legislature was in session. The current language permits a salary payment schedule spread out over a longer period. When the same proposal appeared on the ballot two years earlier, the voters had turned it down.

Throughout all these modifications, one element remained constant: Any change in salary applies only to future legislatures.

SECTION 10

Sessions. The legislature shall convene annually in regular session at 10:00 o'clock A.M. on the third Wednesday in January.

At the written request of two-thirds of the members to which each house is entitled, the presiding officers of both houses shall convene the legislature in special session. At the written request of two-thirds of the members of the senate, the president of the senate shall convene the senate in special session for the purpose of carrying

> out its responsibility established by Section 3 of Article VI. The governor may convene both houses or the senate alone in special session.
>
> Regular sessions shall be limited to a period of sixty days, and special sessions shall be limited to a period of thirty days. Any session may be extended a total of not more than fifteen days. Such extension shall be granted by the presiding officers of both houses at the written request of two-thirds of the members to which each house is entitled or may be granted by the governor.
>
> Each regular session shall be recessed for not less than five days at some period between the twentieth and fortieth days of the regular session. The legislature shall determine the dates of the mandatory recess by concurrent resolution. Any session may be recessed by concurrent resolution adopted by a majority of the members to which each house is entitled. Saturdays, Sundays, holidays, the days in mandatory recess and any days in recess pursuant to a concurrent resolution shall be excluded in computing the number of days of any session.
>
> All sessions shall be held in the capital of the State. In case the capital shall be unsafe, the governor may direct that any session be held at some other place.

The most recent change to this section took place in 1980 when voters approved a legislatively proposed amendment granting the senate president power to convene the senate in special session for the purpose of confirming judicial appointments (a responsibility established under Article VI, Section 3). This afforded the senate an opportunity to consent or to reject judicial appointments on a more timely basis without having to wait until the annual sixty-day session. In effect, it limits gubernatorial power with respect to interim appointments.

A provision regarding a legislative recess first appeared in the 1968 Constitution. It empowered the legislature to call a recess by concurrent resolution. The language requiring a mandatory recess of not less than five days between the twentieth and fortieth days of the regular session was a product of the 1978 convention, where it was adopted without debate. Its purpose is to ensure that about midway through the session both legislators and members of the public have the opportunity to review and discuss all bills that have been introduced.

Later, the legislature unsuccessfully sought to modify this mandatory recess provision. The first attempt, appearing on the 1984 ballot, proposed deleting the requirement that the five-day recess be taken at one time and would have substituted a recess day or days taking place any time after the bill introduction deadline date. The second attempt, on the 1990 ballot, would have increased the length of the recess to six days and allowed it to be taken any time during the session. Voters rejected both.

The 1968 convention addressed other parts of this section and changed much of its detail. The third Wednesday in January, instead of the third Wednesday in February, was set as the legislative starting date. Annual sixty-day sessions replaced the provision in the Statehood Constitution specifying regular sessions of sixty days held in odd-numbered years and thirty-day budget sessions held in even-numbered years.

Under the Statehood Constitution, only the governor was empowered to extend any session, and then for no more than thirty days. The 1968 convention reduced the maximum extension to fifteen days. However, it more significantly bolstered legislative authority by giving the presiding officers of both chambers the power to extend a session, at the written request of two-thirds of the members of each. As a consequence, the legislature is no longer dependent on the governor for extensions; however, the chief executive still has a role to play because extensions "may be granted by the governor."

In like manner, when the constitution was changed in 1968 to give the presiding officers of both chambers the power to call special sessions upon the written request of two-thirds of the members of each house, the scope of executive power was indirectly reduced, although the governor can still convene both houses or the senate alone in special session.

The length of the legislative sessions is an issue that has received a fair amount of attention over the years. Some argue that it should be longer, but an attempt at the 1978 convention to increase the session to seventy-five working days failed. This reflects a generally prevailing view in Hawaii that service in the legislature should be part-time and that any lengthening of the session would negate the concept of a "citizen" legislature. And, yet, each time the legislature extends its session, the issue arises again. In only two of the thirteen sessions from 1980 through 1992, the legislature was able to finish its work on time; the other sessions were extended an average of three days, with the most frequent cause being the need to complete work on the budget.

SECTION 11

Adjournment. Neither house shall adjourn during any session of the legislature for more than three days, or sine die, without the consent of the other.

This section has remained unchanged since the Statehood Constitution; it has not been subject to litigation.

SECTION 12

Organization; Discipline; Rules; Procedure. Each house shall be the judge of the elections, returns and qualifications of its own members and shall have, for misconduct, disorderly behavior or neglect of duty of any member, power to punish such member by censure or, upon a two-thirds vote of all the members to which such house is entitled, by suspension or expulsion of such member. Each house shall choose its own officers, determine the rules of its proceedings and keep a journal. The

> ayes and noes of the members on any question shall, at the desire of one-fifth of the members present, be entered upon the journal.
>
> Twenty days after a bill has been referred to a committee in either house, the bill may be recalled from such committee by the affirmative vote of one-third of the members to which such house is entitled.
>
> Every meeting of a committee in either house or of a committee comprised of a member or members from both houses held for the purpose of making decision on matters referred to the committee shall be open to the public.
>
> By rule of its proceedings, applicable to both houses, each house shall provide for the date by which all bills to be considered in a regular session shall be introduced.

Two major changes to this section were made by the 1978 convention, one of which was subsequently amended in 1984. First, a third paragraph was incorporated requiring open meetings for legislative committees, including conference committees. Although this was normally the practice, the delegates felt that the public's right to observe what their legislators are deciding deserved constitutional protection. But they also made it clear that this change was not meant to open every meeting to the public; they expressly pointed to organizational meetings, partisan caucuses, and hearings where a person's right to privacy might be infringed on as being outside the scope of the provision.

The fourth paragraph, also added in 1978, originally read: "By rule of its proceedings, applicable to both houses, each house shall provide for the date by which all bills to be considered in a regular session shall be introduced. This date shall be after the nineteenth day of the session and shall precede the commencement of the mandatory recess of not less than five days as provided in section 10 of this article." Although there was little discussion about this change, its apparent intent was to make certain that a bill cutoff date furthered the objective of the mandatory recess; that is, a mandatory recess to allow public review of proposed legislation would not make much sense unless all bills had been introduced.

Not long after this amendment went into effect, it became evident that allowing bill introduction through the nineteenth day or later was counterproductive and an earlier date might be in order. A landslide of bills was normally introduced in the final hours before the cutoff, and with the twentieth day as the minimum, fully one-third of the sixty-day session was already over. An amendment was placed on the 1984 general election ballot to allow the legislature the option of setting an earlier cutoff date. Voters approved the deletion of the specific language, leaving the broader wording found today in the last paragraph. However, this language also permits the legislature to set a cutoff day for introduction so late that it vitiates the intent of the provision.

Section 12 must be read in conjunction with another section of the constitution. Although the first sentence of Section 12 specifies that each house shall be the judge of the elections, returns, and qualifications of its own members, Article II, Section 10 specifies that contested elections shall be determined by a court of competent jurisdiction in such manner as shall be provided by law. In resolving the apparent conflict between these two provisions, the Hawaii Supreme Court ruled that the courts, rather than the legislative body, are the final arbiter of a contested election involving a legislative seat. The legislative chamber's function in judging the elections of its members extends only to determining whether the constitution has been followed; that is, "whether the parties have properly invoked the jurisdiction of a competent court to judge the contest" (*Akizaki v. Fong*, 1969).

Because the legislature is empowered by Section 12 to determine the rules of its proceedings, the court has declined to investigate possible violations of legislative rules. In general, the judiciary's role in supervising legislative activity is limited to seeing that such activity does not violate any constitutional provisions. Therefore, it will not "interfere with the conduct of legislative affairs in absence of a constitutional mandate to do so, or unless the procedure or result constitutes a deprivation of constitutionally guaranteed rights" (*Schwab v. Ariyoshi*, 1977).

SECTION 13

Quorum; Compulsory Attendance. A majority of the number of members to which each house is entitled shall constitute a quorum of such house for the conduct of ordinary business, of which quorum a majority vote shall suffice; but the final passage of a bill in each house shall require the vote of a majority of all the members to which such house is entitled, taken by ayes and noes and entered upon its journal. A smaller number than a quorum may adjourn from day to day and may compel the attendance of absent members in such manner and under such penalties as each house may provide.

Unchanged since statehood, this provision mandates a constitutional majority for final passage of a bill; that is, a majority of all members elected to each chamber must vote in favor of the bill. Demanding a constitutional majority for final passage presents a higher hurdle than calling for a majority of those present, as is found in the U.S. and some state constitutions. Notwithstanding, under this section a favorable vote of a majority of those present is sufficient on votes before the final reading of bills.

While Section 12 calls for the recording of the ayes and noes on any question before the legislature only on the desire of one-fifth of the members present, this section requires the ayes and noes on final passage of legislation to be recorded in order to ensure public accountability.

SECTION 14

Bills; Enactment. No law shall be passed except by bill. Each law shall embrace but one subject, which shall be expressed in its title. The enacting clause of each law shall be, "Be it enacted by the legislature of the State of Hawaii."

This section remains as it was in the Statehood Constitution. The language requiring that each law "embrace but one subject, which shall be expressed in its title" is identical to that found in the Organic Act and similar in intent to language found in the pre-territorial constitutions of 1864 and 1887.

In 1977, the state supreme court followed precedent established in Hawaii cases spanning the years 1887 through 1954 in reaffirming that the provision's purpose is to "prevent hodge-podge or logrolling," to "prevent surprise or fraud upon the Legislature by means of provisions in bills of which titles give no intimation," and "to apprise the people of proposed matters of legislation" (*Schwab v. Ariyoshi*, 1977).

The court further stated that the section is mandatory, and a violation of it results in invalid legislation. However, as long as all parts of the act embrace one general subject and "these parts are so connected and related to each other, either logically or in popular understanding, as to be parts of or germane to that general subject," the bill satisfies the one-subject command.

The *Schwab* court also set forth a test for determining whether a bill's title passes constitutional muster: Does the title fairly indicate to the ordinary mind the general subject of the act, is it comprehensive enough to reasonably cover all its provisions, and is it calculated to mislead? With respect to amendments to legislation, the court has said that, even if the title does not refer specifically to them, the title is valid as long as it clearly refers to the general subject matter of those amendments (*Gallas v. Sanchez*, 1965).

SECTION 15

Passage of Bills. No bill shall become law unless it shall pass three readings in each house on separate days. No bill shall pass third or final reading in either house unless printed copies of the bill in the form to be passed shall have been made available to the members of that house for at least forty-eight hours.

Every bill when passed by the house in which it originated, or in which amendments thereto shall have originated, shall immediately be certified by the presiding officer and clerk and sent to the other house for consideration.

Any bill pending at the final adjournment of a regular session in an odd-numbered year shall carry over with the same status to the next regular session. Before the carried-over bill is enacted, it shall pass at least one reading in the house in which the bill originated.

Actions by the 1968 convention resulted in two important additions to this section, one of which was subsequently expanded in 1978. In recognition of the potential for ill-considered decisions due to the hectic pace of a relatively short session, the 1968 revisions included a requirement that printed copies of bills be available for at least twenty-four hours before the third or final reading. In 1978, this was increased to forty-eight hours, reflecting the delegates' stated sensitivity to the increasing numbers of bills being introduced and the expressions of public concern about the difficulty in following a large number of bills during the closing days of a session.

The second of the 1968 convention's actions on Section 15 was the addition of a provision allowing for bills to be carried over from a session in the odd-numbered year to the following session in the even-numbered year. (The Statehood Constitution had not permitted carry-over bills.) However, in order to ensure adequate public and legislative review prior to passage, the section requires that before such bills can be enacted during that second session, they must pass at least one reading in the chamber where they originated.

SECTION 16

Approval or Veto. Every bill which shall have passed the legislature shall be certified by the presiding officers and clerks of both houses and shall thereupon be presented to the governor. If the governor approves it, the governor shall sign it and it shall become law. If the governor does not approve such bill, the governor may return it, with the governor's objections to the legislature. Except for items appropriated to be expended by the judicial and legislative branches, the governor may veto any specific item or items in any bill which appropriates money for specific purposes by striking out or reducing the same; but the governor shall veto other bills, if at all, only as a whole.

The governor shall have ten days to consider bills presented to the governor ten or more days before the adjournment of the legislature sine die, and if any such bill is neither signed nor returned by the governor within that time, it shall become law in like manner as if the governor had signed it.

—**Reconsideration after Adjournment.** The governor shall have forty-five days, after the adjournment of the legislature sine die, to consider bills presented to the governor less than ten days before such adjournment, or presented after adjournment, and any such bill shall become law on the forty-fifth day unless the governor by proclamation shall have given ten days' notice to the legislature that the governor plans to return such bill with the governor's objections on that day. The legislature may convene at or before noon on the forty-fifth day in special session, without call, for the sole purpose of acting upon any such bill returned by the governor. In case the legislature shall fail to so convene, such bill shall not become law. Any such bill may be amended to meet the governor's objections and, if so amended and passed, only one reading being required in each house for such passage, it shall be presented again to the governor, but shall become law only if the governor shall sign it within ten days after presentation.

In computing the number of days designated in this section, the following days shall be excluded: Saturdays, Sundays, holidays and any days in which the legislature is in recess prior to its adjournment as provided in section 10 of this article.

See the commentary following Section 17.

SECTION 17

Procedures upon Veto. Upon the receipt of a veto message from the governor, each house shall enter the same at large upon its journal and proceed to reconsider the vetoed bill, or the item or items vetoed, and again vote upon such bill, or such item or items, by ayes and noes, which shall be entered upon its journal. If after such reconsideration such bill, or such item or items, shall be approved by a two-thirds vote of all members to which each house is entitled, the same shall become law.

Sections 16 and 17 are discussed together as their subject matter is related. Except for one important change made to Section 16, they remain virtually as they were included in the Statehood Constitution. In all fundamental respects, the process by which a bill becomes (or fails to become) law is like that observed in Congress and state legislatures across the country: After passage by both chambers, a bill becomes law if the chief executive signs it, if the latter does not act, or if the legislature overrides a veto. The state does not have any duty to notify individuals personally of the date a law becomes effective, even if such individuals may possibly be affected by that law (*Nachtwey v. Doi*, 1978).

The veto power given the governor in Section 16 is one of the checks and balances built into the American system of separation of powers. But while the veto gives the chief executive the formal authority to "check" the legislative branch, the power is not absolute: The legislature may override a veto.

In contrast to the U.S. president, but like most other state chief executives, Hawaii's governor has the power to veto a specific appropriation item or items while approving the rest of the bill. This line item veto enables the governor to strike out or reduce, but not increase, the monetary amount designated for particular expenditures. Section 16 specifically states that the line item veto applies only to appropriations; except for expenditures, a bill can only be vetoed in its entirety.

Until 1974, the line item veto power granted to Hawaii's governor over appropriations bills was unlimited. However, in that year a constitutional change proposed by the legislature was approved by the voters. It amended Section 16 by specifically excluding appropriations to be expended by the judicial and the legislative branches from the governor's line item veto authority. This change was based on the principle that the chief executive should not be able to use the line item veto as a means for interfering with the ability of the other two branches to perform their responsibilities. This provision does not mean, however, that judicial, legislative, and executive appropriations must be presented in separate bills (*Schwab v. Ariyoshi*, 1977).

While the U.S. president may, in effect, veto a bill by neither approving nor rejecting it by the time the legislature adjourns, Hawaii's governor is precluded from using this "pocket veto." Section 16 establishes distinct procedures that must be followed for bills presented to the governor, depending on whether a bill is delivered at least ten days before adjournment, less than ten days before adjournment, or after adjournment. In the first instance, the governor has ten days to consider the bill, and if he or she does not sign or veto it within that time, it becomes law. In both the second and third cases, the governor has forty-five days after the legislature's adjournment for consideration. The bill becomes law on the forty-fifth day unless the governor issues a proclamation, giving the legislature ten days' prior notice, that the bill is being returned, with objections, on that forty-fifth day. The legislature may convene in special session on or before that day for the sole purpose of acting on the returned bill. Once convened, the legislature may amend the bill to meet the gubernatorial objections, but only if the governor then signs the bill within ten days after presentation will it become law. A vetoed bill dies if the legislature convenes, but takes no action, or if it does not convene.

As in most states, the Hawaii legislature can override a veto by a two-thirds vote of the total membership. Since statehood there have been over 400 vetoes, none was overridden, and the legislature has only met twice in special session to consider vetoed bills, both times amending the bills to meet the governor's objections.

SECTION 18

Punishment of Nonmembers. Each house may punish by fine, or by imprisonment not exceeding thirty days, any person not a member of either house who shall be guilty of disrespect of such house by any disorderly or contemptuous behavior in its presence or that of any committee thereof; or who shall, on account of the exercise of any legislative function, threaten harm to the body or estate of any of the members of such house; or who shall assault, arrest or detain any witness or other person ordered to attend such house, on the witness' or other person's way going to or returning therefrom; or who shall rescue any person arrested by order of such house.

Any person charged with such an offense shall be informed in writing of the charge made against the person and have opportunity to present evidence and be heard in the person's own defense.

No substantive alterations have been made to this section since statehood. Its objective is to give the legislature power to punish nonlegislators who disrupt or interfere with the legislative process.

SECTION 19

Impeachment. The governor and lieutenant governor, and any appointive officer for whose removal the consent of the senate is required, may be removed from office upon conviction of impeachment for such causes as may be provided by law.

The house of representatives shall have the sole power of impeachment of the governor and lieutenant governor and the senate the sole power to try such impeachments, and no such officer shall be convicted without the concurrence of two-thirds of the members of the senate. When sitting for that purpose, the members of the senate shall be on oath or affirmation and the chief justice shall preside. Subject to the provisions of this paragraph, the legislature may provide for the manner and procedure of removal by impeachment of such officers.

The legislature shall by law provide for the manner and procedure of removal by impeachment of the appointive officers.

Judgments in cases of impeachment shall not extend beyond removal from office and disqualification to hold and enjoy any office of honor, trust or profit under the State; but the person convicted may nevertheless be liable and subject to indictment, trial, judgment and punishment as provided by law.

The substance of this section remains unchanged. The two-step process follows that in Article I of the U.S. Constitution. The lower chamber brings the impeachment, while the upper chamber tries and convicts upon a two-thirds vote, with the chief justice presiding. The language found in the last paragraph, like that in the U.S. Constitution, limits the legislature to removal and disqualification from office of any individual impeached and convicted; any criminal prosecution must proceed through the criminal justice system.

Article IV

Reapportionment

Reapportionment has long been a source of political and legal controversy in Hawaii.[48] Although the Organic Act required that it be carried out periodically, the territorial legislature failed to observe that mandate, a failure unsuccessfully challenged in *Territory v. Tam* (1942). A second challenge (*Dyer v. Abe*, 1956) initially succeeded, but was later dismissed as moot (*Dyer v. Abe*, 1958) since in the meantime Congress had reapportioned the territorial legislature by amending the Organic Act. This plan followed provisions adopted by the 1950

[48] Hawaii's reapportionment controversies have been covered extensively. See Anne F. Lee, "Hawaii," in *Redistricting in the 1980's, ed.* Leroy Hardy, Alan Heslop, and George Blair (Claremont, Calif.: Rose Institute of State and Local Government, Forthcoming); Anne F. Lee, "Redistricting in Hawaii," *Comparative State Politics* 13, no. 4 (1992): 47; Robert G. Schmitt, "A History of Recent Reapportionment in Hawaii," *Hawaii Bar Journal* 22 (1990): 171; Anne F. Lee, "Reapportionment in Hawaii, Prospects for the 1990s," *Comparative State Politics* 11, no. 3 (1990): 24; Anne F. Lee and Peter J. Herman, "Ensuring the Right to Equal Representation: How to Prepare or Challenge Legislative Reapportionment Plans," *University of Hawaii Law Review* 5 (1983): 1; Richard H. Kosaki, "Hawaii," in *Reapportionment Politics, The History of Redistricting in the 50 States*, ed. Leroy Hardy, Alan Heslop, and Stuart Anderson (Beverly Hills, Calif.: Sage Publications, 1981), 86; Robert Horwitz, "Reapportionment in the State of Hawaii—Considerations on the Reynolds Decision," in *Representation and Misrepresentation*, ed. Robert A. Goldman (Chicago: Rand McNally, 1968), 21; Harold S. Roberts, *Reapportionment and the Revision and Amending Procedures of the Hawaii State Constitution*, 2d ed. (Honolulu: Department of Political Science, University of Hawaii, 1966).

convention: Districts for the twenty-five senate seats (up from fifteen) created a geographical balance among the islands, while districts for the fifty-one house seats (up from twenty-five) were based on population.

Shortly after statehood and following the landmark reapportionment decisions handed down by the U.S. Supreme Court (*Reynolds v. Sims,* 1964; *Baker v. Carr,* 1962), the state's attorney general issued a series of opinions concluding that the legislature was malapportioned (Op. Att'y Gen. 64-33, 64-34, 64-36, 1964). A period of complex maneuvers and events within the legislature, executive branch, state supreme court, and federal courts followed (*Burns v. Richardson,* 1966; *Holt v. Richardson,* 1965 (*Holt I* and *II*); *Guntert v. Richardson,* 1964). The 1968 convention was born from this struggle, as discussed in detail in Part I.

The 1968 delegates focused considerable attention on reapportionment, and although they retained much of the redistricting language from the Statehood Constitution, they did make significant changes. In 1978, additional modifications were incorporated. This article is new to the 1978 constitution since that year the reapportionment provisions from Article III, where they had been since statehood, were placed in a separate Article IV.

SECTION 1

Reapportionment Years. The year 1973, the year 1981, and every tenth year thereafter shall be reapportionment years.

Each of the earlier constitutions had designated different reapportionment years. As a result of changes adopted in 1978, this section now ensures that Hawaii's reapportionment will coincide with the timing of the nation's decennial census and congressional reapportionment because it specifies "the year 1981, and every tenth year thereafter."

SECTION 2

Reapportionment Commission. A reapportionment commission shall be constituted on or before May 1 of each reapportionment year and whenever reapportionment is required by court order. The commission shall consist of nine members. The president of the senate and the speaker of the house of representatives shall each select two members. Members of each house belonging to the party or parties different from that of the president or the speaker shall designate one of their number for each house and the two so designated shall each select two members of the commission. The eight members so selected shall, promptly after selection, be certified by the selecting authorities to the chief election officer and shall within thirty days thereafter select, by a vote of six members, and promptly certify to the chief election officer the ninth member who shall serve as chairperson of the commission.

Each of the four officials designated above as selecting authorities for the eight members of the commission shall, at the time of the commission selections, also select one person from each basic island unit to serve on an apportionment advisory council for that island unit. The councils shall remain in existence during the life of the commission and each shall serve in an advisory capacity to the commission for matters affecting its island unit.

A vacancy in the commission or a council shall be filled by the initial selecting authority within fifteen days after the vacancy occurs. Commission and council positions and vacancies not filled within the times specified shall be filled promptly thereafter by the supreme court.

The commission shall act by majority vote of its membership and shall establish its own procedures, except as may be provided by law.

Not more than one hundred fifty days from the date on which its members are certified, the commission shall file with the chief election officer a reapportionment plan for the state legislature and a reapportionment plan for the United States congressional districts which shall become law after publication as provided by law. Members of the commission shall hold office until each reapportionment plan becomes effective or until such time as may be provided by law.

No member of the reapportionment commission or an apportionment advisory council shall be eligible to become a candidate for election to either house of the legislature or to the United States House of Representatives in either of the first two elections under any such reapportionment plan.

Commission and apportionment advisory council members shall be compensated and reimbursed for their necessary expenses as provided by law.

The chief election officer shall be secretary of the commission without vote and, under the direction of the commission, shall furnish all necessary technical services. The legislature shall appropriate funds to enable the commission to carry out its duties.

Under the Statehood Constitution, the power to reapportion the state house was placed in the hands of the governor (see *Davis v. Quinn*, 1959), but redistricting the state senate was left to future constitutional amendment (an inappropriate remedy according to *Holt v. Richardson*, 1965 (*Holt I*) and *Guntert v. Richardson* 1964). Reacting to the districting turmoil just experienced, the 1968 convention resolved to take politics out of the process by making a reapportionment commission responsible for redistricting both chambers.

With the selection of commission members placed in the hands of the legislative political parties, eight of the members are equally divided in a bipartisan manner. They have thirty days to select a ninth, who serves as chair; if they are unable to agree, the supreme court makes the appointment. Those who serve are prohibited from becoming state legislative or congressional candidates at the following two elections, thus discouraging eager candidates from serving. Because the plans automatically become effective upon official publication in the newspapers, neither the governor nor the legislature may change or veto them.

The 1978 convention made only two modifications: The commission's responsibility was expanded to include congressional districting, and the time limit for completing its work was increased from 120 to 150 days.

Until November 1992, this section specified that the commission was to be constituted on or before March 1 of each reapportionment year. That starting date, combined with the 150-day limit, caused some difficulties for the 1991 commission because U.S. census data were not available until much of the time period had elapsed. In order to avoid this problem in the future, the 1992 legislature proposed an amendment changing the date to May 1 and it was ratified by the voters at the 1992 general election.

SECTION 3

Chief Election Officer. The legislature shall provide for a chief election officer of the State, whose responsibilities shall be as provided by law and shall include the supervision of state elections, the maximization of registration of eligible voters throughout the State and the maintenance of data concerning registered voters, elections, apportionment and districting.

This section was added in 1978. By statute, the lieutenant governor is designated the chief election officer (Haw. Rev. Stat. § 11-2). In addition to the responsibilities outlined here, Section 2 above stipulates that the lieutenant governor serves the commission as secretary and provides technical services.

SECTION 4

Apportionment Among Basic Island Units. The commission shall allocate the total number of members of each house of the state legislature being reapportioned among the four basic island units, namely: (1) the island of Hawaii, (2) the islands of Maui, Lanai, Molokai and Kahoolawe, (3) the island of Oahu and all other islands not specifically enumerated, and (4) the islands of Kauai and Niihau, using the total number of permanent residents in each of the basic island units and computed by the method known as the method of equal proportions; except that no basic island unit shall receive less than one member in each house.

Most of the language in this section originated in the Statehood Constitution. Until the 1992 general election, however, the document required using the number of registered voters as the apportionment base, a base having a long and controversial history in Hawaii. One of the factors contributing to the territorial legislature's failure to reapportion itself was the Organic Act's mandate to use territorial citizens as the base (a figure difficult to obtain because U.S. census figures did not distinguish territorial citizens from U.S. citizens). To avoid future difficulties, the 1950 convention decided that registered voters should be used because it was an easily obtained figure. This base was used for all districting plans until a court-ordered plan took effect in 1982.

In *Burns v. Richardson* (1966), the U.S. Supreme Court held that, used alone, a registered voter base was not satisfactory. It could be used only if "it was found to have produced a distribution of legislators not substantially different from that which would have resulted from the use of a permissible population base," defined as either (1) total population or (2) total population minus any or all of the following: aliens, transients, short-term or temporary residents, and felons. Satisfied that Hawaii's high voter registration and turnout figures demonstrated an equivalency, the *Burns* Court upheld Hawaii's districting (as did the U.S. district court in *Burns v. Gill*, 1970).

Following the 1981 commission's work, the registered voter basis was again challenged. In *Travis v. King* (1982), the U.S. District Court for the District of Hawaii found the legislative plan unconstitutional because the state was unable to show a substantial equivalency as called for in *Burns v. Richardson*. Hawaii's court-ordered plan for the 1982 election and the subsequent plan drawn by a reconstituted commission (for 1984 through 1990) were based on total population minus an estimated number of temporary residents (primarily nonresident military personnel). The 1991 commission met the problem frontally by ignoring the constitutional mandate and used total population minus nonresidents as the base for state legislative districts. No legal challenge followed.

The 1992 legislature proposed a constitutional amendment deleting the phrase "on the basis of the number of voters registered in the last preceding general election" and substituting "the total number of permanent residents." While similar legislatively proposed amendments placed on the ballot in 1988 and 1990 did not secure voter ratification, this proposal finally received voter approval in November 1992.

The section's requirement for minimum county representation of no less than one member per chamber has always been met, but the provision is unconstitutional. The U.S. district court, in its 1970 *Burns v. Gill* decision, stated quite bluntly that "when the time comes that any one basic island unit is not entitled to be allocated one member in either house, then Hawaii's Constitution simply will have to be amended to set up a different basis."

Where this section calls for use of the method of equal proportions for the basic island units (counties), it is referring to the same method used in allocating the 435 seats in the U.S. House of Representatives. Under this complex method, each unit is initially allocated one seat and then additional seats, if its population warrants, until the total number of seats is distributed. Because of unique geographical, social, and political factors in Hawaii, use of the method of equal proportions has not brought invidious results, and it is constitutionally permissible (*Burns v. Gill*, 1970). But the U.S. Constitution's Fourteenth Amendment equal protection clause supersedes a strict adherence in Hawaii to the method of equal proportions (*Blair v. Ariyoshi*, 1973). The 1991 commission was compelled to ignore this method in allocating seats among the basic island units because it would have resulted in deviations among districts in violation of the one person-one vote guidelines established by the U.S. Supreme Court.

SECTION 5

Minimum Representation for Basic Island Units. The representation of any basic island unit initially allocated less than a minimum of two senators and three representatives shall be augmented by allocating thereto the number of senators or representatives necessary to attain such minimums which number, notwithstanding the provisions of Sections 2 and 3 of Article III shall be added to the membership of the appropriate body until the next reapportionment. The senators or representatives of any basic island unit so augmented shall exercise a fractional vote wherein the numerator is the number initially allocated and the denominator is the minimum above specified.

Added in 1968, and based on longstanding concern for basic island representation, this section is fraught with problems and has not been implemented. It calls for legislators with fractional votes to ensure that each basic island unit has a minimum of two senators and three representatives. Declared impermissible under the one person-one vote principle (*Burns v. Gill*, 1970), it remains in the constitution despite attempts to delete it. The 1978 convention's deletion proposal was ruled not validly ratified in *Kahalekai v. Doi* (1979), and legislatively proposed amendments to do the same failed to receive voter approval in 1988 and 1990.

SECTION 6

Apportionment Within Basic Island Units. Upon the determination of the total number of members of each house of the state legislature to which each basic island unit is entitled, the commission shall apportion the members among the districts therein and shall redraw district lines where necessary in such manner that for each house the average number of permanent residents per member in each district is as nearly equal to the average for the basic island unit as practicable.

In effecting such redistricting, the commission shall be guided by the following criteria:

1. No district shall extend beyond the boundaries of any basic island unit.
2. No district shall be so drawn as to unduly favor a person or political faction.
3. Except in the case of districts encompassing more than one island, districts shall be contiguous.
4. Insofar as practicable, districts shall be compact.
5. Where possible, district lines shall follow permanent and easily recognized features, such as streets, streams and clear geographical features, and, when practicable, shall coincide with census tract boundaries.
6. Where practicable, representative districts shall be wholly included within senatorial districts.
7. Not more than four members shall be elected from any district.
8. Where practicable, submergence of an area in a larger district wherein substantially different socio-economic interests predominate shall be avoided.

Like Section 4 above, this section originally required using a registered voter base. When voters ratified the 1992 legislatively proposed amendment concerning the apportionment base, they also approved substituting "permanent residents" for "registered voters" in the first paragraph of this section. No changes have been made to the eight specified criteria since they were added in 1968, but at least one cannot be observed without violating the U.S. Constitution. The 1978 convention did propose a ninth item—that "no consideration shall be given to holdover senators in effecting redistricting"—but it, too, was ruled not validly ratified by the voters (*Kahalekai v. Doi*, 1979).

The 1982 court-ordered plan included bicounty districts in order to keep population deviations among districts within federally mandated guidelines; for the same reason, plans drawn since then continued to use bicounty districts, thus violating the prohibition (criterion 1) against districts extending beyond county boundaries. In 1990, a legislatively proposed amendment, making the language conform with one person-one vote guidelines, was placed on the ballot, but it was not ratified.

The practice of electing almost all legislators from multi-member districts (allowed by criterion 7), started when Hawaii became a territory, was upheld in the 1966 *Burns v. Richardson* decision and continued until 1982. Though the practice was challenged in *Travis v. King* (1982), the U.S. district court did not address the issue. Nevertheless, the resulting court-ordered plan with only single-member districts brought a dramatic change. While the federal court in *Travis* was acting under judicial constraints that necessitated single-member districts in the absence of a showing to the contrary, the continuation of single-member districts in subsequent state redistricting plans can be explained not because of comparable restrictions, but instead because of political considerations.

SECTION 7

Election of Senators after Reapportionment. Regardless of whether or not a senator is serving a term which would have extended past the general election at which an apportionment plan becomes effective, the term of office of all senators shall end at that general election. The staggered terms of senators in each district shall be recomputed as established by the next section in this article, and the number of senators in a senatorial district under the reapportionment plan of the commission.

See the commentary following Section 8.

SECTION 8

Staggered Terms for the Senate. Any re-elected senator whose prior term was shortened to two years by the occurrence of the reapportionment year shall, after reapportionment, be assigned to serve a four-year term. Any new senator and re-elected senator whose prior term was not shortened by the occurrence of the reapportionment year shall, after reapportionment, be assigned to serve a two-year term.

If the number of senators assigned to serve a two-year term under the previous paragraph exceeds twelve, the number of such senators shall be reduced to twelve by random selection as provided by law.

Sections 7 and 8 concern staggered senate terms and "holdover" senators, and were added in 1978. The language found today is, however, considerably different because of a legislatively proposed amendment ratified in November 1992.

When added in 1978, along with Section 2, Article XVIII (Schedule), these sections reestablished staggered senate terms after they were eliminated by the 1968 convention. The twenty-five senate seats were divided into two classes, one of twelve and one of thirteen. At each election, only one class is up for election. Members of the other class are referred to as holdover senators.

Section 8 was originally titled "Retention of Staggered Terms for the Senate" and contained much detail for initiating the staggered system, for making certain that not all senators in a multi-member district were elected concurrently and that a reapportionment did not disrupt the staggered system. In order to make certain that each holdover senator continued to represent a district for the remaining two years of his or her term, Section 7 (previously titled "Placement of Holdover Senators") gave power to the reapportionment commission to assign holdover senators to new districts, if their districts were eliminated in a new redistricting map. To avoid conflict with Article III, Section 6, requiring legislators to be qualified voters in the district they represent, the section stated that these senators did not have to reside physically in their assigned district.

In response to the 1991 Reapportionment Commission's decision to place two holdover senators in districts they did not reside in (one even being shifted to represent a district on a different island than his original district), the 1992 legislature proposed significant changes that were ratified at the 1992 general election. While staggered terms are retained, the new language in Section 7 means that there will be no holdover senators at the first general election upon a new districting plan becoming effective. All senators will come up for reelection only at that election and this will happen for the first time in 2002. Section 8 now specifies a process for recomputing staggered terms: After a reapportionment some senators will be elected to two-year terms that will be followed by four-year terms, while others will be elected to four-year terms until just before the next redistricting plan comes into effect, at which point they will have two-year terms.

SECTION 9

Congressional Redistricting for United States House of Representatives. The commission shall, at such times as may be required by this article and as may be required by law of the United States, redraw congressional district lines for the districts from which the members of the United States House of Representatives allocated to this State by Congress are elected.

Before this section was added in 1978, the constitution did not assign responsibility for congressional districting; it was assigned, by statute, to the legislature. It is now in the commission's hands. This section is silent with respect to the population base to be used for drawing the districts. Until recently, section 25–2 of Hawaii Revised Statutes required use of the number of registered voters as the base. Such a base is, however, invalid because only total census population can be used for congressional districts, and any other base violates both Article I, Section 2 and the equal protection clause of the Fourteenth Amendment of the U.S. Constitution (*Travis v. King*, 1982). The 1991 Reapportionment Commission expressly ignored the statute, used total population for the state's two congressional districts, and thus avoided legal challenge based on the *Travis* precedent. Future commissions will not have to make such a decision; in 1992, Act 320 amended the statute by replacing the words "registered voters" with "persons in the total population."

SECTION 10

Mandamus and Judicial Review. Original jurisdiction is vested in the supreme court of the State to be exercised on the petition of any registered voter whereby it

> may compel, by mandamus or otherwise, the appropriate person or persons to perform their duty or to correct any error made in a reapportionment plan, or it may take such other action to effectuate the purposes of this section as it may deem appropriate. Any such petition shall be filed within forty-five days of the date specified for any duty or within forty-five days after the filing of a reapportionment plan.

In 1968, the time allowed for filing a petition directly with the state supreme court to challenge redistricting was increased from thirty to forty-five days.

While some of Hawaii's reapportionment challenges have been decided by the state's high court, it is fair to say that those decided by the federal courts have had far greater impact.

Article V

The Executive

Hawaii's tradition of a strong executive began during the monarchy and has been sustained through the Organic Act as well as the state constitution. It is clear from the records of the 1950, 1968, and 1978 conventions that those who played a major role in shaping the executive branch provisions supported continuation of the longstanding pattern of a strong, centralized executive.

In his seminal work on centralization in Hawaii, Norman Meller points to various factors contributing to its acceptance throughout Hawaii's history, including the *Kapu* system, giving arbitrary life-and-death decision-making power to the king and chiefs; the concentration of power in a strong monarchy; the oligarchic structure of missionary institutions; the authoritarian relationship of plantation managers to plantation employees; the importation of foreign-born plantation workers who were "untrained in the American forms of local government" the economic control exerted by five major companies; the concentration of power in one dominant labor union; and, for many years, "the subservience of the Orientals" imported to the islands who had been "bred in a status society in which the extended family and customary conduct overshadowed individualism."[49]

---

[49] Norman Meller, "Centralization in Hawaii: Retrospect and Prospect," *American Political Science Review* 52 (1959): 100–103; for a more recent discussion, see Norman Meller, "Policy Control: Institutionalized Centralization in the Fiftieth State," in Smith and Pratt, eds., *Politics*, 13.

Indices often used to compare the institutionalized powers granted the fifty state governors include tenure potential (length of term and term limitations), appointment and removal powers, budget-making powers, the legislature's budget-changing ability, veto provisions, and the partisan affiliation of a governor vis-à-vis partisan control of the legislative branch. In spite of constitutional modifications over time resulting in some reduction of power, Hawaii's governor remains one of the "strongest" in the nation when examined in these terms.[50]

Previously Article IV, the executive branch article was renumbered to Article V in 1978.

SECTION 1

Establishment of the Executive. The executive power of the State shall be vested in a governor. The governor shall be elected by the qualified voters of this State at a general election. The person receiving the highest number of votes shall be the governor. In case of a tie vote, the selection of the governor shall be determined as provided by law.

The term of office of the governor shall begin at noon on the first Monday in December next following the governor's election and end at noon on the first Monday in December four years thereafter.

No person shall be elected to the office of governor for more than two consecutive full terms.

No person shall be eligible for the office of governor unless the person shall be a qualified voter, have attained the age of thirty years and have been a resident of this State for five years immediately preceding the person's election.

The governor shall not hold any other office or employment of profit under the State or the United States during the governor's term of office.

This section grants executive power to the governor with the same broad strokes as found in Article II of the U.S. Constitution. As a result, it also leaves unresolved the issue of what exactly is meant by "executive power." Although there has been no specific judicial interpretation of this phrase, the Hawaii Supreme Court has stated that the constitution "creates the executive as a coequal branch" (*Deak-Perera v. Department of Transportation*, 1984). The establishment of three distinct and separate branches was intended to preclude a commingling of fundamentally different powers of government in the same hands, even though

---

[50] See, for example, Raymond W. Cox III, "Gubernatorial Politics," in *Politics and Public Policy in the Contemporary American West*, ed. Clive S. Thomas (Albuquerque: University of New Mexico Press, 1991), 253; Thad L. Beyle, "Governors," in *Politics in the American States, A Comparative Analysis*, 5th ed., ed. Virginia Gray, Herbert Jacob, and Robert B. Albritton (Glenview, Ill.: Scott, Foresman, 1990), 201.

these separate powers were not meant to operate with complete independence (*Trustees of OHA v. Yamasaki*, 1987).

Executive power, according to the attorney general, includes delegation of ministerial duties to the lieutenant governor without need of any further legislative act. While the legislature prescribes the duties of the lieutenant governor, in doing so it cannot encroach on the governor's authority or transfer executive power to the lieutenant governor (Op. Att'y Gen. 59–127, 1959).

Where there is an intraexecutive branch dispute of a "peculiarly political nature," the political question doctrine applies, and the matter must be resolved by the legislative and the executive branches instead of the judicial branch of the state (*Trustees of OHA v. Yamasaki*, 1987). However, merely asserting a claim of intrabranch dispute does not make the dispute nonjusticiable (*Board of Education v. Waihee*, 1989).

Until 1978, the constitution allowed a governor to serve an unlimited number of consecutive four-year terms, and of the four governors since statehood, two were elected to three consecutive terms, although one was not able to complete his third term due to death. While expressing the belief that a strong executive should be retained, a standing committee of the 1978 convention proposed a limitation of two consecutive four-year terms in order to prevent an incumbent from building "a political machine to perpetuate reelection" and to "give new candidates a better chance of being elected."[51]

In spite of the significance of this change, no debate accompanied the convention's adoption of it. Because the limitation applies only to two consecutive terms, an individual is not precluded from running again after an intervening period. The language was specifically written so that an individual succeeding to the office of governor upon a vacancy may still be eligible to serve an additional two consecutive terms.

This section requires the legislature to provide a method for resolving a tie vote. Prior to 1990, the statutory provision called for the drawing of lots to determine the winner for all elected positions in the state. As a result of controversy over using that method to resolve a 1988 tie vote between two candidates for the state house, the statute was amended; it now establishes a complicated formula applying "election rate points" based on votes cast per precinct (Haw. Rev. Stat. § 11–57).

Under the Statehood Constitution, the governor had to be a citizen of the United States for twenty years, thirty-five years old, a qualified voter, and a resident of the state for five years. The 1968 convention deleted the twenty-year citizenship requirement, reduced the age to thirty, and retained the qualified voter and residency provisions. No further changes were made by the 1978 convention. In *Hankins v. Hawaii* (1986), the U.S. District Court for the District of

[51] *1978 Proceedings I*, Standing Committee Report no. 32, 573.

Hawaii ruled that the five-year residency requirement is not a violation of the U.S. Constitution's Fourteenth Amendment equal protection clause.

SECTION 2

Lieutenant Governor. There shall be a lieutenant governor who shall have the same qualifications as the governor. The lieutenant governor shall be elected at the same time, for the same term and in the same manner as the governor; provided that the votes cast in the general election for the nominee for governor shall be deemed cast for the nominee for lieutenant governor of the same political party. No person shall be elected to the office of lieutenant governor for more than two consecutive full terms. The lieutenant governor shall perform such duties as may be provided by law.

The position of lieutenant governor originated in the Statehood Constitution, although a corresponding position called the secretary of the territory existed under the Organic Act. A person elected as lieutenant governor must meet the same qualifications as does the governor.

In the very early years of statehood, the governor and lieutenant governor ran independently in both primary and general elections. While it never happened, there was always the possibility that those elected would be from different political parties. The phrase "provided that the votes cast in the general election for the nominee for governor shall be deemed cast for the nominee for lieutenant governor of the same political party" was proposed by the legislature and approved by the voters in 1964. It requires that they run as a team in the general election.

There were many proposals for changing the position of lieutenant governor at the 1978 convention, ranging from abolishing it or making it an appointive position to increasing the mandated responsibilities. The only change agreed upon limited the lieutenant governor to two consecutive terms, consistent with the term limitation imposed on the governor by the same convention.

SECTION 3

Compensation: Governor, Lieutenant Governor. The compensation of the governor and of the lieutenant governor shall be as provided by law, but shall not be less than thirty-three thousand five hundred dollars, and twenty-seven thousand five hundred dollars, respectively, a year. Such compensation shall not be increased or decreased for their respective terms, unless by general law applying to all salaried officers of the State. When the lieutenant governor succeeds to the office of the governor, the lieutenant governor shall receive the compensation for that office.

The figures now set in the constitution as the minimum salaries for the governor and the lieutenant governor were established by the 1968 convention, which increased the smaller amounts found in the Statehood Constitution. By statute (Haw. Rev. Stat. § 26–51), they have since been materially augmented. In order to prevent the use of salary as an incentive or a punishment for executive action, this section also stipulates that the compensation cannot be increased or decreased during the term of office, unless such an action applies to the salaries of all officers of the state.

SECTION 4

Succession to Governorship; Absence or Disability of Governor. When the office of governor is vacant, the lieutenant governor shall become governor. In the event of the absence of the governor from the State, or the governor's inability to exercise and discharge the powers and duties of the governor's office, such powers and duties shall devolve upon the lieutenant governor during such absence or disability.

When the office of lieutenant governor is vacant, or in the event of the absence of the lieutenant governor from the State, or the lieutenant governor's inability to exercise and discharge the powers and duties of the lieutenant governor's office, such powers and duties shall devolve upon such officers in such order of succession as may be provided by law.

In the event of the impeachment of the governor or of the lieutenant governor, the governor or the lieutenant governor shall not exercise the powers of the applicable office until acquitted.

No substantive changes have been made to this section. There has been one occasion when the lieutenant governor succeeded the governor when a vacancy in that office occurred. It is left to the legislature to establish succession to the lieutenant governor's position, and in section 26-2 of Hawaii Revised Statutes, the following order of succession has been set: president of the senate, speaker of the house, attorney general, director of finance, comptroller, director of taxation, and director of personnel services.

SECTION 5

Executive Powers. The governor shall be responsible for the faithful execution of the laws. The governor shall be commander in chief of the armed forces of the State and may call out such forces to execute the laws, suppress or prevent insurrection or lawless violence or repel invasion. The governor shall, at the beginning of each session, and may, at other times, give to the legislature information concerning the affairs of the State and recommend to its consideration such measures as the governor shall deem expedient.

The governor may grant reprieves, commutations and pardons, after conviction, for all offenses, subject to regulation by law as to the manner of applying for the same.

The legislature may, by general law, authorize the governor to grant pardons before conviction, to grant pardons for impeachment and to restore civil rights denied by reason of conviction of offenses by tribunals other than those of this State.

The governor shall appoint an administrative director to serve at the governor's pleasure.

This section, listing executive powers of the governor, has not changed substantively since statehood. Six areas are specified: bearing responsibility for the faithful execution of the laws; serving as commander in chief of the armed forces of the state; presenting a state of the state address to the legislature; recommending legislation to the legislature; granting reprieves, commutations, and pardons; and appointing an administrative director who serves at the governor's pleasure.

SECTION 6

Executive and Administrative Offices and Departments. All executive and administrative offices, departments and instrumentalities of the state government and their respective powers and duties shall be allocated by law among and within not more than twenty principal departments in such a manner as to group the same according to common purposes and related functions. Temporary commissions or agencies for special purposes may be established by law and need not be allocated within a principal department.

Each principal department shall be under the supervision of the governor and, unless otherwise provided in this constitution or by law, shall be headed by a single executive. Such single executive shall be nominated and, by and with the advice and consent of the senate, appointed by the governor. That person shall hold office for a term to expire at the end of the term for which the governor was elected, unless sooner removed by the governor; except that the removal of the chief legal officer of the State shall be subject to the advice and consent of the senate.

Except as otherwise provided in this constitution, whenever a board, commission or other body shall be the head of a principal department of the state government, the members thereof shall be nominated and, by and with the advice and consent of the senate, appointed by the governor. The term of office and removal of such members shall be as provided by law. Such board, commission or other body may appoint a principal executive officer who, when authorized by law, may be an ex officio, voting member thereof, and who may be removed by a majority vote of the members appointed by the governor.

The governor shall nominate and, by and with the advice and consent of the senate, appoint all officers for whose election or appointment provision is not otherwise provided for by this constitution or by law. If the manner or [*sic*] removal of an officer is not prescribed in this constitution, removal shall be as provided by law.

When the senate is not in session and a vacancy occurs in any office, appointment to which requires the confirmation of the senate, the governor may fill the office by

> granting a commission which shall expire, unless such appointment is confirmed, at the end of the next session of the senate. The person so appointed shall not be eligible for another interim appointment to such office if the appointment failed to be confirmed by the senate.
>
> No person who has been nominated for appointment to any office and whose appointment has not received the consent of the senate shall be eligible to an interim appointment thereafter to such office.
>
> Every officer appointed under the provisions of this section shall be a citizen of the United States and shall have been a resident of this State for at least one year immediately preceding that person's appointment, except that this residency requirement shall not apply to the president of the University of Hawaii.

Except for a few changes, this section is fundamentally the same as originally written in 1950. It permits the establishment of no more than twenty principal executive departments in such a manner as to group them according to common purposes and related functions.

When departments carry out their duties pursuant to statutory provisions, they are doing so as a part of the executive branch, under the supervision of the governor, thus fulfilling the executive's duty to execute the law (*Deak-Perera v. Department of Transportation*, 1984). An executive branch department does not have independent budget-making powers (*Board of Education v. Waihee*, 1989).

Prior to 1968, the governor was required to obtain senate advice and consent not only for department head appointments, but for their removal as well. As a result of 1968 convention action, consent is still required for all such appointments, but no longer for removal, except in the case of the attorney general.

Delegates to the 1978 convention entered into spirited debate following the introduction of proposals aimed at removing or limiting the governor's power to appoint the attorney general. One proposal called for the election of the attorney general, while another called for the establishment of a commission to present a list of candidates from which the governor would make the appointment. Both proposals were defeated by similar margins, forty-five to fifty-six for the first and forty-three to fifty-seven for the second. Support for an elected attorney general remains alive. Only seven states do not elect their attorneys general; in four of those states besides Hawaii the position is filled by gubernatorial appointment. A recent editorial in one of the state's two major newspapers pointed out that since the 1978 convention, none of the bills proposing a constitutional amendment to create an elected attorney general has passed in the state legislature. The editorial called upon the public to lobby in favor of such a proposal so that it could be placed before the voters at the 1994 election.[52]

Because legislative sessions last only sixty days, the governor is granted power to make interim appointments. However, an individual appointed on an interim

---

[52] "Isle Should Make Move to Elect Attorney General," *Honolulu Star-Bulletin*, 27 May 1992, A–10.

basis, but not subsequently confirmed by the senate, is ineligible for another interim appointment, thus prohibiting the governor from repeatedly reappointing the same person. The ability of the senate to convene in special session to confirm judicial appointments (Article III, Section 10) further limits the scope of the governor's interim appointment power.

The final paragraph of this section requires all appointed officers to be citizens and residents of the state for at least one year immediately preceding appointment. The 1968 convention not only reduced the three-year residency requirement found in the Statehood Constitution, but also added the exemption for the president of the University of Hawaii to permit recruitment from outside the state.

Article VI

The Judiciary

Unlike most other states, Hawaii has a statewide, centralized judiciary under the administrative control of the supreme court; there are no county or city courts.

From 1966 until 1982, the Hawaii Supreme Court, referred to as the Richardson Court after Chief Justice William S. Richardson, was known for its judicial activism, particularly for breaking new legal ground in the areas of water rights (see Article XI, Section 7) and public access to the shoreline and land created by lava flows (see the introductory remarks to Article XI).

Recently, the *University of Hawaii Law Review*, in a symposium issue on the Hawaii Supreme Court since 1982, focused on the court under Chief Justice Herman Lum. The articles evaluating the Lum Court and comparing it to the earlier Richardson Court are, for the most part, critical in tone. While terms used to describe the Richardson Court include "controversial," "reflective," and "activist," those used to describe the Lum Court include "passive," "caretaker," and "emphasizing efficiency." Specific criticisms center on the court's dramatic increase in the use of memorandum opinions that do not set precedent and do not clarify the law, infrequent dissents with over 80 percent of the decisions decided unanimously, an excessive deference to the legislative and executive branches and "rubber stamp" decisions, protection of labor but not the environment, more conservative land use decisions, conservative interpretation of First Amendment rights, and a failure to protect politically powerless groups with any vigor. On the other hand, the court is applauded for its decisions expanding rights for criminal defendants.[53] The court will, however, soon enter a new era because Chief Justice Lum has made public his intention not to serve another term; a new chief justice will be appointed in 1993.

In addition to exercising the traditional powers granted by most state constitutions to the judiciary, the justices of the supreme court perform a unique function derived not from the constitution, but from a will: The justices as individuals appoint trustees to the Bishop Estate, a charitable trust which is one of the largest private landowners in the state. In this role, the members of the court often find themselves indirectly involved in land politics and native Hawaiian concerns as well as charges of conflict of interest.

This unusual activity dates back to 1883 when Princess Bernice Pauahi Bishop's will became effective. A descendant of King Kamehameha I, the princess inherited an extensive amount of land which her will left in trust, with the income to be used for establishing schools for "the children of Hawaii." While "the children of Hawaii" were not specifically identified, "the first board of trustees, including Mrs. Bishop's husband, established a policy for limiting enrollment to children of Hawaiian and part-Hawaiian ancestry."[54] Whether this policy for the Kamehameha Schools violates the equal protection clause of the U.S. Constitution has never been adjudicated, although Justice Kazuhisa Abe questioned its constitutionality in a concurring opinion (*In Re Bishop Estate*, 1972).

The judiciary article was renumbered from Article V to Article VI in 1978.

SECTION 1

Judicial Power. The judicial power of the State shall be vested in one supreme court, one intermediate appellate court, circuit courts, district courts and in such other courts as the legislature may from time to time establish. The several courts shall have original and appellate jurisdiction as provided by law and shall establish time limits for disposition of cases in accordance with their rules.

In *State v. Moriwake* (1982), the Hawaii Supreme Court pointed out that the exact nature of judicial power is not clarified anywhere in the state constitution and that the "inherent or implied powers of the court are by their nature impracticable if not impossible of all-inclusive enumeration." Nevertheless, the court added that the judiciary's inherent power included protecting itself, administering justice whether or not any previous form of remedy has been

[53] For an overview of this symposium issue, see David Kimo Frankel, "The Hawaii Supreme Court: An Overview," *University of Hawaii Law Review* 14 (1992): 5.

[54] Carol S. Dodd, *The Richardson Years: 1966–1982* (Honolulu: University of Hawaii Foundation, 1985), 50.

granted, promulgating rules of practice, and providing process where none exists.

Like the federal courts, Hawaii's judiciary operates with the understanding that "in a tripartite allocation of power . . . courts will not intrude into areas committed to the other branches of government" (*Trustees of OHA v. Yamasaki*, 1987). The court early stated its adherence to the doctrine of judicial self-restraint in *Koike v. Board of Water Supply* (1960) when it said that, although the judicial branch has the power and the duty to declare laws unconstitutional, there is no question but that laws duly passed by the legislature are presumed constitutional and valid, unless the contrary is clearly evident.

In a similar vein, the court has adopted the political question doctrine whereby it finds certain issues nonjusticiable. In the 1987 *Trustees of OHA* case, the court explained that where political questions are concerned, it follows the teachings of the U.S. Supreme Court and recognizes that it is inappropriate for the judiciary to intrude into matters concerning the political branch of government.

Prior to 1978, this section called only for one supreme court, circuit courts, and "such inferior courts as the legislature may from time to time establish." As a result of action taken by the convention of that year, the section now specifies one supreme court, one intermediate appellate court, circuit courts, district courts, and other courts as established by the legislature.

Although district courts had long existed due to statutory provisions, the convention gave them constitutional status by specifically including them in this section. By statute, Hawaii is divided into four judicial circuits, each with a circuit court, and within each judicial circuit there is a system of district courts. The district and circuit courts comprise the trial level, the former having jurisdiction over misdemeanors and civil cases involving less than $10,000 and the latter having jurisdiction over felonies and civil cases involving more than $10,000. A land court and a tax appeal court have been established by the legislature; there is also a division of family courts.

Until 1980, the supreme court was the only appellate court. However, when the 1978 convention added an intermediate appellate court and its chief judge and two associate judges were sworn in on April 18, 1980, a new era in Hawaii's court system began.

Testimony before the convention's standing committee made it evident that a rapidly increasing caseload resulted in long delays for cases appealed to the supreme court, and the question of a remedy became an important one for the 1978 delegates. Chief Justice William S. Richardson took an active lobbying role in favor of an intermediate appeals court; others argued that the alternative of an enlarged supreme court was a more workable solution. There was apparent agreement, however, on the factors causing congestion, including population growth in the state, a greater number of practicing attorneys, easier access to the courts, the expansion of the rights of criminal defendants, and an increased tendency of litigants to exercise their right of appeal.

In opting in favor of an intermediate court, the convention's standing committee explained that its primary function would be to handle the more routine appeals from lower court decisions, leaving the supreme court with more time for selective review and formulation of decisional law. While the convention did not propose constitutional language defining the jurisdiction of the new court, the standing committee stated its intent that both the supreme court and the intermediate appellate court have jurisdiction to hear all types of cases. Subsequent implementation legislation provides that the intermediate court is to hear matters assigned to it by the chief justice and that its rulings may be appealed to the supreme court only on specified grounds.[55]

While the expanding caseload at the appellate level reached critical proportions during the 1970s, concern with court congestion at the trial level dated back to the period after World War II, while Hawaii was still a territory. Right after the attack on Pearl Harbor on December 7, 1941, the territorial courts were closed under martial law, an action later held unconstitutional in the U.S. Supreme Court's landmark ruling in *Duncan v. Kahanamoku* (1946). Although decided once the war was over, the decision confirmed that as long as civil courts are operating, they are not to be replaced by military courts and set an important precedent governing future relationships between the military and civilians even when there is danger of invasion or rebellion. The *Duncan* decision had immediate impact only on those civilians who had been tried and convicted by military tribunals in Hawaii, but the martial law closure of the civilian courts caused a cumulative backlog in cases still existing almost eighteen years later when Hawaii became a state.[56]

The requirement that the state courts "establish time limits for the disposition of cases" was also added in 1978 to address the problem of court delay, not only at the appellate level, but at the trial level as well. This has been implemented by the judiciary, with a six-month rule for the trial courts and the intermediate court of appeals and a twelve-month rule for the supreme court.[57] Nevertheless, delays caused by court congestion remain an issue in Hawaii.[58]

---

[55] For a discussion of the relationship between the two courts and the suggestion that the number of judges on the intermediate court of appeals should be increased, see Jon C. Yoshimura, "Administering Justice or Just Administration: The Hawaii Supreme Court and the Intermediate Court of Appeals," *University of Hawaii Law Review* 14 (1992): 271.

[56] See D. Nils Tavares, "The Administration of Justice in Hawaii Today," *Hawaii Bar Journal* 5 (1967): 18.

[57] *Hawaii Rules of Penal Procedure*, Rule 48; *Rules of the Intermediate Court of Appeals*, Rule 3; *Rules of the Supreme Court*, Rule 9.

[58] See, for example, Benjamin Seto, "State Courts Battle a Chronic Logjam," *Honolulu Star-Bulletin*, 9 June 1992, A-3.

SECTION 2

Supreme Court; Intermediate Appellate Court; Circuit Courts. The supreme court shall consist of a chief justice and four associate justices. The chief justice may assign a judge or judges of the intermediate appellate court or a circuit court to serve temporarily on the supreme court, a judge of the circuit court to serve temporarily on the intermediate appellate court and a judge of the district court to serve temporarily on the circuit court. As provided by law, at the request of the chief justice, retired justices of the supreme court also may serve temporarily on the supreme court, and retired judges of the intermediate appellate court, the circuit courts, the district courts and the district family courts may serve temporarily on the intermediate appellate court, on any circuit court, on any district court and on any district family court, respectively. In case of a vacancy in the office of chief justice, or if the chief justice is ill, absent or otherwise unable to serve, an associate justice designated in accordance with the rules of the supreme court shall serve temporarily in place of the chief justice.

The provision for a chief justice and four associate justices of the supreme court has remained unchanged since the Statehood Constitution. Because the constitution does not fix the size of the intermediate appellate court, the legislature, by statute, has designated a chief judge and two associate judges.

Section 2 also spells out the power of the chief justice to assign judges to temporary service on a higher level court, a provision originating in the 1968 Constitution. It was not changed by the 1978 convention, although the language was altered then to include the new intermediate court judges. The constitution is "clear and unambiguous" in this mandate to the chief justice, and there "is no provision in the constitution which permits appointment of substitute justices by the drawing of lots" (*Kekoa v. Supreme Court*, 1971).

Language granting the chief justice power to appoint retired supreme court justices to serve temporarily was also added in 1968. In 1986, voters ratified a legislatively proposed amendment extending that power to temporary assignment of retired intermediate appellate, circuit, and district court judges.

SECTION 3

Appointment of Justices and Judges. The governor shall, with the consent of the senate, fill a vacancy in the office of the chief justice, supreme court, intermediate appellate court and circuit courts, by appointing a person from a list of not less than six nominees for the vacancy, presented to the governor by the judicial selection commission.

If the governor fails to make any appointment within thirty days of presentation, or within ten days of the senate's rejection of any previous appointment, the appointment shall be made by the judicial selection commission from the list with the consent of the senate. If the senate fails to reject any appointment within thirty days thereof, it shall be deemed to have given its consent to such appointment. If the senate shall reject any appointment, the governor shall make another appointment from the list within ten days thereof. The same appointment and consent procedure shall be followed until a valid appointment has been made, or failing this, the commission shall make the appointment from the list, without senate consent.

The chief justice shall fill a vacancy in the district courts by appointing a person from a list of not less than six nominees for the vacancy presented by the judicial selection commission. If the chief justice fails to make the appointment within thirty days of presentation, the appointment shall be made by the judicial selection commission from the list. The chief justice shall appoint per diem district court judges as provided by law.

—**Qualifications for Appointment**. Justices and judges shall be residents and citizens of the State and of the United States, and licensed to practice law by the supreme court. A justice of the supreme court, a judge of the intermediate appellate court and a judge of the circuit court shall have been so licensed for a period of not less than ten years preceding nomination. A judge of the district court shall have been so licensed for a period of not less than five years preceding nomination.

No justice or judge shall, during the term of office, engage in the practice of law, or run for or hold any other office or position of profit under the United States, the State or its political subdivisions.

—**Tenure; Compensation; Retirement**. The term of office of justices and judges of the supreme court, intermediate appellate court and circuit courts shall be ten years. Judges of district courts shall hold office for the periods as provided by law. At least six months prior to the expiration of a justice's or judge's term of office, every justice and judge shall petition the judicial selection commission to be retained in office or shall inform the commission of an intention to retire. If the judicial selection commission determines that the justice or judge should be retained in office, the commission shall renew the term of office of such justice or judge for the period provided by this section or by law.

There shall be a salary commission to review and recommend salaries for justices and judges of all state courts. Justices and judges shall have salaries as provided by law. Their compensation shall not be decreased during their respective terms of office, unless by general law applying to all salaried officers of the State. They shall be retired upon attaining the age of seventy years. They shall be included in any retirement law of the State.

This section has been considerably modified since statehood. The first major change occurred in 1968 when the convention lengthened the term of office for supreme court justices from seven to ten years and for circuit court judges from six to ten years. Then, in 1978, language was added providing ten-year terms for intermediate court judges and legislative determination of term length for district court judges (now set at six years by section 604-2 of Hawaii Revised Statutes).

Of particular significance is the 1978 change made to the appointment process. Previously, the governor appointed justices to the supreme court and judges to the circuit courts, limited only by the need to secure senatorial consent. But the 1978 convention altered the process (thereby limiting gubernatorial power) by requiring that the governor appoint them from a list of no less than six presented by a judicial selection commission (see Section 4 below). Senate consent remained a requirement, although in order to avoid the possibility of lengthy judicial vacancies in the event of an impasse, the commission was given the ultimate power to make a selection.

The 1978 convention also altered the appointment process for district court judges. Until that time the chief justice of the supreme court appointed them, pursuant to statute. This was changed so that the chief justice selects from a list of no less than six, presented by the judicial selection commission. In the event that the chief justice fails to make an appointment of a district court judge from the list presented, the commission has the responsibility of doing so.

The requirement that supreme court justices and circuit court judges be licensed to practice law in the state for not less than ten years prior to nomination originated in the Statehood Constitution. In 1978, that same requirement was made applicable to the new intermediate court judges. Another 1978 amendment required that district court judges be licensed to practice law in the state for no less than five years.

In 1990, the legislature proposed a further amendment requiring district court judges to be licensed to practice law in the state for ten years, rather than five, but it was not ratified by the voters. Women's groups, minority groups, and attorney associations opposed it on the grounds that the longer period would limit the pool of women and minorities who could be considered for appointment.[59]

As in the earlier constitutions, judges are prohibited from holding any other office or position of profit or running for any elective office. In 1978, language was added to this section specifically disallowing the practicing of law while a judge. Earlier, in the case of *In re Pioneer Mill* (1972), the Hawaii Supreme Court had addressed the question of what constitutes running for elective office, rejecting the argument that a person becomes a candidate only when formal nomination papers are filed. The court held that when a judge has "availed himself of a campaign headquarters set up for him and has made a public announcement that he will seek office," that judge is a candidate, and any case heard by the judge after that point must be remanded for a new trial.

---

[59] Kevin Dayton, "Women, Minorities Oppose Constitutional Amendment," *Honolulu Advertiser*, 2 November 1990, A–9.

A challenge to the role of the supreme court justices, as individuals, in the appointment of Bishop Estate trustees (see the introductory remarks to this article) put the spotlight on the provision enjoining judges from holding any other office or position of profit. The court did not agree that this ban included their testamentary power of appointment because, however one defines "office or position of profit," it "obviously could not include powers of appointment where no remuneration or compensation is to accrue to the holder of the power" (*Kekoa v. Supreme Court*, 1973).

Starting with the Statehood Constitution, the retirement age for justices and judges has been set at seventy. In May 1991, a judge of the U.S. District Court for the District of Hawaii granted an emergency order blocking the state from forcing a judge into retirement because he had reached seventy.[60] The following month, however, the U.S. Supreme Court ruled in a Missouri case, *Gregory v. Ashcroft* (1991), that such a mandatory retirement age for state judges is permissible under the federal Constitution.

A salary commission for reviewing and recommending salaries for state justices and judges was introduced into this section in 1978. In contrast to the detail provided in Article III, Section 9 regarding the legislative salary commission (also added in 1978), this provision simply states that there shall be such a commission; it is ambiguous even as to who has the responsibility to establish the commission. In 1989, the legislature provided by statute (Haw. Rev. Stat. § 608-1.5) that the commission is to be made up of five members: two appointed by the governor, one by the senate president, one by the house speaker, and one by the chief justice. Members serve terms of four years and do not receive a salary. The commission submits its recommendations to the legislature.

SECTION 4

Judicial Selection Commission. There shall be a judicial selection commission that shall consist of nine members. The governor shall appoint three members to the commission. No more than one of the three members shall be a licensed attorney. The president of the senate and the speaker of the house of representatives shall each respectively appoint one member to the commission. The chief justice of the supreme court shall appoint two members to the commission. No more than one of the two members shall be a licensed attorney. Members in good standing of the bar of the State shall elect two of their number to the commission in an election conducted by the supreme court or its delegate. No more than four members of the commission shall be licensed attorneys.

The commission shall be selected and shall operate in a wholly nonpartisan manner. After the initial formation of the commission, elections and appointments to

[60] "Forced Retirement of Judge, 70, Blocked," *Honolulu Star-Bulletin*, 14 May 1991, A–6.

> the commission shall be for staggered terms of six years each. No member of the commission shall serve for more than one full six-year term on the commission.
>
> Each member of the judicial selection commission shall be a resident of the State and a citizen of the United States. No member shall run for or hold any other elected office under the United States, the State or its political subdivisions. No member shall take an active part in political management or in political campaigns. No member shall be eligible for appointment to judicial office of the State so long as the person is a member of the judicial commission and for a period of three years thereafter.
>
> No act of the judicial selection commission shall be valid except by concurrence of the majority of its voting members.
>
> The judicial selection commission shall select one of its members to serve as chairperson. The commission shall promulgate rules which shall have the force and effect of law. The deliberations of the commission shall be confidential.
>
> The legislature shall provide for the staff and operating expenses of the judicial selection commission in a separate budget. No member of the judicial selection commission shall receive any compensation for commission services, but shall be allowed necessary expenses for travel, board and lodging incurred in the performance of commission duties.
>
> The judicial selection commission shall be attached to the judiciary branch of the state government for purposes of administration.

Added in 1978, this section outlines the composition and internal procedures of the judicial selection commission. Praised for substituting a merit selection system for one characterized by patronage and politics, the idea did not originate in 1978. There was lively and lengthy debate on the issue at both the 1950 and the 1968 conventions, but no agreement was forthcoming; when a strong reform movement again surfaced in 1978, the delegates reached consensus with relative ease.

The power of selecting the nine-member commission is allocated among the governor (appointing three), the chief justice (appointing two), the senate president and the house speaker (each appointing one), and the state bar association (electing two of its members). A major point of contention which did surface centered on whether to limit the number of attorneys serving on the commission in order to ensure public participation. The end result was that only four members can be licensed attorneys, with the governor and the chief justice each limited to appointment of no more than one attorney. Since the bar elects two of its own members, the senate president and house speaker are implicitly limited to appointing nonattorneys.

Whether the utilization of a commission removes politics from the appointment process depends on how one defines the term, as pointed out by the commission's first chair:

> No doubt the system is less "political" in the sense that there is some screening of candidates and the Commission has the sole authority with regard to retention.

> But the Governor, President of the Senate and Speaker obviously appoint commissioners who are likely to agree with their political philosophy and therefore more likely than not to select candidates acceptable to them. Equally apparent, once the list is submitted to the Governor and the Chief Justice, "politics" in the sense of facts not considered by the Commission plays a part, e.g., race, gender, etc., any one of which may be determinative of the question of whether or not a person should be appointed.[61]

Section 4 was the focus of *Richardson v. Koshiba* (1982), wherein the U.S. Court of Appeals for the Ninth Circuit held that members of the judicial selection commission do not have the absolute immunity from liability for judicial actions that judges have under federal law. Based on a distinction between the performance of judicial and executive functions, the court rejected the idea that the commission performed a "judicial" role. It concluded that since the commission's responsibilities were not at all similar to the adjudication of controversies between adversaries, the functions were executive in nature.

Concern about the commission's functioning recently resurfaced when a number of judicial seats became vacant. Although the governor appointed women to the circuit and intermediate courts, he failed to nominate one for the supreme court. Before these nominations were made public, many had argued that the time was ripe for such an appointment; afterward, the governor's failure was roundly criticized. This brought to the fore criticism of the commission's policy of keeping secret the names on the list, as well as whether or not the commission ranked the names. Critics argue in favor of more openness so the public can assess if the governor selects the most qualified. Additionally, they suggest that allowing shorter lists would avoid the possibility that borderline candidates are included just to meet the numerical requirements set in the constitution.[62]

SECTION 5

> **Retirement; Removal; Discipline.** The supreme court shall have the power to reprimand, discipline, suspend with or without salary, retire or remove from office any justice or judge for misconduct or disability, as provided by rules adopted by the supreme court.
>
> The supreme court shall create a commission on judicial discipline which shall have authority to investigate and conduct hearings concerning allegations of

---

[61] James E. T. Koshiba, "Judicial Selection and Retention in the State of Hawaii: Hawaii's Judicial Selection Commission—The First Six Years," *Hawaii Bar Journal* 20 (1986): 8.

[62] See, for example, Richard Borreca, "Is the Fairness Faulty?" *Honolulu Star-Bulletin*, 13 March 1992, A-3; A. A. Smyser, "Judge Selection Process Could Be Improved," *Honolulu Star-Bulletin* 13 March 1992, A-26.

misconduct or disability and to make recommendations to the supreme court concerning reprimand, discipline, suspension, retirement or removal of any justice or judge.

Considerable change characterizes this section. In the Statehood Constitution it was titled "Retirement for Incapacity" and allowed the governor to retire a justice or judge upon certification by an authorized commission or agency that the justice or judge was incapacitated and upon recommendation by a board appointed by the governor to inquire into the circumstances. Another provision also allowed for the removal of a justice or judge upon the two-thirds vote of each legislative chamber, sitting in joint session. The 1968 convention removed the provision relating to the legislature, thus placing these powers in the hands of the governor, subject to certification by a commission and recommendation by a board.

In 1978, the process was again altered. The governor was removed from the process, and the power to reprimand, discipline, suspend, retire, or remove from office any justice or judge for misconduct or disability was transferred to the supreme court, which must establish appropriate rules and create a commission on judicial discipline. In implementing these provisions, the court created a commission (made up of attorneys and lay persons) to investigate complaints. In the words of then Chief Justice William S. Richardson, it also adopted rules that "protect the independence of the individual judge in the decision making process while also assuring public accountability in judicial conduct."[63]

SECTION 6

Administration. The chief justice of the supreme court shall be the administrative head of the courts. The chief justice may assign judges from one circuit court to another for temporary service. With the approval of the supreme court, the chief justice shall appoint an administrative director to serve at the chief justice's pleasure.

See the commentary following Section 7.

SECTION 7

Rules. The supreme court shall have power to promulgate rules and regulations in all civil and criminal cases for all courts relating to process, practice, procedure and appeals, which shall have the force and effect of law.

---

[63] William S. Richardson, "Judicial Independence: The Hawaii Experience," *University of Hawaii Law Review* 2 (1979): 53.

Both Section 7 and Section 8 remain substantively as they were in the Statehood Constitution. As administrative head of the courts, and with approval by whole high court, the chief justice has the power to appoint an administrative director. The chief justice's power to make temporary assignments found in Section 6 differs from that in Section 2. According to Section 2, the chief justice may temporarily assign judges to a higher-level court, whereas Section 6 permits the chief justice to assign circuit court judges to temporary service on another circuit court.

The supreme court's rule-making power is authorized by Section 7. Over the years, questions have arisen about the relationship between statutes regulating court procedures and court-established rules. Three cases suggest that court rules take precedence over conflicting statutes (*Asato v. Furtado*, 1970; *Kudlich v. Ciciarelli*, 1965; *State v. Hawaiian Dredging Co.*, 1964), though the statute under which they were decided was repealed. Requiring that grand jury proceedings be recorded has been judged to fall within the court's rule-making power (*McMahon v. Office of City and County of Honolulu*, 1970).

Article VII

Taxation and Finance

No dramatic amendments were made in 1968 to the taxation and finance provisions of the Statehood Constitution. In contrast, the 1978 convention undertook a major overhaul and produced a greatly expanded article (renumbered from Article VI to Article VII). Starting with eight sections in the Statehood Constitution, the 1968 convention reduced their number by one. In 1978, five new sections were added, and one section was separated into two, yielding thirteen sections in all.

Article VII is as important for what it does not include as for the provisions it does contain. There is no specified tax rate limitation, no earmarking of funds for specific purposes, and no dollar amount specified for the general fund expenditure limit. In addition, no tax exemptions are spelled out. (Another part of the constitution, Article XVI, Section 9, does declare unnecessarily that federal lands and property are exempt.) By leaving such detail to legislative action, this part of the constitution remains comparatively straightforward and flexible, enabling the legislature to make necessary adjustments to the tax laws without requiring recourse to the more difficult constitutional amendment process.

One major change made in 1968 was the deletion of a section titled "Taxation of Non-Resident Citizens," prescribing that "[t]he land and other property belonging to citizens of the United States residing without the State shall never be taxed at a higher rate than the lands and other property belonging to residents thereof." The reason for originally including this provision was to reassure those who worried that under statehood the state government might take discriminatory action against mainlanders or other nonresidents owning land and other property in Hawaii. The delegates to the 1968 convention recognized that this provision was unnecessary since equality of taxation is guaranteed under the equal protection clauses of both the U.S. and the Hawaii constitutions.

More significantly, the 1968 convention substituted a biennial for an annual budgeting process and made a few adjustments regarding public debt. But the bulk of the article was left untouched.

By the time the 1978 convention met, however, new issues had surfaced within a wholly changed fiscal climate:

> The first decade of statehood was largely a prosperous period for Hawaii and, thus, in the last convention [in 1968], there was no discussion of what now appears to be the burning issue in taxation and finance . . . of limits to government spending. Also, full government coffers meant that the executive branch could spend virtually all that the legislature appropriated, whereas, under the leaner times of recent years, executive-legislative fiscal relations have been strained in a collision of the legislative power to appropriate funds vs. the executive power to restrict appropriations.[64]

The stage was set for very spirited and sometimes protracted debate which resulted in substantive changes.

SECTION 1

> **Taxing Power Inalienable.** The power of taxation shall never be surrendered, suspended or contracted away.

There is no need for the constitution to expressly grant taxation and finance powers to the state government; they exist without writing them into the constitution. As a sovereign entity within the federal system, the state has all those powers not delegated to the national government, or prohibited to the states, by the U.S. Constitution. States thus have an inherent power over taxation and finance matters within their own borders, a power on which they can impose self-limitations, but not augment so as to encroach upon federal powers. This section, unchanged since statehood, states very simply that this inalienable power cannot be surrendered, suspended, or contracted away.

While taxing power was not an issue in 1950 and 1968, the 1978 convention focused attention on this section because it was perceived as a prohibition against legislation making Hawaii's tax laws conform automatically with alterations

[64] *Hawaii Constitutional Convention Studies 1978, Article VI: Taxation and Finance* (Honolulu: State of Hawaii, Legislative Auditor, 1978), 2.

made in the federal income tax laws. Such legislation was considered a delegation or "surrender" of power. In order to resolve this uncertainty, the 1978 delegates proposed a new provision which became Section 2.

SECTION 2

Income Taxation. In enacting any law imposing a tax on or measured by income, the legislature may define income by reference to provisions of the laws of the United States as they may be or become effective at any time or from time to time, whether retrospective or prospective in theiroperation. The legislature may provide that amendments to such laws of the United States shall become the law of the State upon their becoming the law of the United States. The legislature shall in any such law set the rate or rates of such tax. The legislature may in so defining income make exceptions, additions, or modifications to any provisions of the laws of the United States so referred to and provide for retrospective exceptions or modifications to those provisions which are retrospective.

There was virtually no debate at the 1978 convention over whether this section should be added. In proposing it, the convention's standing committee made clear its intention of minimizing the burden on state taxpayers that had to cope with two complicated income tax systems, one state and the other federal. This section gives the state legislature the option of, but does not mandate, enacting legislation automatically conforming the state's income tax law to future changes made to the federal income tax code.

SECTION 3

Tax Review Commission. There shall be a tax review commission, which shall be appointed as provided by law on or before July 1, 1980, and every five years thereafter. The commission shall submit to the legislature an evaluation of the State's tax structure, recommend revenue and tax policy and then dissolve.

According to the 1978 standing committee report, neither the legislative nor the executive branch had reviewed the tax system in a systematic way for more than twenty years, resulting in a piecemeal approach to taxation. In line with their general concern about the public's role in the political process, convention delegates adopted this new section establishing a tax review commission not only because a periodic and independent assessment of the tax system would benefit both branches of government, but also because the commission could provide the public with the information necessary to assess executive and legislative policies concerning taxes and revenues. By statute (Haw. Rev. Stat. § 232E-1), the tax review commission is made up of seven members appointed by the governor with the advice and consent of the senate.

SECTION 4

Appropriations for Private Purposes Prohibited. No tax shall be levied or appropriation of public money or property made, nor shall the public credit be used, directly or indirectly, except for a public purpose. No grant shall be made in violation of Section 4 of Article I of this constitution. No grant of public money or property shall be made except pursuant to standards provided by law.

Most of this section originated in the Statehood Constitution; its last sentence was added in 1978. The section's declaration that taxes can be levied and appropriations made only for a public purpose has been given judicial interpretation. In *State v. Anderson* (1976), the state supreme court found that what constitutes a public purpose is generally for the legislature to decide. Although the legislature's determination is not conclusive, the court added, it must be given wide discretion, and courts should not interfere unless the purpose is clearly a private rather than a public purpose.

Expressly prohibited by this section is the granting of any funds in violation of Article I, Section 4, which enjoins the state from passing any law respecting an establishment of religion or prohibiting the free exercise thereof. Read in conjunction with the section's public purpose clause, the due process and equal protection clauses of Article I, Section 5, and the prohibition against appropriating public funds for the support or benefit of sectarian or private schools in Article X, Section 1, it appears that the Constitution takes a more restrictive approach to the separation of church and state than is required under U.S. Supreme Court rulings interpreting Article I of the U.S. Constitution (see also Article X).

In adding the last sentence, the 1978 convention 's standing committee explained that it intended to make the legislature establish standards governing appropriations for those programs, carried out by private organizations, that have been determined by the legislature to be in the public interest. An example of implementation legislation is section 42D-2 of Hawaii Revised Statutes where qualifying standards for an organization requesting a grant or a subsidy or submitting a proposal for the purchase of a service agreement are enumerated.

SECTION 5

Expenditure Controls. Provision for the control of the rate of expenditures of appropriated state moneys, and for the reduction of such expenditures under prescribed conditions, shall be made by law.

No public money shall be expended except pursuant to appropriations made by law. General fund expenditures for any fiscal year shall not exceed the State's current general fund revenues and unencumbered cash balances, except when the governor publicly declares the public health, safety or welfare is threatened as provided by law.

The first sentence of this section has remained intact since statehood. It requires the legislature to establish a system for controlling the rate at which appropriated funds are expended and for reducing expenditures should specified conditions occur. Such controls are intended to ensure an orderly flow of expenditures spread out over a designated period of time, with a reduction of expenditures when there are insufficient revenues to meet legislative appropriations.

The second paragraph was added in 1978 and must be considered in conjunction with the expenditure ceiling provision, added to Section 9 at the same time. It is meant to prevent the state from circumventing the expenditure ceiling by engaging in deficit spending. While provisions in Section 8 merely imply that the governor must submit a balanced budget, this language explicitly calls for balanced budgeting. The one exception allowed occurs when the governor publicly declares an emergency; the state can then continue to operate, even if this means deficit spending.

SECTION 6

Disposition of Excess Revenues. Whenever the state general fund balance at the close of each of two successive fiscal years exceeds five percent of general fund revenues for each of the two fiscal years, the legislature in the next regular session shall provide for a tax refund or tax credit to the taxpayers of the State, as provided by law.

The 1978 convention did not spend much time on this provision for a tax rebate when it was proposed from the floor. It found its way into the constitution as a result of what could be called a populist taxpayers' uprising among delegates who had earlier tried, without success, to have the proposal included among the standing committee proposals. The section leaves the fixing of the specific amount of any refund to legislative determination. The effect of this section to date has been nominal: Like most other years, the tax rebate set for each taxpayer in 1992 equaled $1.00. In 1984, the voters turned down a legislatively proposed amendment deleting the tax rebate provision.

SECTION 7

Council on Revenues. There shall be established by law a council on revenues which shall prepare revenue estimates of the state government and shall report the estimates to the governor and the legislature at times provided by law. The estimates shall be considered by the governor in preparing the budget, recommending appropriations and revenues and controlling expenditures. The estimates shall be considered by the legislature in appropriating funds and enacting revenue measures. All revenue estimates submitted by the council to the governor and the legislature shall be made public. If the legislature in appropriating funds or if the governor in preparing the budget or recommending appropriations exceeds estimated revenues due to proposed expenditures, this fact shall be made public including the reasons therefor.

This section was also added in 1978. It calls for instituting a council on revenues to prepare revenue estimates for both the governor and the legislature to consider during the budget-making process.

Recognizing that tension always exists between the executive and the legislative branches during the budget process, the delegates intended this section to minimize conflict by making certain that both branches would work with the same set of revenue estimates, thereby reducing the role politics played in making revenue estimates.

The work of the council is advisory, rather than binding, but to make certain that it does not engage in useless work, the section specifies that if budget proposals or actual appropriations exceed the estimated revenues presented by the council, this information and the reasons therefor must be made public. By statute (Haw. Rev. Stat. § 37–111), the council consists of seven members: The governor appoints three (for four-year terms), the senate president appoints two (for two-year terms), and the house speaker appoints two (for two-year terms).

SECTION 8

The Budget. Within such time prior to the opening of each regular session in an odd-numbered year as may be provided by law, the governor shall submit to the legislature a budget in a form provided by law setting forth a complete plan of proposed expenditures of the executive branch, estimates as provided by law of the aggregate expenditures of the judicial and legislative branches, and anticipated receipts of the State for the ensuing fiscal biennium, together with such other information as the legislature may require. A complete plan of proposed expenditures of the judicial branch for the ensuing fiscal biennium shall be submitted by the chief justice to the legislature in a form and within such time prior to the opening of each regular session in an odd-numbered year as shall be provided by law. The budget prepared by the governor and the plan of proposed expenditures prepared by the chief justice shall also be submitted in bill form. The governor shall also, upon the opening of each such session, submit bills to provide for such proposed expenditures and for any recommended additional revenues or borrowings by which the proposed expenditures are to be met. The proposed general fund expenditures in the plan of proposed expenditures, including estimates of the aggregate expenditures of the judicial and legislative branches, submitted by the governor shall not exceed the general fund expenditure ceiling established by the legislature under section 9 of this article; provided that proposed general fund expenditures in the plan may exceed such ceiling if the governor sets forth the dollar amount and the rate by which the ceiling will be exceeded and the reasons therefor.

Until 1968, this section required the governor to submit the state budget on an annual basis and compiled in two parts. One part was to set forth all proposed operating expenditures, while the other was to present all proposed capital improvements expenditures. The 1968 convention changed the budget process to a biennial one and deleted the requirement for a two-part budget.

Other important alterations were again made in 1978, motivated, to some extent, by a desire to ensure that the governor presents a realistic budget.

Whereas the earlier provisions merely required the governor to submit "a complete plan of proposed expenditures and anticipated receipts of the State," the constitution now requires that the expenditure portion include the proposed spending of the executive branch, but only the estimates of the aggregate expenditures for the judicial and the legislative branches. Its effect is to deny the executive any ability to specify particulars for the budgets of the other two branches of government.

In an additional provision, the governor's proposed budget is tied in with the general fund expenditure ceiling found in Section 9. This ceiling as set by the legislature cannot be exceeded unless the governor specifically states the amount and rate of the excess and provides a rationale for it.

SECTION 9

Legislative Appropriations; Procedures; Expenditure Ceiling. In each regular session in an odd-numbered year, the legislature shall transmit to the governor an appropriation bill or bills providing for the anticipated total expenditures of the State for the ensuing fiscal biennium. In such session, no appropriation bill, except bills recommended by the governor for immediate passage, or to cover the expenses of the legislature, shall be passed on final reading until the bill authorizing operating expenditures for the ensuing fiscal biennium, to be known as the general appropriations bill, shall have been transmitted to the governor.

In each regular session in an even-numbered year, at such time as may be provided by law, the governor may submit to the legislature a bill to amend any appropriation for operating expenditures of the current fiscal biennium, to be known as the supplemental appropriations bill, and bills to amend any appropriations for capital expenditures of the current fiscal biennium, and at the same time the governor shall submit a bill or bills to provide for any added revenues or borrowings that such amendments may require. In each regular session in an even-numbered year, bills may be introduced in the legislature to amend any appropriation act or bond authorization act of the current fiscal biennium or prior fiscal periods. In any such session in which the legislature submits to the governor a supplemental appropriations bill, no other appropriation bill, except bills recommended by the governor for immediate passage, or to cover the expenses of the legislature, shall be passed on final reading until such supplemental appropriations bill shall have been transmitted to the governor.

—**General Fund Expenditure Ceiling**. Notwithstanding any other provision to the contrary, the legislature shall establish a general fund expenditure ceiling which shall limit the rate of growth of general fund appropriations, excluding federal funds received by the general fund, to the estimated rate of growth of the State's economy as provided by law. No appropriations in excess of such ceiling shall be authorized during any legislative session unless the legislature shall, by a two-thirds vote of the members to which each house of the legislature is entitled, set forth the dollar amount and the rate by which the ceiling will be exceeded and the reasons therefor.

What was originally a one-sentence section has over time become quite lengthy, and its impact has considerably changed. That original sentence remains as the second sentence in the first paragraph. It specifies that, with stated exceptions, no appropriation bill can be passed by the legislature until after the general appropriations bill has been sent to the governor. It is meant to prevent the legislature from considering a flurry of appropriations before definitively dealing with the task of financing the running of the government as embodied in the governor's proposed budget.

In 1968, the second paragraph, setting out the process for supplemental budgets, was added. As Section 8 calls for biennial rather than annual budgets, this change allows budget adjustments to be made in the second year of the two-year cycle.

After this paragraph came into effect, an apparent typographical error was discovered. Where it should have read supplemental appropriation "bill," it read "bills," though the convention clearly intended only one supplemental appropriation bill. A proposal correcting the mistake, placed on the 1972 ballot, received voter approval.

The subsection entitled "General Fund Expenditure Ceiling" was added by the 1978 convention in response to wide public support for adopting some mechanical method of limiting state government spending. It requires the legislatureto establish a ceiling on the rate of growth of general fund appropriations-based on the estimated rate of growth of the state's economy. Although theceiling may be exceeded, serious hurdles must first be surmounted. A two-thirdsvote of each chamber is required, as is setting forth the actual amount and rateof excess along with the reasons why it is necessary to exceed the ceiling.

The ceiling applies only to the general fund. In referring only to general fund revenues, the amendment excludes special fund revenues (i.e., those earmarked for special purposes and received from specific taxes or other earmarked revenues) from the ceiling provisions. Also, federal funds, normally included in a general fund, are specifically excluded because they are not reflective of the state's ability to generate revenue.

SECTION 10

Auditor. The legislature, by a majority vote of each house in joint session, shall appoint an auditor who shall serve for a period of eight years and thereafter until a successor shall have been appointed. The legislature, by a two-thirds vote of the members in joint session, may remove the auditor from office at any time for cause. It shall be the duty of the auditor to conduct post-audits of the transactions, accounts, programs and performance of all departments, offices and agencies of the State and its political subdivisions, to certify to the accuracy of all financial statements issued by the respective accounting officers and to report the auditor's findings and recommendations to the governor and to the legislature at such times as shall be provided by law. The auditor shall also make such additional reports and conduct such other investigations as may be directed by the legislature.

This section remains almost the same as it was in the Statehood Constitution.In recognition of actual practice, the language was changed in 1978, but onlyto clarify that post-audits should evaluate programs and performance as well aswhether public funds are being used in authorized ways.

The auditor is appointed by the legislature in joint session, with a majority-vote of the members of each chamber, but can be removed from office only by a two-thirds vote. The legislature may also designate additional duties for the auditor. As an example, it has under what is known as the sunset law given the auditor responsibility for evaluating boards, commissions, and regulatory programs to determine if they should be continued, modified, or permitted to expire at the time of their required repeal date (Haw. Rev. Stat. § 26H–5).

SECTION 11

Lapsing of Appropriations. All appropriations for which the source is general obligation bond funds or general funds shall be for specified periods, and no such appropriation shall be made for a period exceeding three years. Any such appropriation or any portion of any such appropriation which is unencumbered at the close of the fiscal period for which the appropriation is made shall lapse; provided that no appropriation for which the source is general obligation bond funds nor any portion of any such appropriation shall lapse if the legislature determines such appropriation or any portion of such appropriation is necessary to qualify for federal aid financing and reimbursement. Where general obligation bonds have been authorized for an appropriation, the amount of the bond authorization shall be reduced in an amount equal to the amount lapsed.

Any appropriation for which the source is general obligation bond funds or general funds or any portion of any such appropriation which is effective on the date of ratification of this amendment and which is unencumbered on June 30, 1980 shall lapse on that date unless earlier lapsed by law; provided that no appropriation for which the source is general obligation bond funds nor any portion of any such appropriation shall lapse if the legislature determines such appropriation or any portion of such appropriation is necessary to qualify for federal aid financing and reimbursement. Where general obligation bonds have been authorized for an appropriation, the amount of the bond authorization shall be reduced in an amount equal to the amount lapsed on June 30, 1980.

Added in 1978, this section provides for the automatic lapsing of appropriated-funds if they are not actually encumbered within three years. This lapsing mechanism is intended to bring about ongoing review of projects and programs, by the executive branch, to determine if they are still viable, if more funds are needed, or if they should be cancelled.

SECTION 12

Definitions; Issuance of Indebtedness. For the purposes of this article:

1. The term "bonds" shall include bonds, notes and other instruments of indebtedness.
2. The term "general obligation bonds" means all bonds for the payment of the principal and interest of which the full faith and credit of the State or a political subdivision are pledged and, unless otherwise indicated, includes reimbursable general obligation bonds.
3. The term "net revenues" or "net user tax receipts" means the revenues or receipts derived from a public undertaking, improvement or system remaining after the costs of operation, maintenance and repair of such public undertaking, improvement or system and the required payments of the principal of and interest on all revenue bonds issued therefor have been made.
4. The term "person" means an individual, firm, partnership, corporation, association, cooperative or other legal entity, governmental body or agency, board, bureau or other instrumentality thereof, or any combination of the foregoing.
5. The term "rates, rentals and charges" means all revenues and other moneys derived from the operation or lease of a public undertaking, improvement or system, or derived from any payments or return on security under a loan program or a loan thereunder.
6. The term "reimbursable general obligation bonds" means general obligation bonds issued for a public undertaking, improvement or system from which revenues, or use taxes, or a combination of both, may be derived for the payment of the principal and interest as reimbursement to the general fund and for which reimbursement is required by law, and, in the case of general obligation bonds issued by the State for a political subdivision, general obligation bonds for which the payment of the principal and interest as reimbursement to the general fund is required by law to be made from the revenue of the political subdivision.

7. The term "revenue bonds" means all bonds payable from the revenues, or user taxes, or any combination of both, of a public undertaking, improvement, system or loan program and any loan made thereunder and secured as may be provided by law.
8. The term "special purpose revenue bonds" means all bonds payable from rental or other payments made to an issuer by a person pursuant to contract and secured as may be provided by law.
9. The term "user tax" means a tax on goods or services or on the consumption thereof, the receipts of which are substantially derived from the consumption, use or sale of goods and services in the utilization of the functions or services furnished by a public undertaking, improvement or system.

The legislature, by a majority vote of the members to which each house is entitled, shall authorize the issuance of all general obligation bonds, bonds issued under special improvement statutes and revenue bonds issued by or on behalf of the State and shall prescribe by general law the manner and procedure for such issuance. The legislature by general law shall authorize political subdivisions to issue general obligation bonds, bonds issued under special improvement statutes and revenue bonds and shall prescribe the manner and procedure for such issuance. All such bonds issued by or on behalf of a political subdivision shall be authorized by the governing body of such political subdivision.

Special purpose revenue bonds shall only be authorized or issued to finance facilities of or for, or to loan the proceeds of such bonds to assist, manufacturing, processing or industrial enterprises, utilities serving the general public, health care facilities provided to the general public by not-for-profit corporations or low and moderate income government housing programs, each of which is hereinafter referred to in this paragraph as a special purpose entity. The legislature, by a two-thirds vote of the members to which each house is entitled, may enact enabling legislation for the issuance of special purpose revenue bonds separately for each special purpose entity, and, by a two-thirds vote of the members to which each house is entitled and by separate legislative bill, may authorize the State to issue special purpose revenue bonds for each single project or multi-project program of each special purpose entity; provided that the issuance of such special purpose revenue bonds is found to be in the public interest by the legislature. The legislature may enact enabling legislation to authorize political subdivisions to issue special purpose revenue bonds. If so authorized, a political subdivision by a two-thirds vote of the members to which its governing body is entitled and by separate ordinance may authorize the issuance of special purpose revenue bonds for each single project or multi-project program of each special purpose entity; provided that the issuance of such special purpose revenue bonds is found to be in the public interest by the governing body of the political subdivision. No special purpose revenue bonds shall be secured directly or indirectly by the general credit of the issuer or by any revenues or taxes of the issuer other than receipts derived from payments by a person under contract or from any security for such contract or special purpose revenue bonds and no moneys other than such receipts shall be applied to the payment thereof. The governor shall provide the legislature in November of each year with a report on the cumulative amount of all special purpose revenue bonds authorized and issued, and such other information as may be necessary.

See the commentary following Section 13.

SECTION 13

Debt Limit; Exclusions. General obligation bonds may be issued by the State; provided that such bonds at the time of issuance would not cause the total amount of principal and interest payable in the current or any future fiscal year, whichever is higher, on such bonds and on all outstanding general obligation bonds to exceed: a sum equal to twenty percent of the average of the general fund revenues of the State in the three fiscal years immediately preceding such issuance until June 30, 1982; and thereafter, a sum equal to eighteen and one-half percent of the average of the general fund revenues of the State in the three fiscal years immediately preceding such issuance. Effective July 1, 1980, the legislature shall include a declaration of findings in every general law authorizing the issuance of general obligation bonds that the total amount of principal and interest, estimated for such bonds and for all bonds authorized and unissued and calculated for all bonds issued and outstanding, will not cause the debt limit to be exceeded at the time of issuance. Any bond issue by or on behalf of the State may exceed the debt limit if an emergency condition is declared to exist by the governor and concurred to by a two-thirds vote of the members to which each house of the legislature is entitled. For the purpose of this paragraph, general fund revenues of the State shall not include moneys received as grants from the federal government and receipts in reimbursement of any reimbursable general obligation bonds which are excluded as permitted by this section.

A sum equal to fifteen percent of the total of the assessed values for tax rate purposes of real property in each political subdivision, as determined by the last tax assessment rolls pursuant to law, is established as the limit of the funded debt of such political subdivision that is outstanding and unpaid at any time.

All general obligation bonds for a term exceeding two years shall be in serial form maturing in substantially equal installments of principal, or maturing in substantially equal installments of both principal and interest. The first installment of principal of general obligation bonds and of reimbursable general obligation bonds shall mature not later than five years from the date of issue of such series. The last installment on general obligation bonds shall mature not later than twenty-five years from the date of such issue and the last installment on general obligation bonds sold to the federal government, on reimbursable general obligation bonds and on bonds constituting instruments of indebtedness under which the State or a political subdivision incurs a contingent liability as a guarantor shall mature not later than thirty-five years from the date of such issue. The interest and principal payments of general obligation bonds shall be a first charge on the general fund of the State or political subdivision, as the case may be.

In determining the power of the State to issue general obligation bonds or the funded debt of any political subdivision under section 12, the following shall be excluded:

1. Bonds that have matured, or that mature in the then current fiscal year, or that have been irrevocably called for redemption and the redemption date has occurred or will occur in the then fiscal year, or for the full payment of which moneys or securities have been irrevocably set aside.
2. Revenue bonds, if the issuer thereof is obligated by law to impose rates, rentals and charges for the use and services of the public undertaking, improvement or system or the benefits of a loan program or a loan thereunder or to impose a user tax, or to impose a combination of rates, rentals and charges and user tax, as the case may be, sufficient to pay the cost of operation, maintenance and repair, if any, of the public undertaking, improvement or system or the cost of maintaining a loan program or a loan thereunder and the required payments of the principal of and interest on all revenue bonds issued for the public undertaking, improvement or system or loan program, and if the issuer is obligated to deposit such revenues or tax or a combination of both into a special fund and to apply the same to such payments in the amount necessary therefor.
3. Special purpose revenue bonds, if the issuer thereof is required by law to contract with a person obligating such person to make rental or other payments to the issuer in an amount at least sufficient to make the required payment of the principal of and interest on such special purpose revenue bonds.
4. Bonds issued under special improvement statutes when the only security for such bonds is the properties benefited or improved or the assessments thereon.
5. General obligation bonds issued for assessable improvements, but only to the extent that reimbursements to the general fund for the principal and interest on such bonds are in fact made from assessment collections available therefor.
6. Reimbursable general obligation bonds issued for a public undertaking, improvement or system but only to the extent that reimbursements to the general fund are in fact made from the net revenue, or net user tax receipts, or combination of both, as determined for the immediately preceding fiscal year.
7. Reimbursable general obligation bonds issued by the State for any political subdivision, whether issued before or after the effective date of this section, but only for as long as reimbursement by the political subdivision to the State for the payment of principal and interest on such bonds is required by law; provided that in the case of bonds issued after the effective date of this section, the consent of the governing body of the political subdivision has first been obtained; and provided further that during the period that such bonds are excluded by the State, the principal amount then outstanding shall be included within the funded debt of such political subdivision.
8. Bonds constituting instruments of indebtedness under which the State or any political subdivision incurs a contingent liability as a guarantor, but only to the extent the principal amount of such bonds does not exceed seven percent of the

principal amount of outstanding general obligation bonds not otherwise excluded under this section; provided that the State or political subdivision shall establish and maintain a reserve in an amount in reasonable proportion to the outstanding loans guaranteed by the State or political subdivision as provided by law.

9. Bonds issued by or on behalf of the State or by any political subdivision to meet appropriations for any fiscal period in anticipation of the collection of revenues for such period or to meet casual deficits or failures of revenue, if required to be paid within one year, and bonds issued by or on behalf of the State to suppress insurrection, to repel invasion, to defend the State in war or to meet emergencies caused by disaster or act of God.

The total outstanding indebtedness of the State or funded debt of any political subdivision and the exclusions therefrom permitted by this section shall be made annually and certified by law or as provided by law. For the purposes of section 12 and this section, amounts received from on-street parking may be considered and treated as revenues of a parking undertaking.

Nothing in section 12 or in this section shall prevent the refunding of any bond at any time.

Provisions concerning debt limitations and bonds were combined in one section in both the Statehood Constitution and the 1968 Constitution. The 1968 convention made some additions regarding debt limitations. Although keeping much of what was already included, the 1978 convention made extensive changes and separated the provisions into two sections: Section 12, covering "Definitions; Issuance of Indebtedness"; and Section 13, covering "Debt Limit; Exclusions."

Public bonds are ordinarily sold to obtain funds for major projects, while spreading the cost to the taxpayers over a period of time. Bonds are debts of the state and must be repaid, with interest, within a specified period of time (thus, the phrase "issuance of indebtedness"). General obligation bonds are repaid from the state's general revenues, while revenue bonds are repaid from the earnings of a specific project or from user taxes.

Section 12 defines nine important terms relating to bonds and requires authorization by majority vote of the total membership in each chamber of the legislature for the issuance of general obligation bonds. In addition, it is the legislature that grants the four counties the authority to issue bonds. The last, and lengthy, paragraph outlines the conditions for authorizing special purpose revenue bonds.

Section 13 establishes a ceiling for bonded debt, stated not as a dollar amount, but as a percentage of the average general fund revenues of the state in the three fiscal years immediately preceding a proposed issuance (18.5 percent after 1982). This limit can be exceeded only if an emergency condition is declared and two-thirds in each legislative chamber approve. For county indebtedness, a ceiling is set at 15 percent of the total assessed valuation for tax purposes of real property within the county.

Section 13 also lists the types of bonds that are excluded when computing the funded debt of the state and its political subdivisions. The scope of such exclusions has twice come before the Hawaii Supreme Court. In *Employees' Retirement System v. Budget Director Ho* (1960), the court held that, while the 1950 convention did not consider highway revenue bonds specifically, there was no reason to exclude them from the state debt since the "literal meaning of the term 'funded' debt includes such bonds" and the constitution requires including such bonds in the state debt. Sixteen years later, in *State v. Anderson* (1976), the court found that anti-pollution revenue bonds were chargeable against the state debt limitation since they did not fall within the exclusion provisions.

Article VIII

Local Government

In contrast to other states, with their layers of political subdivisions, Hawaii has the simplest of political systems. The only local governments are one combined city/county unit and three counties: The city and county of Honolulu and the counties of Hawaii, Kauai, and Maui. (A fifth area called a county, Kalawao, encompasses Kalaupapa Settlement on the island of Molokai. It does not have its own government and falls under the jurisdiction of the state department of health as its primary purpose is the care and treatment of people with Hansen's disease).

During the monarchy, the four groups of islands corresponding to today's four local units each had a governor reporting to the monarch and his or her government. Power remained in the monarchical government, and this centralization continued during the short-lived republic as well as during the early years of territorial status. In 1905, because of local complaints and "Congressional rumblings of disapproval" regarding the existence of only one governmental unit for the whole territory, the territorial legislature created counties, a system of subdivisions that remains basically unchanged.[65]

Notwithstanding the existence of counties, Hawaii, as pointed out in other sections of this work, is still characterized as having a strong centralized form of state government, and this is particularly evident in the context of local government.

[65] See Meller, "Centralization," 98–99.

Although called counties, Hawaii's units of local government are somewhat unique in the American context. Many functions usually carried out by political subdivisions in other states are performed instead by the state government. For example, the state government administers all public education and has responsibility for furnishing public welfare services, and a single state judicial system includes the circuit and the district courts. At the same time, Hawaii's counties The Hawaii Constitution and Commentary bear a resemblance to cities in other states in providing such services as fire and police protection, garbage collection, and street maintenance and construction.

Two major changes have been made to this article (renumbered from Article VII to Article VIII in 1978). In response to a state supreme court ruling that county charters were subject to continuing legislative control (*Fasi v. City and County of Honolulu* 1968), the 1968 convention expanded Section 2 to enhance county autonomy. Then, in 1978, because of criticism that the state government imposed functions and services on local government without aiding in their financing, the convention of that date added Section 5, directing that the state share the cost of newly mandated or expanded programs and services.

These changes reflect a continuous conflict centering on the question of how much power the subdivisions ought to have (i.e., the scope of home rule). Since there are no incorporated or unincorporated cities, towns, or villages and no other functional districts common on the mainland, the battle is clearly joined. On the one side is the state government and on the other the four counties, which formed their own lobbying group in 1959 called the Hawaii State Association of Counties. Over the years, the association has sought constitutional amendments and statutory changes to increase county powers.

A particular bone of contention between the state and the counties concerns land use under Hawaii's unique statewide zoning system. In an attempt to reduce conflict over this issue, a 1978 convention standing committee proposed a new section, stating that "[r]eclassification of land to urban use shall be subject to approval by the county in which the land exists." While sitting as a committee of the whole, the convention amended and approved this proposal. But only a few days later, after contentious debate during the plenary session, it was deleted entirely from the proposed constitution. Those arguing that the provision was unnecessary and not an improvement over the existing shared state/county responsibility for planning and regulation narrowly defeated those contending that, because of rapid urbanization, the counties ought to have a stronger voice in land use matters.

SECTION 1

Creation; Powers of Political Subdivisions. The legislature shall create counties, and may create other political subdivisions within the State, and provide for the government thereof. Each political subdivision shall have and exercise such powers as shall be conferred under general laws.

This section, giving the legislature the power to create subdivisions and determine the powers they can exercise, has remained unchanged since statehood. The number of counties has not been altered, and although the idea of dividing the City and County of Honolulu into two counties recently came before the legislature, it died an early death.

According to the 1950 framers, the purpose of the section's last sentence was to allow the counties some self-government with a minimum of legislative interference. By specifying that the powers can be conferred only under general laws, they intended to prohibit discrimination against particular localities. General laws are distinguished from special laws which concern a specific or local area. In *Bulgo v. County of Maui* (1967), the Hawaii Supreme Court found that, in its broadest meaning, the term *general laws* means laws applying uniformly throughout the state's political subdivisions. But it also explained there that "a law may apply to less than all of the political subdivisions and still be a general law, if it applies uniformly to a class of political subdivisions, which, considering the purpose of the legislation, are distinguished by sufficiently significant characteristics to make them a class by themselves."

SECTION 2

Local Self-Government; Charter. Each political subdivision shall have the power to frame and adopt a charter for its own self-government within such limits and under such procedures as may be provided by general law. Such procedures, however, shall not require the approval of a charter by a legislative body.

Charter provisions with respect to a political subdivision's executive, legislative and administrative structure and organization shall be superior to statutory provisions, subject to the authority of the legislature to enact general laws allocating and reallocating powers and functions.

A law may qualify as a general law even though it is inapplicable to one or more counties by reason of the provisions of this section.

Section 2 is a partial grant of home rule to the counties; that is, it allows them a measure of self-government. In the Statehood Constitution, this section consisted of only one sentence: "Each political subdivision shall have power to frame and adopt a charter for its own self-government within such limits and under such procedures as may be prescribed by law."

Just a few months before the 1968 convention met, the Hawaii Supreme Court decided *Fasi v. City and County of Honolulu*, holding that a county charter "is no more than a statutory charter" and that nothing in the constitution prohibits the legislature from amending a charter provision after a political subdivision has adopted it.[66] In reaction, the 1968 convention significantly altered Section 2, and the amendments adopted then remain.

First, a sentence was added making it clear that county charters are not conditional upon receiving legislative ratification since any procedures the legislature establishes governing how counties are to frame and adopt a charter cannot require subsequent legislative approval of the charter itself.

Second, by including what is referred to as a "superior" clause, county charters, with respect to their executive, legislative, and administrative structure and organization, are granted a status superior to that of any statutory provision the legislature may pass (i.e., county charters are protected against legislative interference in those areas).

However, the section specifically exempts general laws allocating and reallocating powers and functions. The state can thus interfere with charter provisionsby transferring a power or function from the counties to the state or vice versa.The language of the last paragraph, also added in 1968, defines a general law, within the context of this section, as one that does not have to cover all counties.

Since 1968, various provisions of county charters have been challenged as violating Section 2. Underlying the ensuing supreme court rulings is the premise that while "each political subdivision has the power to frame and adopt its own charter, the provisions in the charter must be limited to the self-government of the political subdivision and the provisions must further be within such limits and procedure as is prescribed by general law" (*Kunimoto v. Kawakami*, 1976). This was expanded upon in *Hawaii Government Employees' Association v. County of Maui* (1978), where the court found "the constitutional protection afforded county governments against legislative intrusion is far from total" because the constitutional provisions on local government only grant limitedfreedom from legislative control, rather than complete home rule.

In ruling on specific charter provisions, the court has considered the provisions of Section 2 in conjunction with Section 6, which states that none of the provisions in Article VIII limits the legislature's power to pass laws of statewide concern. In *Hawaii Government Employees' Association*, it held that county charter provisions concerning the Maui board of water supply and its liquor and police commissions involved the county's executive and administrative structure and organization and were thus of local, not statewide, concern. However, sections of the county charter relating to matters of civil service and compensation were invalid because this is an area of statewide, rather than local, concern. Pointing to the 1968 convention, the court emphasized that in amending Section 2 the delegates specifically excluded issues of statewide concern from

[66] *Fasi* is discussed in Recent Developments, "Marsland v. First Hawaiian Bank: Home Rule and the Scope of the County Prosecutor's Power," *University of Hawaii Law Review* 12 (1990): 267–71.

the scope of home rule. The framers, it concluded, thus clearly intended the legislature to retain final authority on all civil service and compensation matters.[67]

Justice Baird H. Kidwell, concurring in part and dissenting in part in the *Hawaii Government Employees' Association* case, argued that the test for determining "the essential difference between matters which pertain to county self-government and those which are of state-wide concern lies in whether the choices which a county makes are of significance only to the people of the county or are also of significance to the people of the state who do not reside in the county." Use of this test led him to agree with the court's decision, except with respect to the liquor commission, which he felt was a statewide rather than a local concern.

Not many years passed before the court again dealt with the scope of Section 2. *City and County of Honolulu v. Ariyoshi* (1984) concerned a 1982 law increasing the salaries of some governmental officials and freezing the salaries of others in order to alleviate existing pay inequities. At issue was whether this law invalidated an ordinance passed a few years before by the City and County of Honolulu regarding the salaries of certain county officials.

Relying on *Hawaii Government Employees' Association,* the court again found that personnel matters, including civil service and compensation, remain subject to legislative control because the "area of compensation of county officials is a matter of statewide concern where a salary structure integrated with that of the state structure will provide for more efficient and effective government for the people of Hawaii." The court did not believe the law intruded on county executive, legislative, or administrative structure or organization.

One commentator views *Ariyoshi* as contributing to the "erosion" of home rule in Hawaii.[68] Another, however, points out that the decision appears to qualify the legislature's ability to interfere with county structure and organization.[69] This latter view of *Ariyoshi* leads the commentator to conclude that it is unclear whether a subsequent decision, *Marsland v. First Hawaiian Bank* (1988), demonstrated a retreat from, or simply a clarification of, *Ariyoshi* In *Marsland,* the court invalidated a provision in the Honolulu Charter, authorizing subpoena powers for the county prosecutor that were broader than or inconsistent with the subpoena powers authorized for the state attorney general under state law.

A charter provision permitting zoning by initiative within the county was ruled not superior to a contrary state statute because it did not fall under a county's executive, legislative, or administrative structure and organization (*Kaiser Hawaii Kai Development Co. v. City and County of Honolulu,* 1989).[70] But Justice

---

[67] See Recent Developments, "Marsland v. First Hawaiian," 271–74 for discussion of *Hawaii Government Employees' Association.*

[68] Comment, "The Erosion of Home Rule in Hawaii: City and County of Honolulu v. Ariyoshi," *University of Hawaii Law Review* 7 (1985): 503.

[69] Recent Developments, "Marsland v. First Hawaiian," 261.

[70] See Note, "Kaiser Hawaii Kai Development Company v. City and County of Honolulu," 181.

Edward Nakamura dissented, emphasizing that the local government's legislative structure does include "the people and their power to enact legislation through popular vote" and that the state legislature had never exercised its power, granted under Article VIII, Section 2, to pass a general law limiting the local government's power to make zoning amendments.

SECTION 3

Taxation and Finance. The taxing power shall be reserved to the State, except so much thereof as may be delegated by the legislature to the political subdivisions, and except that all functions, powers and duties relating to the taxation of real property shall be exercised exclusively by the counties, with the exception of the county of Kalawao. The legislature shall have the power to apportion state revenues among the several political subdivisions.

This section reflects the basic relationship between a state and its subdivisions. Local governments, as creatures of state government, do not have an inherent power to tax. Any taxation power that they enjoy must be granted through constitutional provision or delegated by statute.

Until 1978, the constitution simply stated that, without any exceptions, the taxing power was reserved to the state which had the power to apportion revenues among the counties. Though the 1968 convention considered changing this section, no amendments were placed before the voters. However, in 1978, in line with an effort to enhance county home rule, this section was amended to transfer complete power over real property taxation to the counties.

Previously, the legislature had given the counties authority to set the rate of real property taxes within their jurisdictions, but had reserved the power to assess the value of real property as well as to collect the taxes. While the monies so collected were returned to the counties, the state charged an administrative fee. This split responsibility allowed each side to blame the other for high property taxes. With the change adopted in 1978, the counties took control of the assessment, rate setting, and collection of real property taxes, thus becoming accountable to the voters for the real property taxes they have to pay. (See Article XVIII, Section 6 regarding the effective date and application of this transfer.)

SECTION 4

Mandates; Accrued Claims. No law shall be passed mandating any political subdivision to pay any previously accrued claim.

See the commentary following Section 5.

SECTION 5

Transfer of Mandated Programs. If any new program or increase in the level of service under an existing program shall be mandated to any of the political subdivisions by the legislature, it shall provide that the State share in the cost.

Sections 4 and 5 concern statutory or administrative provisions requiring a local government to carry out a designated activity or provide a service satisfying standards established by the state.

Section 4 originated in the Statehood Constitution and has not been changed since. It prohibits the state from passing one particular type of mandate; that is, the legislature cannot compel a county to make payments on an accrued claim made, at an earlier time, against the county.

Section 5 requires that, when the state mandates any new program or an increase in the level of service under an already existing program, it must share the cost with the county or counties affected. It was added in 1978 in response to complaints best summed up by the words of a county mayor: "One of the distinct ways in which the state has hindered local government has been the imposition of functions and services without offsetting allotment of revenues."[71] Not only was the section meant to prevent the state from placing such burdens on the counties that they would find themselves facing a financial crisis, but also the section was intended to keep the state from transferring state functions to the counties, or requiring the counties to assume new programs, in order to circumvent the expenditure ceiling (added to Article VII, Section 9 at the same time).

SECTION 6

Statewide Laws. This article shall not limit the power of the legislature to enact laws of statewide concern.

Unaltered substantively since statehood, this section declares that even though the counties have some powers under the constitution, the legislature retains the power to pass statutes dealing with statewide concerns. "In order to give effect to section 6, the power of the legislature to enact laws of statewide concern regarding local self-government cannot be diminished" (*City and County of Honolulu v. Ariyoshi*, 1984). However, "on functions of statewide interest and concern, the general rule is that if the counties are not given specific authority to take over the function, the counties cannot thwart the State from performing its duty" (*Kunimoto v. Kawakami*, 1976).

---

[71] Statement by former Mayor Malapit of Kauai, quoted in *Hawaii Constitutional Convention Studies 1978, Article VII: Local Government* (Honolulu: State of Hawaii, Legislative Reference Bureau, 1978), 15.

Article IX

Public Health and Welfare

Hawaii has long been in the forefront of the public health field. Its department of public health, existing when Hawaii was a territory, is the nation's oldest; its Prepaid Health Care Act of 1974 and the recently implemented State Health Insurance Program are models Congress and other states are considering following in their deliberations on comprehensive health plans.

When delegates met in 1950 to draft the Statehood Constitution, there was no question but that they would include a separate article on public health and welfare, although considerable debate occurred over the generality or specificity of provisions to be incorporated. In the end, the article's first section mandating the state to provide for the protection and promotion of the public health was followed by four sections giving the state power to act in as many areas: care of handicapped persons; public assistance; slum clearance, rehabilitation, and housing; and public sightliness and good order.

Although the 1968 convention left the article as originally written, a number of important changes have been made since, with the first occurring in 1976 when voters approved a legislatively proposed amendment broadening the state's responsibility over housing.

This signaled the frame of mind evident among delegates to the 1978 convention.They were disposed to amend the article significantly, reflecting the desire for an expanded governmental role. Two major alterations were made to existing provisions, and five new sections were added, covering economic security of the elderly, management of state population growth, preservation of a healthful environment, cultural resources, and public safety.

Two of the present ten sections are more than empowering for they mandate state action. The 1978 delegates considered and decided against including comparable mandatory language in any of the other eight sections. Instead, those sections leave it to the state, first, to determine whether action is needed and, if so, then to take action. In 1978, this article was renumbered from Article VIII to Article IX.

SECTION 1

Public Health. The State shall provide for the protection and promotion of the public health.

This section remains as it was in the Statehood Constitution. The 1978 convention debated a recommendation by a standing committee to alter the language to the following: "The State shall *have power to* provide for the protection and promotion of the public health" (proposed addition in italics). This would have removed the mandate and simply granted the legislature full discretion to determine whether state resources should be allocated for public health. There was, however, clear consensus against such a major change in emphasis, and after perfunctory debate, the convention, sitting as a committee of the whole, left the original mandatory language.

SECTION 2

Care of Handicapped Persons. The State shall have the power to provide for the treatment and rehabilitation of handicapped persons.

When the section on the care of handicapped persons was placed in the Statehood Constitution, the framers took what was then a forward-thinking approach in emphasizing not only governmental responsibility for handicapped persons, but also concern for their treatment and rehabilitation.

While maintaining the essential thrust of the section, the 1978 convention made an important change by deleting, as out of date, the following bracketed words from the original section: "The State shall have power to provide for the treatment and rehabilitation[, as well as domiciliary care,] of [mentally or physically] handicapped persons." In so doing, the delegates made it clear that they did not mean to remove any type of handicapped persons from the section's coverage. Rather, they intended to broaden it so that all categories of handicaps were included.

SECTION 3

Public Assistance. The State shall have the power to provide financial assistance, medical assistance and social services for persons who are found to be in need of and are eligible for such assistance and services as provided by law.

This section authorizes assistance for those "who are found to be in need of and are eligible for such assistance and services as provided by law." The language differs in two significant ways from that found prior to 1978 which read: "The State shall have power to provide assistance for persons unable to maintain a standard of living compatible with decency and health."

In order to recognize the types of assistance actually provided by government agencies and to allow more flexibility for future programs and services, the 1978 convention expanded "assistance" to encompass financial and medical assistance and social services. The original language referring to "persons unable to maintain a standard of living compatible with decency and health" was considered too vague, and the delegates believed the new wording would allow the legislature to develop precise definitions covering qualifications for assistance and services.The current language is very broad, allowing the legislature to define "need" beyond the previous "decency and health" standard.

SECTION 4

Economic Security of the Elderly. The State shall have the power to provide for the security of the elderly by establishing and promoting programs to assure their economic and social well-being.

This section was added in 1978 because the convention delegates wanted to emphasize the importance of the economic security and social well-being of the elderly, as well as to encourage the legislature to give a high priority to appropriating funds for services to the elderly.

SECTION 5

Housing, Slum Clearance, Development and Rehabilitation. The State shall have the power to provide for, or assist in, housing, slum clearance and the development or rehabilitation of substandard areas. The exercise of such power is deemed to be for a public use and purpose.

The 1968 convention did not alter the original language of this section found in the Statehood Constitution: "The State shall have power to provide for, or assist in, slum clearance and the development or rehabilitation of substandard areas, including housing for persons of low income."

Its present language is almost identical to that adopted in 1976 when voters ratified a legislatively proposed amendment inserting the word "housing" in the first part and substituting "and the exercise of such power is deemed to be for a public use and purpose" in place of "including housing for persons of low income." These changes were intended to expand the state's power by giving it greater flexibility to deal with housing and by removing the limitation, implied in the original language, that the power could be used only with respect to persons of low income.

This section of the constitution must also be read with others in the document having a bearing on housing. These include Article I, Section 2 on the right to acquire and possess property; Article I, Section 20 on eminent domain; Article IX, Section 6 on the state's responsibility to manage state population growth (see below); and Article XI, Section 10 on farm and home ownership. Cumulatively, all of these provisions, including Section 5, demonstrate the saliency of land and housing throughout Hawaii's history and indicate that the constitutional framers "recognized the significance of home ownership and intended the state to exercise considerable authority in providing adequate housing for its citizens."[72] (See Article I, Section 20, "Eminent Domain," for more about land and housing issues in Hawaii.)

SECTION 6

Management of State Population Growth. The State and its political subdivisions, as provided by general law, shall plan and manage the growth of the population to protect and preserve the public health and welfare; except that each political subdivision, as provided by general law, may plan and manage the growth of its population in a more restrictive manner than the State.

When this section was added in 1978, it caused considerable controversy among the delegates. Some argued that it should not be in the document. After spirited debate, a motion to leave it out was defeated in a twenty-four to seventy-three vote, demonstrating that a large majority believed it necessary to mandate the planning and management of population growth. Although the phrase "plan and manage the growth of the population" is extremely broad and ill-defined, most ongoing activity at the state and the county levels focuses on the distribution of population through zoning decisions and development plans.

There was also much discussion among the delegates about whether the section should apply only to the state government or include the counties as well. The language finally adopted not only incorporates the counties, but also permits

[72] Comment, "Resolving a Conflict—Ohana Zoning & Private Covenants," *University of Hawaii Law Review* 6 (1983): 208.

them to plan and manage population growth in a more restrictive manner than does the state; to date, the counties have not taken advantage of the possibilities implied by this clause.

SECTION 7

Public Sightliness and Good Order. The State shall have the power to conserve and develop objects and places of historic or cultural interest and provide for public sightliness and physical good order. For these purposes private property shall be subject to reasonable regulation.

While novel in 1950 so that much discussion accompanied the adoption of this section by the convention that proposed the Statehood Constitution, its language was retained in 1968 and changed only slightly in 1978.

Hawaii is unique in that it has a long history of banning billboards due, in large measure, to the efforts of the Outdoor Circle, an interest group active sincethe early 1900s. In its landmark *State v. Diamond Motors* (1967) decision upholding a county ordinance banning billboards, the Hawaii Supreme Court interpreted this section of the constitution as a broad grant of legislative power. Acknowledging that it was breaking with precedent set by other courts in the country, the court proceeded to do so because this section permitted it to "accept beauty as a proper community objective, attainable through the use of the police power." Thus, a regulation based solely on aesthetic considerations was constitutionally permissible. Refusing to accept the argument that billboards should be allowed in industrial areas, the justices clarified the ambiguous phrase "sightliness and physical good order" by holding that the "natural beauty of the Hawaiian Islands is not confined to mountain areas and beaches [for the] term 'sightliness and physical good order' does not refer only to junk yards, slaughter houses, sanitation, cleanliness, or incongruous business activities in residential areas."

Although presented with a claim that the ban on billboards constituted a denial of freedom of speech, the *Diamond Motors* court dismissed it as without merit, considering only the issue of regulation for aesthetic purposes. However, subsequent state and federal court decisions suggest that, in certain circumstances, the right to freedom of speech in the U.S. and Hawaii constitutions outweighs a governmental interest in aesthetics. These decisions raise questions about the constitutionality of Hawaii's statewide ban on billboards (Haw. Rev. State § 445-111 *et seq.*) as well as similar county ordinances.[73] For example, in ruling unconstitutional an ordinance banning the distribution of handbills in Waikiki, the center of Hawaii's tourist industry, Hawaii's high court found that while "preventing nuisances to enhance the attractiveness of tourism is

[73] See Note, "Metromedia, Inc. v. City of San Diego," 79.

important, on balance, this rationale is not sufficient to justify the total suppression of commercial speech" (*State v. Bloss*, 1981; the same result was reached in *State v. Hawkins*, 1982). More recently, the U.S. District Court for the District of Hawaii held that "[l]ess drastic means than a *complete ban on the posting of political signs outdoors* are clearly available to promote the City's interest in . . . aesthetic beauty" and that such an ordinance violates the U.S. constitutional guarantee of freedom of speech (*Runyon v. Fasi*, 1990 (emphasis in original)).

SECTION 8

Preservation of a Healthful Environment. The State shall have the power to promote and maintain a healthful environment, including the prevention of any excessive demands upon the environment and the State's resources.

The 1978 Constitutional Convention added this section based on the belief that protecting the environment is directly related to the public health and welfare. Although recognizing that already existing governmental bodies could go far in preserving and maintaining a healthful environment, the delegates felt that giving constitutional status to this public policy issue served to make the state's power explicit.

SECTION 9

Cultural Resources. The State shall have the power to preserve and develop the cultural, creative and traditional arts of its various ethnic groups.

Added in 1978, this section reflects the strong sense of pride among convention delegates in Hawaii's ethnic heritage and diversity. It was just one of many changes incorporated to acknowledge and give constitutional status to the multi-cultural, and in particular the native Hawaiian, traditions so important to the islands. Other amendments to the 1978 Constitution, growing out of what was referred to as the Hawaiian affairs package, added Section 10, the law of the splintered paddle (see below); changed the Preamble; created an Office of Hawaiian Affairs (Article XII); required a Hawaiian education program in public schools (Article X); added Hawaiian as an official language (Article XV); and added the state motto, written in Hawaiian (Article XV).

SECTION 10

Public Safety. The law of the splintered paddle, mamala-hoe kanawai, decreed by Kamehameha I—Let every elderly person, woman and child lie by the roadside in safety—shall be a unique and living symbol of the State's concern for public safety.

> The State shall have the power to provide for the safety of the people from crimes against persons and property.

Although a constitutional provision specifying that the state has "the power to provide for the safety of the people from crimes against persons and property" is unnecessary, the 1978 convention added it as a policy statement to address increasing public concern over the growing crime rate. In addition, it also served a more important symbolic purpose. Like other changes resulting from the Hawaiian affairs package, it officially recognized the significant contribution nativeHawaiian culture makes to contemporary society in Hawaii.

The reference to the law of the splintered paddle is to an episode in the life of Kamehameha I, who eventually united the islands and reigned from 1795 to 1819. While there are different versions of the incident, said to have taken place sometime around 1782 to 1784, the major elements are summarized here.

As a young chief, Kamehameha embarked on a raid into enemy territory along the Puna coast of the island of Hawaii, taking along only the crew of his war canoe. Arriving at Puna, he saw some fishermen and decided to take their catch. Leaping from his canoe in order to chase them, his foot became caught in a crevice of lava rock near the shore. Seeing that Kamehameha was defenseless, but not knowing his identity, one of the fishermen turned back and, using a paddle, hit him on the head with such force that the paddle splintered. Saved from further injury when his crew came to his assistance, Kamehameha eventually recognized that his attempt to attack and rob the fishermen was wrong.

Years later Kamehameha commemorated the experience when he proclaimed the *mamala-hoe kanawai*—the law of the splintered paddle—translated as "Let every elderly person, woman and child lie by the roadside in safety." From early on, according to authorities Abraham Fornander and Ralph S. Kuykendall, the law was seen as protecting the helpless from unprovoked physical attack and robbery.[74] This interpretation was probably the basis for the 1978 convention's use of the law of the splintered paddle as the focal point to emphasize concerns about increasing crime rates.

But there are other significantly different interpretations, suggesting that the law implies more than a right to be protected against crime. For example, in his 1973 book, *The Warrior King, Hawaii's Kamehameha The Great,* Richard Tregaskis writes that it "protected innocent citizens from the depredations of rampaging men-at-arms and government officials bent on looting and pillaging."[75] In this respect he echoes two writers from the early 1900s. William D. Westervelt

---

[74] Ralph S. Kuykendall, *The Hawaiian Kingdom* (Honolulu: University of Hawaii Press, 1938), vol. 1, *1778–1854*, 33–34; Abraham Fornander, *Hawaiian Antiquities and Folklore*, vol. V, part II (Honolulu: Bishop Museum Press, 1919; Millwood, N.Y.: Kraus Reprint, 1986), 468–70.

[75] Richard Tregaskis, *The Warrior King, Hawaii's Kamehameha The Great* (New York: Macmillan Publishing Co., 1973), 150.

suggests that the law was especially important as a decree against the "plunder of the weak by the powerful."[76] The Reverend Herbert H. Gowen states that the law decreed "that any chief who should henceforth engage in a raid upon unarmed and helpless people should be surely put to death."[77]

On the other hand, in *Ka Po'e Kahiko, The People of Old* (a series of newspaper articles published in Hawaiian from 1866 to 1871), Samuel Manaiakalani Kamakau interprets the law as the power to pardon, for it gave the king "unlimited power while ruler of his kingdom [and] [a]nyone so unfortunate as to be taken captive and about to be killed could be saved by Kamehameha pronouncing the Mamalahoa law; it was consecrated to the saving of lives and fortunes."[78] Writing just after the turn of the century, N. B. Emerson comments that behind the law "there loom up the unknown possibilities of a powerful autocratic will, that is at once a law-giver, judge and executioner."[79]

However interpreted, the *mamala-hoe kanawai* is a unique Hawaiian heritage adding not only richness, but a human dimension as well, to the state's basic law.

---

[76] William D. Westervelt, *Hawaiian Historical Legends* (1923; reprint, Rutland, Vt.: Charles E. Tuttle Co., 1977), 174–75.

[77] Herbert H. Gowen, *Hawaiian Idylls of Love and Death* (New York: Cochrane Publishing Co., 1908), 32.

[78] Samuel Manaiakalani Kamakau, *Ka Po'e Kahiko, The People of Old* (Honolulu: Bishop Museum Press, 1964), 16–17.

[79] N. B. Emerson, "Mamala-Hoa," *Hawaiian Historical Society Report* 10 (1903): 26.

Article X

Education

Hawaii's public school system, one of the oldest in the nation, dates from 1840 during the reign of Kamehameha III. It has always been unique in its highly centralized nature, a characteristic often criticized. At the 1978 convention, those who favored decentralization in some form put up a valiant, but losing, fight. Abolition of the statewide system in favor of a completely decentralized one was never seriously considered, but the convention sitting as a committee of the whole spent a good deal of time debating proposals aimed at establishing a two-tiered approach, with constitutionally mandated local boards of education in addition to a single statewide board. That such proposals failed demonstrates a reluctance to change the basic nature of the state's school system, a reluctance flowing from the more general acceptance of and support for centralized powers lodged in the state government.

Nevertheless, this education article has undergone considerable alteration. Between statehood and the 1968 convention, it was amended more than any other article, the result of changes ratified by voters in 1964. It was unaltered by the 1968 convention, but the convention of 1978 made significant modifications; it is one of the few articles to have been amended since then. In 1978, it was renumbered from Article IX to Article X.

SECTION 1

Public Education. The State shall provide for the establishment, support and control of a statewide system of public schools free from sectarian control, a state university, public libraries and such other educational institutions as may be deemed desirable, including physical facilities therefor. There shall be no discrimination in public educational institutions because of race, religion, sex or ancestry; nor shall public funds be appropriated for the support or benefit of any sectarian or private educational institution.

The language of this section is fundamentally the same as in the Statehood Constitution. In 1978, however, the first clause of the second sentence was amended, and though only one word was changed and one word added, the alteration is telling. The clause previously read: "There shall be no segregation in public educational institutions because of race, religion or ancestry." "No discrimination" was substituted for "no segregation" because it was a more encompassing term, including an implicit prohibition against segregation. In addition, "sex" was incorporated into the list of characteristics that could not be the basis for such discrimination. This latter change was consistent with a strong movement within the state to recognize equality based on gender; Article I, Section 3, the equality of rights provision, forbidding discrimination on the basis of gender, had already been added in 1972.

The unique statewide system of public schools is established by the first sentence, with the result that funds are appropriated by the state legislature, from the state's general fund, covering all public schools within the state. The Hawaii Supreme Court held, in 1976, that where the section calls for providing for the establishment, support, and control of a statewide system, it means that the legislature has the power over, "among other things, the selection and location of public school and state university sites" (*Kunimoto v. Kawakami*, 1976).

Following similar wording in the Organic Act, the Statehood Constitution included two provisions, unchanged since then, regarding the separation of church and state. The first sentence states that the system of public schools is to be free from sectarian control, while the final clause prohibits public funds from being appropriated for the support or benefit of any sectarian or private educational institution.

In *Spears v. Honda* (1968), the court found that the language in the section's last clause "is unequivocal," and it invalidates legislation providing transportation for both public and nonpublic school students, as well as a program furnishing subsidized bus transportation for all school children. Appropriations made just for the transportation of public school students are valid.

Hawaii's high court found the U.S. Supreme Court's landmark 1947 ruling in *Everson v. Board of Education of Ewing Township* inapplicable. *Everson* held bus transportation for nonpublic school students valid as a benefit to school children, rather than to the institution they attend. The Hawaii court, on the other hand, found that the 1950 convention specifically rejected this child benefit theory with respect to bus transportation and similar general welfare programs for nonpublic school students and that Section 1 clearly prohibits the type of program challenged in *Spears*. In basing its decision on this section, the court left open consideration of such programs under two other provisions in the state constitution, the establishment clause in Article I, Section 4 and the prohibition of appropriations in violation of the establishment clause in Article VII, Section 4. The court has not, however, considered the issue in relation to those sections in any subsequent case.

SECTION 2

Board of Education. There shall be a board of education composed of members who shall be elected in a nonpartisan manner by qualified voters, as provided by law, from two at-large school board districts. The first school board district shall be comprised of the island of Oahu and all other islands not specifically enumerated. The second school board district shall be comprised of the islands of Hawaii, Maui, Lanai, Molokai, Kahoolawe, Kauai and Niihau. Each at-large school board district shall be divided into departmental school districts, as may be provided by law. There shall be at least one member residing in each departmental school district. The Hawaii State Student Council shall select a public high school student to serve as a nonvoting member on the board of education.

This section establishes a board of education (BOE), elected on a nonpartisan basis from two at-large districts, within which the legislature must create smaller departmental districts. Some of the BOE members must reside within such departmental districts. In addition, the BOE includes a nonvoting student selected by the Hawaii State Student Council.

Although based on a provision in the Statehood Constitution, this section now differs considerably from the original language.

Prior to 1964, the board of education was appointed by the governor from lists submitted by local school advisory councils, with the appointment subject to the advice and consent of the senate. In 1964, voters ratified a legislatively proposed amendment turning the BOE into an elected body. This amendment did not, however, alter language requiring that at least part of the membership of the board represent geographical subdivisions of the state.

No changes were made four years later when the 1968 convention met, and, in 1970, the voters rejected a legislatively proposed amendment changing this section so that the legislature would determine, by statute, the method of selecting BOE members. While the 1978 convention supported continuation of an elected board, it amended the section to make those elections nonpartisan in order to take party politics out of the process.

Attempts to alter the method of selecting school board members and/or the superintendent continue, however. Two alternative constitutional amendment proposals came out of the 1992 legislature: (1) a school board and superintendent appointed by the governor, and (2) an elected school board with a superintendent appointed by the governor. In proposing these two options, the legislature called for a two-step process where the voters would decide at the primary election which alternative would then appear on the general election ballot for ratification or rejection. But because the Hawaii Supreme Court found this process, never before used in Hawaii, in violation of the Article XVII amendment and revision provisions, the school governance issue did not come before the voters (*Blair v. Cayetano*,1992) (see also the discussion under Article XVII).

The 1978 delegates faced a dilemma: They did not want to change the basic principle of BOE representation based on geography, a concept incorporated in the Statehood Constitution. But they were very aware of the need to meet one person-one vote districting guidelines because a 1970 opinion of the attorney general (Op. Att'y Gen. 70-5, 1970) had concluded that the BOE districts were malapportioned and that the legislature had failed to take corrective action. A subsequent court order issued by the U.S. District Court for the District of Hawaii June 19, 1974, reapportioned the board districts.

In order to reconcile geographic representation and the one person—one vote principle, the convention devised an election framework resulting in a system best characterized as confusing to the voters. Two at-large school board districts are constitutionally established, Oahu (the City and County of Honolulu) being the "first" and the neighbor islands comprising the "second." The legislature then defines "departmental" districts within each at-large district. This allows the legislature to make periodic adjustments in response to population shifts. The section further requires at least one member to reside in each of these departmental districts.

The number of members on the BOE has never been specified in the constitution and is thus left to legislative discretion. By statute, the number is currently set at thirteen (Haw. Rev. Stat. § 13-1). The statutory provision further specifies that ten members are to be elected at large from the "first" school board district; one member must reside in each of the four legislatively defined districts. The "second" school board district elects three at-large members, with each residing in one of the three departmental districts. The term of office served by BOE members is also left up to the legislature, which has, by statute, established staggered four-year terms.

The final sentence, giving constitutional status to a nonvoting public high school student member, was added in 1988 when voters ratified a legislatively proposed amendment.

SECTION 3

Power of the Board of Education. The board of education shall have the power, as provided by law, to formulate policy and to exercise control over the public school system through its executive officer, the superintendent of education, who shall be appointed by the board; except that the board shall have jurisdiction over the internal organization and management of the public school system, as provided by law, and shall exercise its jurisdiction in a manner consistent with general laws.

Like several other sections in this article, Section 3 was amended in 1964. The term "superintendent of public instruction" was replaced with "superintendent of education." In addition, the original language making the superintendent an ex officio voting member was changed so that the superintendent could no longer vote and was only the BOE "secretary." This latter provision was subsequently removed in 1978. The superintendent's appointment by the board and the title of "executive officer" of the public school system have remained constant over the years. In 1970, a legislatively proposed amendment allowing the legislature to determine the method of selecting the superintendent was rejected by the voters.

According to the Hawaii Supreme Court, the first part of this section grants the BOE "broad discretionary powers in formulating and enacting educational programs for the State's public schools" and does not require any specific authorization from the legislature before the board can establish policies or adopt programs (*Medeiros v. Kiyosaki*, 1970). This approach was reiterated in *Shorba v. Board of Education* (1978), where the court held that "formulation of policy and control over the public school system rests with the Board of Education."

Despite these broad decisions, the 1978 convention delegates believed it necessary to make clear that the BOE should have, to the fullest extent possible, jurisdiction over the internal organization and management of the public school system. But at the same time they wanted to clarify that the legislature determines which matters relating to internal organization and management are to be within the board's jurisdiction. As a result, the language stating "except that the board shall have jurisdiction over the internal organization and management of the public school system, as provided by law, and shall exercise its jurisdiction in a manner consistent with general laws" was added. The convention records state, moreover, that this change was not intended to impact on the governor's authority over the BOE with regard to policies implemented through the budget and that board requests for appropriations would continue to be reviewed by the executive before being submitted to the legislature.

This clause was at issue in the 1989 case *Board of Education v. Waihee*, when the BOE argued that its ability to plan and efficiently implement programs, to set priorities, to hire needed personnel, and to carry out repairs and maintenance of school facilities had been limited or destroyed because of the governor's authority over the budget process. Although the case was dismissed by the trial court as a nonjusticiable political question, the Hawaii Supreme Court disagreed. The latter concluded that, in contrast to some situations, this particular intra-executive dispute was capable of judicial resolution. A review of the 1978 convention records led the court to rule against the BOE, concluding that the language added at that time could "hardly be characterized as a constitutional declaration emancipating the Board of Education from all executive direction" because the framers did not intend to take away the governor's statewide policy-making and executive powers or his or her authority over the executive budget.

SECTION 4

Hawaiian Education Program. The State shall promote the study of Hawaiian culture, history and language.

The State shall provide for a Hawaiian education program consisting of language, culture and history in the public schools. The use of community expertise shall be encouraged as a suitable and essential means in furtherance of the Hawaiian education program.

This section was added in 1978, reflecting the commitment on the part of delegates to preserving the state's native Hawaiian heritage. As stated in the convention records, its purposes were to "insure that there is a comprehensive Hawaiian education program" within the public schools' regular curriculum, "to provide for the employment in the public school system of persons who have knowledge of Hawaiian language, culture and history but not necessarily the necessary formal educational achievements," to assure "the general diffusion of Hawaiian history on a wider basis," and to "recognize and preserve the Hawaiian culture which has contributed to, and in many ways forms the basis and foundation of, modern Hawaii."[80]

SECTION 5

University of Hawaii. The University of Hawaii is hereby established as the state university and constituted a body corporate. It shall have title to all the real and personal property now or hereafter set aside or conveyed to it, which shall be held in public trust for its purposes, to be administered and disposed of as provided by law.

See the commentary following Section 6.

SECTION 6

Board of Regents; Powers. There shall be a board of regents of the University of Hawaii, the members of which shall be nominated and, by and with the advice and

[80] *1978 Proceedings I*, Standing Committee Report no. 57, 637.

> consent of the senate, appointed by the governor. At least part of the membership of the board shall represent geographic subdivisions of the State. The board shall have the power, as provided by law, to formulate policy, and to exercise control over the university through its executive officer, the president of the university, who shall be appointed by the board; except that the board shall have exclusive jurisdiction over the internal organization and management of the university. This section shall not limit the power of the legislature to enact laws of statewide concern.

Sections 5 and 6 concern the University of Hawaii and its board of regents (BOR). Section 5, establishing the University of Hawaii, is virtually the same as when it was included in the Statehood Constitution. The phrase "body corporate" means that the university is granted some autonomy from the executive branch and is presumed to have certain independent powers of its own.

Section 6 provisions covering gubernatorial appointment of regents, requiring geographic representation among regents, and leaving the number of members up to the legislature (set at eleven by statute) remain as originally found in the Statehood Constitution. First amended in 1964, when voters approved deleting a sentence that made the president of the university and the superintendent of public instruction ex officio voting members of the BOR, this section was not changed again until 1978.

Using language similar to that added to Section 3, "Power of the Board of Education," the 1978 convention modified Section 6 to ensure the BOR's exclusive jurisdiction over the internal organization and management of the university. It differs from Section 3 by not including a directive that the legislature define what matters are to be included within that exclusive jurisdiction. However, the BOR is constrained by the last clause, stating that the provisions shall not limit the power of the legislature to enact laws of statewide concern.

While the 1989 *Board of Education v. Waihee* decision concerned the language in Section 3 above, the corresponding provision in Section 6 has not been the subject of judicial interpretation. Nevertheless, it is possible to speculate that were such a case to arise, the ruling in *Board of Education v. Waihee*, sustaining the governor's authority over the BOE's budget, would probably be held applicable to the board of regents under Section 6. In practice, the university's budget is subject to the same executive branch control that was unsuccessfully challenged by the board of education.

Such speculation is strengthened by the reasoning used in *Levi v. University of Hawaii* (1981), in which the Hawaii Supreme Court emphasized that Section 6 clearly makes the BOR's authority to formulate policy subject to the clause "as provided by law." In addition, the court said, the regents' exclusive power over internal matters does not limit legislative power to enact laws of statewide concern. This means that policies adopted by the BOR must be consistent with those laws. In *Levi*, the court ruled that retirement is such a statewide concern and that the board exceeded its authority in setting the university retirement age at sixty-five when the legislature had, by statute, established the retirement age for all public employees at seventy. (That statutory provision was subsequently repealed in 1984.)

However, two years after *Levi*, the court found that the BOR does have "exclusive jurisdiction over matters such as setting the criteria for determining tenure, promotion, and other areas of faculty employment, as well as establishing the procedure by which such matters are to be reviewed and grievances resolved" (*University of Hawaii Professional Assembly v. University of Hawaii*, 1983). The board's power in this area also includes delegating, to the university president, authority to make negative decisions in tenure cases (*Abramson v. Board of Regents*, 1976).

Article XI

Conservation, Control and Development of Resources

During the decade leading up to the 1978 convention, the preservation of the environment became a critical and controversial issue in Hawaii. The title of this article, formerly Article X, read only Conservation and Development of Resources. However, when the 1978 delegates inserted the word "Control," they signaled a heightened awareness of the need to protect the environment and scarce resources. Not only were changes made for the first time to the five original sections, but also the article was significantly expanded by the addition of five new sections.

There would have been one more addition if a section introduced from the floor, titled "Shoreline Access and Parks," had not been defeated by only one vote. The convention records do not clearly indicate why there was opposition. Implied, however, is that delegates found the section unnecessary in light of the path-breaking decisions handed down over the previous ten years by the Hawaii Supreme Court. In those cases, the court redefined the shoreline boundary line separating private and public lands, holding that private ownership of shoreline property ended at the vegetation line, which was further up on the beach than had been the precedent in Hawaii and the nation. The decisions had the effect of expanding the shoreline areas to which the public had access.

In the first of these cases, *In re Ashford* (1968), the court held that the Hawaiian term *ma ke kai* (along the sea) means the "upper reaches of the wash of the waves, usually evidenced by the edge of vegetation or by the line of debris left by the wash of waves" rather than the lower "mean high water" line (sometimes referred to as the seaweed line). In *County of Hawaii v. Sotomura* (1973), the court explained that "[p]ublic policy as interpreted by this court, favors extending to public use and ownership as much of Hawaii's shoreline as is reasonably possible" and ruled that private land ended and public land began at the vegetation line. This was reaffirmed in *In re Sanborn* (1977). Shortly thereafter, in another path-breaking decision, the court ruled that land created by lava flows belonged to the public (*State v. Zimring*, 1977). Although continuing to expand the public's domain, the *Zimring* court claimed that it was taking a cautious approach. It pointed out that the case was one of first impression since "[n]o court sitting at common law had occasion to deal with the question of lava extensions" and that it was very much aware of the decision's potential impact for the future.[81]

A new *Sotomura* case brought in the U.S. District Court for the District of Hawaii rekindled the whole issue. The state's motion to dismiss was denied (*Sotomura v. County of Hawaii*, 1975) and was followed by a ruling enjoining enforcement of the boundary line as established by the 1973 state court decision. The federal court then found that the state court had not only taken private property for public use in violation of the U.S. Constitution's due process and just compensation clauses, but had also gone against all precedent that established the seaweed line as the correct boundary (*Sotomura v. County of Hawaii*, 1978). In a strong rebuke, the federal judge wrote: "The [state court's 1973] decision in *Sotomura* was contrary to established practice, history and precedent and, apparently, was intended to implement the [state] court's conclusion that public policy favors extension of public use and ownership of the shoreline. A desire to promote public policy, however, does not constitute justification for a state taking private property without compensation [nor violating due process]."

This conflict in interpretation between the federal court and the state court has not been resolved.[82] Nevertheless, the Hawaii Supreme Court has continued to define the upper boundary of the public beach as it did in the *Ashford* and 1973 *Sotomura* decisions (*Littleton v. State*, 1982), and the shoreline is defined by state statute in those same terms as well (see, e.g., Haw. Rev. Stat. § 200-1).

Article XI is one of the few articles amended since the convention of 1978: In 1988, voters approved an additional section, now numbered [11], affirming the state's rights over its "exclusive economic zone."

---

[81] See Michael Anthony Town and William Wai Lim Yuen, "Public Access to Beaches in Hawaii: 'A Social Necessity,'" *Hawaii Bar Journal* 10 (1973): 5.

[82] See Dennis J. Hwang, " Shoreline Setback Regulations and the Taking Analysis," *University of Hawaii Law Review* 13 (1991): 1.

SECTION 1

Conservation and Development of Resources. For the benefit of present and future generations, the State and its political subdivisions shall conserve and protect Hawaii's natural beauty and all natural resources, including land, water, air, minerals and energy sources, and shall promote the development and utilization of these resources in a manner consistent with their conservation and in furtherance of the self-sufficiency of the State.

All public natural resources are held in trust by the State for the benefit of the people.

Prior to 1978, this section consisted of only one sentence: "The legislature shall promote the conservation, development and utilization of agricultural resources, and fish, mineral, forest, water, land, game and other natural resources."

Believing this placed too little emphasis on preservation, doing no more than empowering the state to promote conservation, the 1978 convention substituted much stronger language. The section now mandates the state and the counties to "conserve and protect Hawaii's natural beauty and all natural resources." Although the development and utilization of natural resources is to be promoted "in a manner consistent with their conservation," this is to be balanced with furthering "the self-sufficiency of the State."

The opening phrase, "For the benefit of present and future generations," was included to affirm the ethical obligations of each generation to those that follow, while the last sentence places a special obligation on the state, by specifying that it holds the public natural resources in trust for the benefit of the people.

SECTION 2

Management and Disposition of Natural Resources. The legislature shall vest in one or more executive boards or commissions powers for the management of natural resources owned or controlled by the State, and such powers of disposition thereof as may be provided by law; but land set aside for public use, other than for a reserve for conservation purposes, need not be placed under the jurisdiction of such a board or commission.

The mandatory provisions of this section shall not apply to the natural resources owned by or under the control of a political subdivision or a department or agency thereof.

No substantive changes have been made to this section since it was placed in the Statehood Constitution. By requiring the establishment of one or more boards or commissions to manage and dispose of state-owned natural resources, it gives the legislature discretion to establish a centralized or decentralized administrative system. Since, for the most part, the management responsibility called for by this section falls under the authority of the State Department of Land and

Natural Resources (see Haw. Rev. Stat. tit. 12, Conservation and Resources), the legislature has centralized its administration.

The second clause of the first paragraph gives the legislature the option of placing certain public lands (e.g., for airports or schools) under the jurisdiction of other governmental entities. The second paragraph exempts from state jurisdiction natural resources owned by or under the control of the counties. This adds an element of decentralization to the otherwise centralized management of natural resources in the state.

SECTION 3

Agricultural Lands. The State shall conserve and protect agricultural lands, promote diversified agriculture, increase agricultural self-sufficiency and assure the availability of agriculturally suitable lands. The legislature shall provide standards and criteria to accomplish the foregoing.

Lands identified by the State as important agricultural lands needed to fulfill the purposes above shall not be reclassified by the State or rezoned by its political subdivisions without meeting the standards and criteria established by the legislature and approved by a two-thirds vote of the body responsible for the reclassification or rezoning action.

By the late 1970s, urban development had seriously encroached on agricultural lands, thus raising concerns about the future of agriculture in the islands. This section, added in 1978, directs the state to conserve and protect such lands, promote diversified agriculture, increase agricultural self-sufficiency, and make sure that agriculturally suitable lands are available. That this was of critical importance in the minds of the 1978 delegates is indicated in the language of the second paragraph, which places particular obstacles in the path of reclassi-fying or rezoning agricultural lands (e.g., changing their permitted use to urban development). After the state has specifically identified "important agricultural lands," they cannot be reclassified or rezoned without a two-thirds vote of the body responsible for such decisions. This is an extremely controversial area, and the legislature has, to date, been unable to reach consensus on identifying important agricultural lands; therefore, the section has not been implemented.

The "self-sufficiency" clause in the first paragraph was challenged in *Safeway v. Board of Agriculture* (1984), when Safeway was denied a permit to sell fresh milk produced on the mainland. While the U.S. district court did not rule the provision unconstitutional as a violation of the U.S. Constitution's commerce clause, as Safeway argued, it did hold that Section 3 could not be used to deny the license, "for to do so would have an unconstitutional discriminatory effect of excluding out-of-state goods from Hawaii for no other reason than the fact that they travel in interstate commerce."

The 1978 convention proposed that this section replace a section entitled "Farm and Home Ownership." However, since *Kahalekai v. Doi* (1979) held that the decision proposal was not validly ratified, that section (see Section 10) remains.

SECTION 4

Public Land Banking. The State shall have the power to acquire interests in real property to control future growth, development and land use within the State. The exercise of such power is deemed to be for a public use and purpose.

Added in 1978, this section represents an attempt to counteract the fact that "[i]n Hawaii's land economy, a few major landowners and large developers exercise a predominant influence in land development and land marketing decisions."[83] It gives the state power to acquire land in fee or through leases that second parties hold on land "for the specified purpose of asserting the State's ownership interests in shaping the growth and development of entire regions, in advance of any immediate need for a particular public use."[84]

SECTION 5

General Laws Required; Exceptions. The legislative power over the lands owned by or under the control of the State and its political subdivisions shall be exercised only by general laws, except in respect to transfers to or for the use of the State, or a political subdivision, or any department or agency thereof.

This section remains substantively the same as it was in the Statehood Constitution. Legislative provision for specific individuals is precluded, and any laws passed regarding state-owned lands (e.g., selling land to private persons) must be general; that is, they must apply equally to everyone. However, the section permits special laws, granting special treatment, when transferring lands between governmental entities.

SECTION 6

Marine Resources. The State shall have the power to manage and control the marine, seabed and other resources located within the boundaries of the State, including the archipelagic waters of the State, and reserves to itself all such rights outside state boundaries not specifically limited by federal or international law.

---

[83] *1978 Proceedings I*, Standing Committee Report no. 77, 689.

[84] Ibid.

> All fisheries in the sea waters of the State not included in any fish pond, artificial enclosure or state-licensed mariculture operation shall be free to the public, subject to vested rights and the right of the State to regulate the same; provided that mariculture operations shall be established under guidelines enacted by the legislature, which shall protect the public's use and enjoyment of the reefs. The State may condemn such vested rights for public use.

Prior to 1978, this section was entitled "Sea Fisheries" and provided only that "[a]ll fisheries in the sea waters of the State not included in any fish pond or artificial inclosure [sic] shall be free to the public, subject to vested rights and the right of the State to regulate the same." Although the 1978 convention retained this language as a core element, it expanded the section's coverage with the intent of clarifying Hawaii's longstanding interest in marine resources and asserting the state's right to manage and control those resources. The new title, "Marine Resources," reflects this new emphasis.

The provision regarding vested rights to fisheries stems from Sections 95 and 96 of the Organic Act which repealed exclusive fishing rights, called *konohiki* fishing rights, originating during the Hawaiian monarchy.

In *State v. Hawaiian Dredging Co.* (1964), the Hawaii Supreme Court found that, in enacting those sections, Congress intended to destroy, "so far as it was in its power to do so, all private rights of fishery and to throw open the fisheries to the people." The court found that the language of the sections was unambiguous in requiring that any claim of a vested right be registered in order to preserve it and that where claims were not preserved, the "vested rights which were surrendered to the public continue to be free to the public."

Prior to 1978, the constitution also included a related section (in the article titled Schedule), giving the state condemnation power, upon payment of just compensation, so that those waters not registered with vested rights could be established as public waters. However, the 1978 convention eliminated the need for such a separate section by incorporating a final sentence in Section 6, stating that the state may condemn such vested rights for public use. However, one must note an important difference: Previously, the state was required to carry out the condemnation, while the current wording makes condemnation optional. As stated in the 1978 convention record, this change was based on the belief that condemnation of all *konohiki* rights might not be in the public's interest.

Section 6 incorporates another aspect of native Hawaiian tradition. Although all fisheries in the sea waters are for public use, fishponds are specifically excluded. A fishpond, called *loko kuapa* in Hawaiian, is an area of sea water enclosed by the shoreline and a stone wall constructed in the sea water. In its 1976 decision, in *United States v. Kaiser Aetna*, the U.S. district court summarized the history of fishponds as follows:

> [T]he status of fishponds from Hawaiian prerecorded history up through the Great Mahele [of 1848] was clearly that of private property, appropriated by successive

> conquerors, and given by and to chiefs, with the commoners excluded from the lands, the pond waters and the fish therein, under every regime. The distribution of land in the Great Mahele made no change in the rights of private ownership of fishponds, as the Hawaii Supreme Court recognized in a series of pre-annexation cases. The Organic Act of 1900 . . . repealed all prior laws conferring private rights in "seawater" fisheries (subject to vested rights) but specifically exempted fishponds from its scope. A similar provision appears in the Hawaii Constitution. . . . Opinions since annexation and statehood confirm the private nature of fishponds in Hawaii.

In *Kaiser Aetna*, the U.S. district court held that Kuapa Pond (originally a fishpond on the island of Oahu) had been transformed into navigable waters used for commerce and was thus subject to regulation by Congress and that the United States could not appropriate those waters for a public use without just compensation. Upheld in part and reversed in part by the U.S. Court of Appeals for the Ninth Circuit (*United States v. Kaiser Aetna*, 1978), the case eventually reached the U.S. Supreme Court which, in 1979, agreed with the district court's ruling (*Kaiser Aetna v. United States*, 1979).[85]

When the 1978 convention included the concept of mariculture operations in this section, it specifically did so to allow development of sea farming in addition to traditional fishing operations; testimony before the subject matter committee convinced delegates that the success of future commercial fisheries lay in this direction.

SECTION 7

> **Water Resources.** The State has an obligation to protect, control and regulate the use of Hawaii's water resources for the benefit of its people.
>
> The legislature shall provide for a water resources agency which, as provided by law, shall set overall water conservation, quality and use policies; define beneficial and reasonable uses; protect ground and surface water resources, watersheds and natural stream environments; establish criteria for water use priorities while assuring appurtenant rights and existing correlative and riparian uses and establish procedures for regulating all uses of Hawaii's water resources.

This section was added in 1978 in the belief, shared by many in the state, that the use and conservation of water had become a critical issue. The language of the first paragraph was phrased so as to declare that the state has a duty and a responsibility to care for water resources as distinguished from merely being granted power to do so.

The second paragraph requires the legislature to establish an agency to set water policies and procedures in such areas as conservation, quality, and

[85] See Note, "Kaiser Aetna v. United States: Private Property Rights in a Navigable Marina," *University of Hawaii Law Review* 2 (1980–1981): 589.

use regulation. Appurtenant rights and existing correlative and riparian rights to water use are to be assured when setting water use priorities. Surrounded by controversy and opposing views regarding the public or private ownership of water, the mandate to provide a water resources agency was not implemented until 1987. The State Water Code (Haw. Rev. Stat. ch. 174C) establishes the Commission on Water Resources Management and covers such areas as regulation of water use, water quality, and native Hawaiian water rights.

Water rights were at the core of litigation ongoing at the time of the 1978 convention. These cases have taken what can be best characterized as a long and tortuous journey yet to be concluded.

McBryde Sugar Co. v. Robinson (1973) involved a dispute between landowners over water rights in the Hanapepe Valley on the island of Kauai. It resulted in one of the Hawaii Supreme Court's most significant and controversial decisions. Overturning precedent, the court (in a four-to-one decision) unexpectedly held that the water at issue was not privately owned because the state owned all flowing surface waters. It based this conclusion on Hawaii's history as a monarchy where "the King was the sole owner of all the land in the Hawaiian Kingdom and also sole owner of the water, which is considered part of the land, and . . . he could do whatever he wanted." Even when Kamehameha III issued the Great *Mahele*, proclaiming "that he was sharing the lands in the Hawaiian Kingdom with his people," and when the *Mahele* was subsequently implemented, the "right to water was not intended to be, could not be, and was not transferred to [landowners], and the ownership of water in natural watercourses, streams and rivers remained in the people of Hawaii for their common good." The court did find, nevertheless, that landowners had some rights to use the water, although they could not transport water into other watersheds. Later in 1973 the court, after a rehearing, reaffirmed its decision (by a vote of three to two). The U.S. Supreme Court summarily denied certiorari and dismissed an appeal (*McBryde Sugar Co. v. Robinson*, 1974).

In the meantime, however, the issue was brought to the U.S. district court where, in *Robinson v. Ariyoshi* (1977), the state was enjoined from enforcing *McBryde* because the assertion of state ownership of water was invalid and the landowners were deprived of property without compensation and due process.[86] In sharply worded language, the federal judge criticized the state court:

> From the manner in which the court wrote the majority opinion in *McBryde* . . ., it was obvious that the court determined, without notice to any party of its intent, that

[86] See Note, "Hawaii Surface Water Law: An Analysis of Robinson v. Ariyoshi," *University of Hawaii Law Review* 8 (1986): 603; Williamson B. C. Chang, "Unraveling Robinson v. Ariyoshi: Can Courts 'Take' Property?" *University of Hawaii Law Review* 2 (1979): 57. See also Douglas W. MacDougal, "Testing the Current: The Water Code and the Regulation of Hawaii's Water Resources," *University of Hawaii Law Review* 10 (1988): 205; Comment, "Groundwater Rights in Hawaii: Status and Suggested Change," *University of Hawaii Law Review* 8 (1986): 513.

> it was going to completely restructure what was universally thought to be the well settled law of waters in Hawaii. The court sua sponte decided that all the flowing waters of the streams in the State should belong entirely to the State, subject only to appurtenant use under the English common law doctrine of riparian rights. It was strictly a "public-policy" decision with no prior underlying "legal" justification therefor.

"The entire rationale of the majority" was, he added, "one of the grossest examples of unfettered judicial construction used to achieve the result desired."

While *Robinson* was on appeal to the Ninth Circuit, a unanimous Hawaii Supreme Court handed down a ruling in *Reppun v. Board of Water Supply* (1982), which indicated that it had no intention of changing its mind and declined the invitation to overrule *McBryde*.

The Hawaii Supreme Court also answered six certified questions for the federal court and reiterated its position that the state owned the water (*Robinson v. Ariyoshi*, 1982). The Ninth Circuit concluded to the contrary. While the state, through its legislature or courts, has the power to change its laws, a new law could not divest rights that were vested before the court announced that new law (*Robinson v. Ariyoshi*, 1985). With respect to the specifics of the case, the Ninth Circuit held that since landowners had acquired a "vested right to divert water from their lands within the Hanapepe watershed to their own or related lands outside the watershed," they could only be divested of that right if there was just compensation.

Next, the U.S. Supreme Court granted certiorari, vacated the lower court's judgment, and remanded the case without a written opinion (*Ariyoshi v. Robinson*, 1986). On remand, the U.S. district court reaffirmed the earlier federal decisions of 1977 and 1985, finding that (1) the equal protection and due process claims made by the property owners were ripe for decision and (2) the state's Water Code, enacted in 1987, did not settle the matter (*Robinson v. Ariyoshi*, 1987).

The conflicting approaches taken by the state and the federal courts remain unresolved. The state has not tried to enforce its ownership of water established by *McBryde*, and any attempt to do so would rekindle the controversy and bring the issue before the courts once again.

SECTION 8

> **Nuclear Energy**. No nuclear fission power plant shall be constructed or radioactive material disposed of in the State without the prior approval by a two-thirds vote in each house of the legislature.

Introduced from the floor of the 1978 convention, this section became part of the constitution only after much delegate debate. The question of approving construction of a nuclear fission power plant or disposal of radioactive material has never been voted on by the legislature.

SECTION 9

Environmental Rights. Each person has the right to a clean and healthful environment, as defined by laws relating to environmental quality, including control of pollution and conservation, protection and enhancement of natural resources. Any person may enforce this right against any party, public or private, through appropriate legal proceedings, subject to reasonable limitations and regulation as provided by law.

As expressed by the delegates in 1978, the addition of this section was based on the premise that every citizen enjoys a right to a clean and healthful environment and that this right deserves constitutional protection. But what constitutes a "clean and healthful environment" is not specifically spelled out, and its definition is left to the legislature through laws relating to environmental quality. That such laws are to include "control of pollution and conservation" and "protection and enhancement of natural resources" suggests that these at least are to be the core elements of any definition adopted.[87]

By expressly granting this right to each person, the framers intended to remove barriers that would otherwise deny individuals any standing to sue. The delegates did intend, however, that the legislature be allowed to establish reasonable regulations covering procedure, jurisdiction, and a statute of limitations regarding this private enforcement right.

In the 1982 decision, *Stop H–3 Association v. Lewis*, the U.S. district court commented in a footnote that Section 9 is not an entitlement to a private right of action. The following year, the Ninth Circuit found that Section 9 was not an attempt to enlarge the subject matter jurisdiction of the federal courts (which the states had no power to do), but rather an attempt to remove barriers to standing to sue (*Fiedler v. Clark*, 1983).

SECTION 10

Farm and Home Ownership. The public lands shall be used for the development of farm and home ownership on as widespread a basis as possible, in accordance with procedures and limitations prescribed by law.

---

[87] See Comment, "Environmental Protection Based on State Constitutional Law: A Call for Reinterpretation," *University of Hawaii Law Review* 12 (1990): 123. For recent discussions of environmental concerns in Hawaii, see Callies, Kalama, and Kellelt, "The Lum Court, Land Use and the Environment," 119; and Richard J. Tobin and Dean Higuchi, "Environmental Quality in America's Tropical Paradise," in Smith and Pratt, eds., *Politics*, 113.

The 1978 convention proposed removing this section and replacing it with the new provision (now Section 3) on agricultural lands because the phrase "farm and home ownership" had been interpreted as meaning either farm or home ownership. Delegates believed this interpretation could lead to diverting farm lands to housing and that the section was thus inconsistent with a need to preserve valuable and important agricultural lands. Since the deletion proposal was ruled not validly ratified by the voters (*Kahalekai v. Doi*, 1979), it remains in the document as written in 1950. (Following the court's decision it was redesignated as Section 10.)

The language of this section refers expressly to farm and home ownership; it does not apply to state-leased public pasture lands according to the decision in *Big Island Small Ranchers Association v. State* (1978).

SECTION [11]

Exclusive Economic Zone. The State of Hawaii asserts and reserves its rights and interest in its exclusive economic zone for the purpose of exploring, exploiting, conserving and managing natural resources, both living and nonliving, of the seabed and subsoil, and superadjacent waters.

This section carries brackets around the number because the legislatively proposed amendment that voters approved in November 1988 did not indicate any section number. It asserts the state's interest in offshore waters in order to indicate that the state, and not the federal government alone, has power to determine how any resources found there can be used. The Exclusive Economic Zone (EEZ) extends 200 miles around the major and outlying islands, a stretch of some 1,500 miles, and is defined by statute as having "the meaning set forth in Presidential Proclamation 5030 issued March 10, 1983, whereby the United States proclaimed jurisdiction from the seaward boundary of the State out to two hundred nautical miles from the baseline from which the breadth of the territorial sea is measured" (Haw. Rev. Stat. § 228–3). Among the resources of interest are cobalt-rich manganese nodules on the ocean floor, corals, and fishing. Ambiguous at best, the possible impact of this section for the future is not clear.[88]

---

[88] See Comment, "State-Federal Jurisdiction Conflict over the Internal Waters and Submerged Lands of the Northwestern Hawaiian Islands," *University of Hawaii Law Review* 4 (1982): 139; Kent M. Keith, "Laws Affecting the Development of Ocean Resources in Hawaii," *University of Hawaii Law Review* 4 (1982): 227.

Article XII

Hawaiian Affairs

Article XII traces its genesis to a series of events dating from at least the first western contact with Hawaii. Those events are complex, are associated with controversy, and record the tragic near-demise of an ethnic group.

Basic to an understanding of this article is the designation of certain lands in Hawaii as "ceded lands," "available lands," and "public lands." When Hawaii was annexed in 1898 and become a territory in 1900, it ceded and transferred to the United States ownership of all government and crown lands. Congress specified, in the Joint Resolution of Annexation of July 7, 1898, that the territory was to administer these ceded lands and use the proceeds "solely for the benefit of the inhabitants of the Hawaiian islands for educational and other public purposes."

Uncertainty accompanies the estimates of the indigenous population at the time Cook arrived in 1778. The conventional estimations fall between 200,000 and 400,000, though a recent analysis placing the range at 800,000 to 1 million has prompted considerable controversy.[89] No uncertainty, however, exists with

[89] See Andrew W. Lind, *Hawaii's People*, 4th ed. (Honolulu: University Press of Hawaii, 1980); Eleanor C. Nordyke, *The Peopling of Hawaii*, 2d ed. (Honolulu: University of Hawaii Press, 1989). The recent controversy has been fueled by David E. Stannard, *Before the Horror, The Population of Hawaii on the Eve of Western Contact* (Honolulu: Social Science Research Institute, University of Hawaii, 1989); in Part I, Stannard presents his arguments for the much larger estimate, while Part II contains critical commentaries by Nordyke and Robert C. Schmitt as well as a reply by Stannard.

respect to the fact that the indigenous population rapidly declined: By 1896, it had decreased to around 39,500, including those of mixed ancestry, and not until 1920 did census figures indicate growth rather than decline in their numbers.

Hoping to reverse the terrible impact that contact with the West had on native Hawaiians, Congress passed the Hawaiian Homes Commission Act (HHCA) in 1920. It classified approximately 200,000 acres of the ceded lands as available lands and set them aside to provide rehabilitation for "native Hawaiians" through homesteading. However, the HHCA is seen by most commentators as a compromise more beneficial to business interests than to the people it was meant to help.[90] For example, the available lands were for the most part of extremely poor quality, while superior, productive lands were left for continued leasing by sugar planters.

It is important to point out that the HHCA defined native Hawaiians as "any descendant of not less than one-half part of the blood of the races inhabiting the Hawaiian Islands previous to 1778." This definition has not been altered, and the term *native Hawaiian* has a legal meaning resulting in important political and legal consequences in Hawaii.

The 1950 convention adopted two sections relating to Hawaiian homelands because it wanted to ensure continuation of the program and also because Congress was likely to require inclusion of the HHCA as part of any proposed statehood constitution. In fact, the Hawaii Admission Act of 1959 did contain such a requirement. Congress also insisted that a third section, further clarifying the compact, be added as well, and it became a part of the Statehood Constitution upon approval by voters at the statehood election of June 1959. Thus, the state assumed the trust obligations for the available lands.

At statehood, the federal government gave up title to most of the ceded lands. Referred to as the public lands, they consist of the ceded lands excluding the available lands. The Hawaii Admission Act prescribed that the public lands be held by the state as a public trust, with the income and proceeds to be used for five public purposes (see the commentary following Section 4 below). In stipulating that the state assume the trustee role over those lands, the national government took a step "without precedent in United States history and one wholly contrary to established congressional public land policy."[91]

The 1968 convention did not devote much attention to the subject of Hawaiian homelands, and the three constitutional provisions covering the state's trust obligations for the available lands were left untouched. In contrast, the 1978 convention spent more time as a committee of the whole on proposals

---

[90] See, for example, Lawrence H. Fuchs, *Hawaii Pono: A Social History* (New York: Harcourt, Brace & World, Inc., 1971), 173–74; Gavan Daws, *Shoal of Time, A History of the Hawaiian Islands* (Honolulu: University of Hawaii Press, 1968), 298.

[91] Comment, "Hawaii's Ceded Lands," *University of Hawaii Law Review* 3 (1981): 102.

concerning Hawaiian affairs than on any other subject area. All part of the Hawaiian affairs package, as it was called at the time, the constitutional provisions resulting from those debates are scattered throughout the document. But the bulk of this part of the convention's work transformed what is now Article XII. Previously designated Article XI and titled Hawaiian Home Lands, its new title, Hawaiian Affairs, reflects the fact that four new sections broadened it far beyond the subject of Hawaiian homelands. The changes made were significant and flowed from a heightened ethnic identity and concern for their rights that developed among persons of Hawaiian ancestry in the 1970s, often referred to as the Hawaiian renaissance.

SECTION 1

Hawaiian Homes Commission Act. Anything in this constitution to the contrary notwithstanding, the Hawaiian Homes Commission Act, 1920, enacted by the Congress, as the same has been or may be amended prior to the admission of the State, is hereby adopted as a law of the State, subject to amendment or repeal by the legislature; provided that if and to the extent that the United States shall so require, such law shall be subject to amendment or repeal only with the consent of the United States and in no other manner; provided further that if the United States shall have been provided or shall provide that particular provisions or types of provisions of such Act may be amended in the manner required for ordinary state legislation, such provisions or types of provisions may be so amended. The proceeds and income from Hawaiian home lands shall be used only in accordance with the terms and spirit of such Act. The legislature shall make sufficient sums available for the following purposes: (1) development of home, agriculture, farm and ranch lots; (2) home, agriculture, aquaculture, farm and ranch loans; (3) rehabilitation projects to include, but not limited to, educational, economic, political, social and cultural processes by which the general welfare and conditions of native Hawaiians are thereby improved; (4) the administration and operating budget of the department of Hawaiian home lands; in furtherance of (1), (2), (3) and (4) herein, by appropriating the same in the manner provided by law.

Thirty percent of the state receipts derived from the leasing of cultivated sugarcane lands under any provision of law or from water licenses shall be transferred to the native Hawaiian rehabilitation fund, section 213 of the Hawaiian Homes Commission Act, 1920, for the purposes enumerated in that section. Thirty percent of the state receipts derived from the leasing of lands cultivated as sugarcane lands on the effective date of this section shall continue to be so transferred to the native Hawaiian rehabilitation fund whenever such lands are sold, developed, leased, utilized, transferred, set aside or otherwise disposed of for purposes other than the cultivation of sugarcane. There shall be no ceiling established for the aggregate amount transferred into the native Hawaiian rehabilitation fund.

The two first sentences of this section remain virtually the same as in the Statehood Constitution: (1) the Hawaiian Homes Commission Act is adopted as a law of the state; (2) the legislature may amend or repeal it, limited by conditions established by the U.S. government; and (3) the proceeds and income from Hawaiian homelands are to be used according to the terms of the HHCA.

Prior to 1978, the section ended with a clause giving the legislature discretion to appropriate, from time to time, additional sums for carrying out the purposes of the HHCA. The 1978 convention, however, substituted for that clause the requirement that the legislature "shall make sufficient sums available" for four specific purposes listed at the end of the first paragraph. The standing committee report included considerable detail to show that the Hawaiian homes program had failed to accomplish its intent, pointing out that during the fifty-seven years since the HHCA's passage, less than 12.5 percent of the total available lands had in fact been turned over to native Hawaiians. The specification of the four purposes was intended to make absolutely clear what the program is (and was) meant to bring about.

In addition, a final paragraph was added, writing into the constitution the requirement that 30 percent of state receipts derived from the lease (or sale, etc.) of cultivated sugar cane lands and from the sale of water licenses are to be transferred to a Native Hawaiian Rehabilitation Fund. This was a fund created by the 1978 convention and incorporated at the same time into the HHCA itself. All the amendments to the HHCA proposed by the convention were also voted on, and approved, by voters at the November 1978 ratification election. Although funding by 30 percent of the receipts from leasing cane lands and selling water licenses already existed in the HHCA, the creation of this fund redefined an administrative component of the program.

Over the years, some have questioned whether the HHCA itself, because it benefits only "native Hawaiians," is unconstitutionally discriminatory under the Fourteenth Amendment of the U.S. Constitution and/or under the due process and equal protection section in Hawaii's bill of rights. At the time of its consideration by Congress, the solicitor of the U.S. Department of the Interior, the territorial attorney general, and the U.S. House Committee on Territories concluded that it did not violate the equal protection clause of the Fourteenth Amendment. Relying on those opinions, the 1950 convention came to the same conclusion; it also decided that there was no violation of the state bill of rights that it was proposing. However, there were delegates who objected, and one, Marguerite K. Ashford, refused to sign the final document in part because of her belief that it was unconstitutional to incorporate a classification based on accident of birth (see also Section 2).

Later conventions did not consider the HHCA provision a major issue; it has never been subjected to judicial review. Though the issue was recently before the U.S. District Court for the District of Hawaii, the court did not address it directly; the court found that the native Hawaiian plaintiffs were beneficiaries of the

HHCA and thus lacked standing to challenge it in terms of the Fourteenth Amendment (*Naliielua v. Hawaii*, 1991).

Nevertheless, the question is now central to a controversy between the state government and the U.S. Justice Department because of the latter's recently adopted position that use of federal housing funds for Hawaiian homelands programs constitutes illegal discrimination against non-Hawaiians. State officials have said publicly that the state is prepared to take legal action if the disagreement cannot be resolved through the political process.[92]

SECTION 2

> **Acceptance of Compact**. The State and its people do hereby accept, as a compact with the United States, or as conditions or trust provisions imposed by the United States, relating to the management and disposition of the Hawaiian home lands, the requirement that section 1 hereof be included in this constitution, in whole or in part, it being intended that the Act or acts of the Congress pertaining thereto shall be definitive of the extent and nature of such compact, conditions or trust provisions, as the case may be. The State and its people do further agree and declare that the spirit of the Hawaiian Homes Commission Act looking to the continuance of the Hawaiian homes projects for the further rehabilitation of the Hawaiian race shall be faithfully carried out.

The language of this section remains almost identical with that originally written in 1950. Having entered into a compact on the Hawaiian homes program with the United States, the state has an obligation to ensure, as the last sentence states, that the rehabilitation of the Hawaiian race is faithfully undertaken.

In *Ahuna v. Department of Hawaiian Home Lands* (1982), the Hawaii Supreme Court reviewed the history of the HHCA, concluding that "the federal government set aside certain public lands to be considered Hawaiian home lands to be utilized in the rehabilitation of native Hawaiians, thereby undertaking a trust obligation benefiting the aboriginal people," and "the State of Hawaii assumed this fiduciary obligation upon being admitted into the Union as a state." It found the Hawaiian Homes Commission to be the specific state administrative entity obligated to carry out the fiduciary duty under the HHCA on behalf of eligible native Hawaiians. However, in making a decision regarding one particular land parcel, that commission breached its "fiduciary duty to eligible native Hawaiian beneficiaries collectively and individually" when it "gave undue weight to the interest of the State, the County of Hawaii and the citizens or taxpayers of

---

[92] Kevin Dayton, " 'Discrimination' Snag in Home Lands Funds," *Honolulu Advertiser*, 20 November 1991, A-3.

Hawaii in general." The commissioners thus "violated the trust obligations imposed by the Hawaii Constitution."

A major question that arose at the 1950 convention centered on whether the compact might be a violation of the U.S. constitutional provision granting Congress the power to admit new states, which is generally thought to require that all new states be admitted on equal terms with the old states. While a few 1950 delegates objected to the compact and one delegate declined to sign the final document, in part because of her belief that it infringed on Hawaii's equal status and sovereign powers (see also Section 1 above), the question is now essentially moot. It did not become an issue at later conventions, nor has it ever been specifically litigated.

In 1985, the U. S. Court of Appeals for the Ninth Circuit found that "Congress' role in the formation of a compact between the United States and a State is at least as great as Congress' role in approving a compact between two States," and that "federal law is 'an essential element' of a suit that charges a violation of a compact incorporating 'the spirit of the Hawaiian Homes Commission Act looking to the continuance of the Hawaiian homes projects'" (*Price v. Hawaii*, 1985).

SECTION 3

Compact Adoption; Procedures After Adoption. As a compact with the United States relating to the management and disposition of the Hawaiian home lands, the Hawaiian Homes Commission Act, 1920, as amended, shall be adopted as a provision of the constitution of this State, as provided in section 7, subsection (b), of the Admission Act, subject to amendment or repeal only with the consent of the United States, and in no other manner; provided that (1) sections 202, 213, 219, 220, 222, 224 and 225 and other provisions relating to administration, and paragraph (2) of section 204, sections 206 and 212 and other provisions relating to the powers and duties of officers other than those charged with the administration of such Act, may be amended in the constitution, or in the manner required for state legislation, but the Hawaiian home-loan fund, the Hawaiian home-operating fund and the Hawaiian home-development fund shall not be reduced or impaired by any such amendment, whether made in the constitution or in the manner required for state legislation, and the encumbrances authorized to be placed on Hawaiian home lands by officers other than those charged with the administration of such Act, shall not be increased, except with the consent of the United States; (2) that any amendment to increase the benefits to lessees of Hawaiian home lands may be made in the constitution, or in the manner required for state legislation, but the qualifications of lessees shall not be changed except with the consent of the United States; and (3) that all proceeds and income from the "available lands," as defined by such Act, shall be used only in carrying out the provisions of such Act.

Required by Congress as a condition for statehood, this section was added verbatim from the Hawaii Admission Act upon voter approval at the 1959 statehood election. It has been characterized as highly unusual and even of questionable validity because Congress had never before required a "parallel restriction upon the self-government of an American state" as a condition for statehood.[93] No substantive modifications have been made since then.

Intended to clarify the compact, this section specifies what provisions in the HHCA may be changed with or without congressional approval. In general, the state may increase benefits for lessees and alter administrative provisions for the Hawaiian homes program without congressional consent, but must obtain such consent if it desires to decrease lessee benefits or alter lessee qualifications.

Perhaps most troublesome has been the requirement that any change to the qualifications of lessees occur only with the consent of the U.S. government. The HHCA defines a native Hawaiian as "any descendant of not less than one-half part of the blood of the races inhabiting the Hawaiian Islands previous to 1778." Recognizing that the number of individuals satisfying this blood quantum qualification is rapidly and dramatically declining, some in the state would like to change the definition. Although they discussed the need to do so, delegates to the 1978 convention decided not to introduce such a change to the HHCA. No formal action on this matter has taken place.

There is uncertainty about whether and to what extent the substance of this constitutional section can be amended. Some believe that because it also exists in the Hawaii Admission Act as a condition of statehood, any substantive change would require congressional amendment of that act as well. The question remains unanswered.

During the early years of statehood, confusion arose about a related issue: Is the entire HHCA, through this section, actually a part of the constitution? In 1961, the attorney general opined that it was not because to include it would "create a difficult, cumbersome and time consuming process for effectuating amendments" and because Congress only intended to ensure the continuation of the HHCA under state law (Op. Att'y Gen. 61-21, 1961).

SECTION 4

Public Trust. The lands granted to the State of Hawaii by Section 5(b) of the Admission Act and pursuant to Article XVI, Section 7, of the State Constitution, excluding therefrom lands defined as "available lands" by Section 203 of the Hawaiian Homes Commission Act, 1920, as amended, shall be held by the State as a public trust for native Hawaiians and the general public.

[93] Paul C. Bartholomew and Robert M. Kamins, "The Hawaiian Constitution: A Structure for Good Government," *American Bar Association Journal* 45 (1959): 1222.

Added in 1978, this section states that the ceded lands, excluding the available lands covered by Sections 1, 2, and 3, are held as a public trust for native Hawaiians and the general public. Approximately 1.5 million acres, referred to as the public lands, fall under this section's coverage.

This provision is based on Section 5(b) of the Hawaii Admission Act which, with certain exceptions, granted Hawaii title to the ceded lands and Section 5(f) which stipulated that the public lands are to be held by the state as a public trust, with the proceeds and income to be used for five purposes: (1) the support of the public schools and other public educational institutions, (2) the betterment of the conditions of native Hawaiians, (3) the development of farm and home ownership on as widespread a basis as possible, (4) the making of public improvements, and (5) the provision of lands for public use.

At the heart of the 1978 convention's decision to add Section 4 was the recognition that in addition to being beneficiaries of the Hawaiian homelands trust, covered in sections 1, 2, and 3 (available lands), native Hawaiians are also designated as beneficiaries, along with the general public, of the public lands trust. Prior to 1978, the constitutional provisions relating to public lands were very general: One section called for use of the public lands for widespread farm and home development (see Article XI, Section 10), and another required the state to comply with any trust provisions concerning lands through appropriate legislation (see Article XVI, Section 7). Because there were no statutory provisions providing constraining detail, the state used the funds derived from the public lands for only one of the five purposes specified in Section 5(f) of the Hawaii Admission Act—public education. As a result, Hawaiians and researchers of Section 5(f) argued that the state was remiss in carrying out its responsibilities as trustee of the public lands trust.[94]

SECTION 5

Office of Hawaiian Affairs; Establishment of Board of Trustees. There is hereby established an Office of Hawaiian Affairs. The Office of Hawaiian Affairs shall hold title to all the real and personal property now or hereafter set aside or conveyed to it which shall be held in trust for native Hawaiians and Hawaiians. There shall be a board of trustees for the Office of Hawaiian Affairs elected by qualified voters who are Hawaiians, as provided by law. The board members shall be Hawaiians. There shall be not less than nine members of the board of trustees; provided that each of the following Islands have one representative: Oahu, Kauai, Maui, Molokai and Hawaii. The board shall select a chairperson from its members.

See the commentary following Section 6.

---

[94] Jocelyn Fujii, "Hawaiian Land Concerns," in *Issues 1978* (Honolulu: O Ka Po'e Ke Kumu O Ke Kanawai, A Project of the League of Women Voters of Hawaii Education Fund, Inc., 1978), 99.

SECTION 6

Powers of Board of Trustees. The board of trustees of the Office of Hawaiian Affairs shall exercise power as provided by law: to manage and administer the proceeds from the sale or other disposition of the lands, natural resources, minerals and income derived from whatever sources for native Hawaiians and Hawaiians, including all income and proceeds from that pro rata portion of the trust referred to in section 4 of this article for native Hawaiians; to formulate policy relating to affairs of native Hawaiians and Hawaiians; and to exercise control over real and personal property set aside by state, federal or private sources and transferred to the board for native Hawaiians and Hawaiians. The board shall have the power to exercise control over the Office of Hawaiian Affairs through its executive officer, the administrator of the Office of Hawaiian Affairs, who shall be appointed by the board.

As both Sections 5 and 6 concern the Office of Hawaiian Affairs (OHA), they are discussed together. In adding them to the constitution, the 1978 convention intended to provide for "accountability, self-determination, methods for self-sufficiency through assets and a land base, and the unification of all native Hawaiian people."[95]

Section 5 creates the Office of Hawaiian Affairs, which, according to convention records, is to have the anomalous status of being a state agency, but independent from the executive and other branches of the state government. OHA holds title to all the real and personal property set aside or conveyed to it in trust for "native Hawaiians" and "Hawaiians" (see the definitions below). OHA is administered by a board of at least nine trustees, with five elected from as many specific islands. Though the language of this section permits a board larger than nine members, the legislature has chosen to leave it at nine (Haw. Rev. Stat. § 13D–5). Members of the board must be ethnic Hawaiians, and voting for them is limited to qualified voters who are of Hawaiian ancestry, a provision which, according to the attorney general, does not violate the equal protection and right to vote provisions found in Article I, Section 5 and Article II, Section 1 of the Hawaii Constitution or the Fourteenth and Fifteenth Amendments to the U.S. Constitution (Op. Att'y Gen. 80–8, 1980).

Section 6 broadly outlines the powers of the OHA board of trustees and specifies that OHA will receive a pro rata portion of the public lands trust referred to in Section 4. It is left to the legislature to provide the detail governing the board's powers and to establish what the pro rata share will be. By statute, the latter is now set at 20 percent.

In *Trustees of OHA v. Yamasaki*, (1987), the Hawaii Supreme Court determined that a dispute regarding OHA's claim of entitlement to receive 20 percent from certain lands held in trust was a nonjusticiable political question. Although the

---

[95] *1978 Proceedings I*, Standing Committee Report no. 59, 646.

issue of OHA's constitutionality was raised in a companion case, the court did not address the issue.[96] In 1992, the major conflicts giving rise to the case were resolved when the board of trustees ratified a settlement with the state administration for $112 million as back payments owed OHA for the revenues on those lands.

In order to ensure that OHA would benefit all persons of Hawaiian ancestry and not just those meeting the restrictive 50 percent blood quantum definition in the HHCA, Sections 5 and 6 specifically use the terms *native Hawaiians* and *Hawaiians*. The 1978 convention also proposed another new section, titled "Definition: Hawaiian; Native Hawaiian" to define these terms. Its text read:

> The term "Hawaiian" means any descendant of the races inhabiting the Hawaiian Islands, previous to 1778. The term "native Hawaiian" means any descendant of not less than one-half part of the blood of races inhabiting the Hawaiian Islands previous to 1778 as defined by the Hawaiian Homes Commission Act, 1920, as amended or may be amended.

This proposal did not become part of the 1978 Constitution because in the 1979 *Kahalekai v. Doi* decision it was ruled not validly ratified. The definitions were, however, codified as statutory law in 1979 (Haw. Rev. Stat. § 10–2). When inclusion of the definition of "Hawaiian" was later challenged, the U.S. district court found that defining "Hawaiian" without regard to blood quantum "has a rational basis and reasonably furthers the legislature's legitimate purpose to address the needs of Hawaii's aboriginal descendants"; it does not violate the equal protection clause of the Fourteenth Amendment to the U.S. Constitution (*Hoohuli v. Ariyoshi*, 1986).

Although the purpose of OHA was to benefit all ethnic Hawaiians, the revenues it receives from the trust lands can be used only on behalf of "native Hawaiians" (pursuant to Section 5(f) of the Hawaii Admission Act). Since the constitutional provisions do not specify a separate source of funds to be used for "Hawaiians," such funding is left to legislative discretion. This, one commentator points out, raises questions about whether OHA can be as independent from the other branches of government as the 1978 convention envisioned; she also contends that, while to date the legislature is the main source of such funding, "OHA has been burdened by a legislative process that mandates the submission

---

[96] See Note, "The Trustees of the Office of Hawaiian Affairs v. Yamasaki: The Application of the Political Question Doctrine to Hawaii's Public Land Trust Dispute," *University of Hawaii Law Review* 10 (1988): 345. For opposing views on OHA's legal status, see Jon Van Dyke, "The Constitutionality of the Office of Hawaiian Affairs," *University of Hawaii Law Review* 7 (1985): 63; James H. Dannenberg, "The Office of Hawaiian Affairs and the Issue of Sovereign Immunity," *University of Hawaii Law Review* 7 (1985): 95.

of expenditures of general and public funds to the legislature, thereby limiting OHA's financial independence."[97]

Other unsettled issues remain. There is disagreement among Hawaiian groups about priorities. The very difficult question about how to dispose of lands in ways that do not terminate the age-old linkage between Hawaiians and their land continues to be a troublesome one.[98] In addition, a very complex, and as yet unresolved, area has to do with their right to sue over various aspects of native Hawaiian lands (see *Price v. Akaka*, 1990; *Price v. Hawaii*, 1990; *Hoohuli v. Ariyoshi*, 1986; *Hoohuli v. Ariyoshi*, 1984).

SECTION 7

> **Traditional and Customary Rights.** The State reaffirms and shall protect all rights, customarily and traditionally exercised for subsistence, cultural and religious purposes and possessed by ahupua'a tenants who are descendants of native Hawaiians who inhabited the Hawaiian Islands prior to 1778, subject to the right of the State to regulate such rights.

Added in 1978, this section was intended to "reaffirm, for descendants of native Hawaiians, rights customarily and traditionally exercised for subsistence, cultural and religious purposes" and to give the state power to regulate them.[99] The rights referred to include access to certain land areas as well as fishing, hunting, gathering, trail use, and water rights. But the standing committee explicitly decided against listing specific categories in order to avoid constraining either the legislature or the courts.

Although some delegates at the convention suggested the section might be constitutionally vulnerable on equal protection grounds, this specific issue has never come before the courts. In *Kalipi v. Hawaiian Trust Co.* (1982), the state supreme court did find, however, that Article XII, Section 7 established a state obligation to preserve and enforce traditional rights and that the court was bound to follow the policy expressed in it.

---

[97] MacKenzie, ed., *Native Hawaiian Rights*, 89. For criticism of OHA, see Trask, "Kūpa'a 'Aina," in Smith and Pratt, eds. *Politics*, 250–52.

[98] For discussion about ethnic Hawaiians and their land, see Linda S. Parker, *Native American Estate: The Struggle over Indian and Hawaiian Lands* (Honolulu: University of Hawaii Press, 1989); Ramon Lopez-Reyes, "The Demise of the Hawaiian Kingdom: A Psycho-cultural Analysis and Moral Legacy (Something Lost, Something Owed)," *Hawaii Bar Journal* 18 (1983): 3; Patrick W. Hanifin, "Hawaiian Reparations: Nothing Lost, Nothing Owed," *Hawaii Bar Journal* 17 (1982): 107; Karen N. Blondin, "A Case for Reparations for Native Hawaiians," *Hawaii Bar Journal* 16 (1981): 13; Neil M. Levy, "Native Hawaiian Land Rights," *California Law Review* 63 (1975): 848.

[99] *1978 Proceedings I*, Standing Committee Report no. 57, 639.

In adding Section 7, the 1978 delegates recognized that a conflict might arise between traditional rights and those observed by modern society, but they believed that it was possible to protect both. This was at issue in *Kalipi,* where the court held that gathering rights in an *ahupuaa* (a land division usually wedge-shaped, and extending from the mountains at its narrowest to the sea at its widest) existed for those residing there, although simply owning land within the *ahupuaa* was not sufficient. The "retention of a Hawaiian tradition should in each case be determined by balancing the respective interests and harm once it is established that the application of the custom has continued in a particular area." According to the court, its *Kalipi* decision conformed "traditional rights born of a culture which knew little of the rigid exclusivity associated with the private ownership of land, with a modern system of land tenure in which the right of an owner to exclude is perceived to be an integral part of fee simple title."

A decade later, in *Pele Defense Fund v. Paty* (1992), the court noted that "*Kalipi* defined the rudiments of native Hawaiian rights protected by [this section], commonly known as *Kalipi* rights." The court's *Pele Defense Fund* decision is highly significant because it extended these rights to land areas abutting an ahupuaa. As it explained:

> If . . . the customary and traditional rights associated with tenancy in an ahupua'a extended beyond beyond the boundaries of the ahupua'a, then [A]rticle XII, [Section] 7 protects those rights as well. The drafters of the constitutional amendment emphasized that *all* such rights were reaffirmed and that they did not intend for the provision to be narrowly construed. We therefore hold that native Hawaiian rights protected by [this section] may extend beyond the ahupua'a in which a native Hawaiian resides where such rights have been customarily and traditionally exercised in this manner, (emphasis in original).

Article XIII

Organization; Collective Bargaining

SECTION 1

Private Employees. Persons in private employment shall have the right to organize for the purpose of collective bargaining.

See the commentary following Section 2.

SECTION 2

Public Employees. Persons in public employment shall have the right to organize for the purpose of collective bargaining as provided by law.

After spending considerable time deliberating whether and where to include provisions on employee rights, and their possible contents, the 1950 convention adopted a separate article of two sections in lieu of adding provisions to Article I, Bill of Rights. In 1978, this article was renumbered from Article XII to Article XIII.

The first section grants private employees the right to organize for the purpose of collective bargaining. With minimal discussion, both the 1968 and the 1978 conventions retained this section as it was originally written.

The language adopted by the 1950 convention for Section 2 only gave public employees the "right to organize and to present and make known their grievances and proposals to the State, or any political subdivision or any department or agency." After lively debate, the 1968 convention adopted the significantly different language found today; while the section was the focus of spirited discussion again in 1978, the convention of that year made no substantive changes.

Almost all delegates at the three conventions agreed that the rights of public and private employees should be treated differently in the constitution. This is clear with respect to the language adopted in 1950. But while the current language of the two sections is very similar, the phrase "as provided by law," which is now found at the end of Section 2, results in a critical difference. Private employees have a constitutional right to bargain collectively, while the scope of that right for public employees is to be determined legislatively. Proposals made at the 1968 and the 1978 conventions to eliminate this difference were unsuccessful.

The crux of the distinction revolves around the right to strike. Concern about the new language proposed for Section 2 led the 1968 convention president to seek an opinion from the attorney general on whether it would force the legislature to recognize that public employees had a right to strike. It would not, the opinion stated, because "the scope and extent of the right of collective bargaining for public employees, including the right to strike, and the manner in which it is to be exercised, shall be as determined by the Legislature" (Op. Att'y Gen. 68-27,1968).

At the time of statehood, the Hawaii Constitution was one of a very few state constitutions to include provisions addressing the right to organize and to bargain collectively. Two years after the new language was adopted for Section 2, the legislature passed the 1970 collective bargaining statute for public employees (see Haw. Rev. Stat. ch. 89). It allows public employees the right to strike under certain conditions, making Hawaii one of the first states to legalize strikes by public workers.

Public employee unions have long played an exceptionally strong role in state politics. The 1968 constitutional amendment mirrored their strength, and the fact that they continued to be a significant factor is evidenced by the ease with which the 1978 convention defeated proposals to curtail the thrust of Section 2, particularly in light of the fact that in the early 1970s some public employees did strike. In the process of those strikes, the Hawaii Supreme Court had occasion to rule on both Section 2 and the 1970 law. Because the section enables the legislature to prescribe the right to strike, and to define its scope, the court upheld certain limitations and procedures found in the statute (*Board of Education v. Hawaii Public Employment Relations Board*, 1974; *Hawaii Public Employment Relations Board v. Hawaii State Teachers Association*, 1974; *Hawaii Public Employment Relations Board v. Hawaii State Teachers Association*, 1973).[100]

---

[100] See Benjamin C. Sigal, "Public Employee Arbitration in Hawaii, A Study in Erosion," *University of Hawaii Law Review* 2 (1981): 477. See also Deborah S. Jackson and Elizabeth Jubin Fujiwara, "Employee Rights under Judicial Scrutiny: Prevalent Policy Discourse and the Hawaii Supreme Court," *University of Hawaii Law Review* 14 (1992): 189; Ronald C. Brown, "Commentary on Selected Employment and Labor Law Decisions under the Lum Court," *University of Hawaii Law Review* 14 (1992): 423.

Article XIV

Code of Ethics

The people of Hawaii believe that public officers and employees must exhibit the highest standards of ethical conduct and that these standards come from the personal integrity of each individual in government. To keep faith with this belief, the legislature, each political subdivision and the constitutional convention shall adopt a code of ethics which shall apply to appointed and elected officers and employees of the State or the political subdivision, respectively, including members of the boards, commissions and other bodies.

Each code of ethics shall be administered by a separate ethics commission, except the code of ethics adopted by the constitutional convention which shall be administered by the state ethics commission. The members of ethics commissions shall be prohibited from taking an active part in political management or in political campaigns. Ethics commissioners shall be selected in a manner which assures their independence and impartiality.

Each code of ethics shall include, but not be limited to, provisions on gifts, confidential information, use of position, contracts with government agencies, post-employment, financial disclosure and lobbyist registration and restriction. The financial disclosure provisions shall require all elected officers, all candidates for elective office and such appointed officers and employees as provided by law to make public financial disclosures. Other public officials having significant discretionary or fiscal powers as provided by law shall make confidential financial disclosures. All financial disclosure statements shall include, but not be limited to, sources and amounts of income, business ownership, officer and director positions, ownership of real property, debts, creditor interests in insolvent businesses and the names of persons represented before government agencies.

A provision mandating codes of ethics first appeared in the 1968 Constitution when a short section was added to the General and Miscellaneous Provisions (Article XVI). It read: "The legislature and each political subdivision shall adopt a code of ethics which shall apply to appointed and elected officers and employees of the State or the political subdivision, including members of the boards, commissions and other bodies." Believing this to be ineffective, the 1978 convention expanded it considerably and made it into a separate article.

Opening with a policy statement that public officers and employees must exhibit the highest standards of ethical conduct, the first paragraph incorporates the original language mandating the state and counties to enact codes of ethics applying to public officials. In addition, the provisions were extended to cover future constitutional conventions.

The second paragraph requires the establishment of state and county ethics commissions to administer their respective codes, with a constitutional convention's code administered by the state ethics commission. It prohibits commission members from active political participation, and, while not detailing how members will be selected, it insists on a selection process assuring their independence and impartiality. The legislature has implemented this article: The state's code of ethics and provisions for a state ethics commission are found in chapter 84 of Hawaii Revised Statutes. All four counties have similarly carried out the mandate for their respective jurisdictions.

The final paragraph states that codes must, at a minimum, regulate the specific activities listed and distinguishes between individuals who must make public financial disclosures and those who can make confidential financial disclosures. In *Nakano v. Matayoshi* (1985), Hawaii's high court ruled that the financial disclosure requirements do not violate the right to privacy in Article I, Section 6. The court found significance in the fact that the same convention, that of 1978, not only added a right to privacy section to the bill of rights, but also included constitutional language that made a code of ethical conduct applicable to public officials. Therefore, it concluded, while "the people of Hawaii have a legitimate expectation of privacy where their personal financial affairs are concerned," state or county employees cannot reasonably expect that their interest in avoiding disclosure of financial affairs "is protected to the same extent as that of other citizens."

One provision of the state statutes concerning the state ethics commission makes it a felony to disclose information about a complaint filed with the commission, including making public the fact that a complaint was filed. Upon challenge as a violation of the right to free speech, the state and the plaintiff settled the lawsuit without going to trial; the U.S. District Court for the District of Hawaii approved a stipulation of settlement, stating that the so-called "gag rule" was unconstitutional and unenforceable under the First Amendment of the U.S. Constitution (*Roe v. Akamine*, 1991).

Article XV

State Boundaries; Capital; Flag; Language and Motto

In 1978, two new sections, one making Hawaiian and English official languages (Section 4) and one incorporating the state motto (Section 5), were added to this article. They, and a change to Section 1, reflect the convention's desire to pay respect to the state's Hawaiian heritage. Formerly Article XIII, it was renumbered in 1978 to Article XV.

Though none did so in 1978, delegates to earlier conventions had introduced proposals giving constitutional status to symbols such as a state flower, seal, colors, song, and bird; none was approved because of an apparent consensus against cluttering up the document.

SECTION 1

Boundaries. The State of Hawaii shall consist of all the islands, together with their appurtenant reefs and territorial and archipelagic waters, included in the Territory of Hawaii on the date of enactment of the Admission Act, except the atoll known as Palmyra Island, together with its appurtenant reefs and territorial waters; but this State shall not be deemed to include the Midway Islands, Johnston Island, Sand Island (offshore from Johnston Island) or Kingman Reef, together with their appurtenant reefs and territorial waters.

As it now reads, this section varies from that originally written because modification was required by Congress as a precondition to statehood. The 1950 convention draft read: "The State of Hawaii shall include the islands and territorial waters heretofore constituting the Territory of Hawaii." However, when Hawaii's citizens voted on whether to become a state (in June 1959), they also voted on the amendment to this section posited by Congress, changing the definition so that Palmyra atoll would be specifically excluded. The language today is almost identical to what was thus approved at the time of statehood, except for one significant change made since. When the 1978 convention inserted the words "and archipelagic" between "territorial" and "waters," it took a step of potentially far-reaching impact.

The term *archipelagic* means an expanse of water with many scattered islands. By inserting this into the constitution, the delegates intended that all the waters between the islands be included within the state's boundaries. That is, they redefined seaward boundaries so as to supersede earlier actions establishing a three-mile limit around each island. The Submerged Lands Act passed by Congress in 1953 had set the seaward boundaries of the states at three miles, and this act was considered incorporated into the Hawaii Admission Act.

In 1963, the Hawaii Supreme Court discussed the issue of the state's seaward boundaries, but reached no conclusion (*In re Island Airlines,* 1963). However, the next year the U.S. District Court for the District of Hawaii held that the statehood act did not establish the channels between islands as being within the state's boundaries and that neither when Hawaii was annexed nor when it became a state did it consider or insist that such channels were historic waters falling within its boundaries. Therefore, the seaward boundaries "were fixed at three nautical miles from the line of ordinary low water surrounding each and every one of the islands composing the State of Hawaii" (*Civil Aeronautics Board v. Island Airlines,* 1964). This was affirmed by the U.S. Court of Appeals for the Ninth Circuit in *Island Airlines v. Civil Aeronautics Board* (1965).[101]

Reaching back into Hawaiian history, a standing committee of the 1978 convention nevertheless determined that the kingdom of Hawaii had in fact regarded its waters as archipelagic and that the concept applied to the state; thus, it concluded that all channel waters fell within its boundaries. Comments made during committee-of-the-whole debate indicated uncertainty as to the full range of implications that might follow from the change: For example, could the boundaries be changed without congressional approval? But virtually no opposition to the amendment surfaced. The delegates' action was based on the premise that the document ought to state what they believed to be the correct interpretation of Hawaii's historical boundaries.

[101] See Keith, "Laws Affecting the Development," 239–40.

SECTION 2

Capital. Honolulu, on the island of Oahu, shall be the capital of the State.

This section is substantively the same as it was in the Statehood Constitution. The 1950 convention did consider the possibility of another location, but ended up retaining Honolulu, which had long served as the capital city. Since then, the capital's location has not been an issue.

Because of the state's island nature and its distribution of population, the capital city is unique within the country. As of the 1990 census, 75 percent of the state's population resides in the City and County of Honolulu on Oahu and thus in very close proximity to the seat of government; in the past, the proportion has been as high as 80 percent.

SECTION 3

State Flag. The Hawaiian flag shall be the flag of the State.

No changes have been made to this section since it was included in the Statehood Constitution. It is, however, unusual to give constitutional status to a state flag, for most states make such a designation by statute.

There is uncertainty about the exact origin of the Hawaiian flag, though there is agreement on the following: "The Hawaiian flag dates from the reign of Kamehameha I. The 8 stripes represent the 8 major islands of the Hawaiian archipelago. The designer of the flag was an Englishman, which explains, in part, the incorporation of the British Union Jack in the flag."[102]

Although faced with proposals to change the design either in part or in its entirety, the 1950 convention decided to keep the territorial flag as the state flag because of its historical and sentimental value. It has not been an issue at the subsequent constitutional conventions.

SECTION 4

Official Languages. English and Hawaiian shall be the official languages of Hawaii, except that Hawaiian shall be required for public acts and transactions only as provided by law.

This section was added in 1978 with virtually no debate among the delegates. The convention's Standing Committee on Hawaiian Affairs proposed it "to give

---

[102] *Hawaii Constitutional Convention Studies 1978, Article XIII: State Boundaries, Capital, Flag; Article XIV: General and Miscellaneous Provisions; Article XVI: Schedule* (Honolulu: State of Hawaii, Legislative Reference Bureau, 1978), 14.

full recognition and honor to the rich cultural inheritance that Hawaiians have given to all ethnic groups of this State."[103] A point made in the report issued by the committee of the whole adds depth to its historical significance: The provision was also intended to "overcome certain insults of the past where the speaking of Hawaiian was forbidden in the public school system."[104] It should be noted, however, that, until 1968, the ability to speak, read, and write English or Hawaiian was a constitutional requirement for voting (see Article II, Section1).

Delegates supporting the addition of this section did recognize the practical problems entailed and explained that it was written so as to give the legislature discretion to determine when the Hawaiian language would be officially required. The legislature has, by statute, specified that the Hawaiian language will not be required for public acts and transactions (Haw. Rev. Stat. § 1–13). In 1992, this was amended with new statutory language encouraging the use of diacritical marks (macrons and glottal stops) for Hawaiian words when they are used in official publications (Haw. Rev. Stat. § 1–13.5).

SECTION 5

Motto. The motto of the State shall be, "Ua mau ke ea o ka aina i ka pono."

In adding this new section, the 1978 convention gave constitutional status to what was already established by statute as the state's motto. It was placed in the constitution in order to remove the legislature's power to adopt any other motto. A motion to include the English translation, in parentheses, was defeated after emotional arguments by those believing the Hawaiian language ought to stand alone on its beauty and symbolic value.

The motto was born out of traumatic events during the reign of Kamehameha III, 1825–1854, and its translation is "The life of the land is perpetuated in righteousness." (Sometimes the word "preserved" is used.) Under threat of imminent attack by Lord Paulet, commander of the British ship *Carysfort*, the King agreed to a provisional cession of Hawaii to Britain. On February 25, 1843, the Hawaiian flag was lowered and replaced by that of Great Britain. Almost five months of British rule ended when Admiral Thomas arrived, informing the King that Lord Paulet had gone beyond his authority. Hawaii's independence was restored in return for an agreement protecting the interests of British subjects living in the islands. On July 31 the Hawaiian flag again flew over an independent Hawaii. At a ceremony to give thanks, the King announced that, as he had hoped, the life of the land had been restored. His emotion-laden words live on in the motto.

---

[103] *1978 Proceedings I*, Standing Committee Report no. 57, 638.

[104] *1978 Proceedings I*, Committee of the Whole Report no. 12, 1016.

Article XVI

General and Miscellaneous Provisions

This article is aptly described as "the rug of the constitution under which all the disparate and distinctive provisions are swept."[105]

In 1968, only two changes were made: The section on disqualifications from public office or employment (Section 3) was modified; and a new section, titled "Codes of Ethics," was added. Ten years later it was renumbered from Article XIV to Article XVI and underwent noteworthy alterations, including deletion of the section on ethics because that provision was incorporated into a new article devoted solely to that subject.

SECTION 1

Civil Service. The employment of persons in the civil service, as defined by law, of or under the State, shall be governed by the merit principle.

Since this section was placed in the Statehood Constitution, it has remained unchanged. Two concepts it incorporates are particularly important: "civil service" and "the merit principle." Civil service refers generally to government employment. In designating that the civil service is to be governed by the merit principle, the section implicitly prohibits patronage as the basis for such employment.

[105] *Hawaii Constitutional Convention Studies 1978, Article XIII,* 27.

Under a patronage system, employment may depend on such factors as friendship or political support, whereas under a merit system, employment is to be based on competence as established by objective standards and procedures.

What comprises the civil service is to be defined by law. The statute (Haw. Rev. Stat. ch. 76) covering state civil service, besides identifying the employees covered, incorporates a wide range of procedures and policies. The statute also identifies the positions excluded from civil service requirements, based on the recognition that Section 1 does not mandate employment of every state employee under the merit system; such exclusions include appointees to the cabinet and to boards and commissions, as well as legislative staff positions.

SECTION 2

Employees' Retirement System. Membership in any employees' retirement system of the State or any political subdivision thereof shall be a contractual relationship, the accrued benefits of which shall not be diminished or impaired.

This section, carried over intact from the Statehood Constitution, does not mandate the state, or any county, to establish a retirement system for public employees. It does require, however, that in the event a system is set up, the benefits accrued (i.e., accumulated or due after a period of time) by those enrolled cannot be reduced retroactively.

When the Hawaii Supreme Court considered this provision in *Chun v. Employees' Retirement System of the State of Hawaii* (1980), it relied heavily on the purpose expressed by the 1950 framers—namely, that the legislature would determine benefits and conditions, but could not change benefits attributable to past services. According to the court, "the extent of such benefits as well as the conditions under which an employee should receive benefits, are governed by applicable statutory provisions."

SECTION 3

Disqualifications from Public Office or Employment. No person shall hold any public office or employment who has been convicted of any act to overthrow, or attempt to overthrow, or conspiracy with any person to overthrow the government of this State or of the United States by force or violence.

A sensitivity to congressional opposition to statehood, based to a large extent on alleged communist influence in the islands, led the framers of the 1950 document to include this loyalty section. Subsequent conventions retained it, although the language was significantly altered by each one.

Initially, the section in the Statehood Constitution, titled "Disqualification for Disloyalty," read:

> No person who advocates, or who aids or belongs to any party, organization or association which advocates, the overthrow by force or violence of the government of this State or of the United States shall be qualified to hold any public office or employment.

When the 1968 convention met, delegates recognized that rulings by the U.S. Supreme Court had made this language unconstitutional, as violative of the rights to association and belief guaranteed by the First Amendment to the U.S. Constitution. In spite of suggestions to delete the section, the delegates determined that it should be retained, but with constitutionally permissible language. After amendment, the section in the 1968 Constitution stated:

> No person shall hold any public office or employment who, knowingly and intentionally, does any act to overthrow, or attempts to overthrow, or conspires with any person to overthrow the government of this State or of the United States by force or violence.

This new language in effect removed mere advocacy as a sufficient condition for disqualification. Actual acts or attempts had to be committed knowingly and intentionally.

While the 1978 delegates believed the section passed constitutional muster, they wanted to avoid the implication that a person could be disqualified "based on vague standards of determining loyalty, [on] procedures which do not meet due process requirements, or [on] inadequate evidence."[106] To correct this shortcoming, the delegates established a more stringent test for determining disqualification based on disloyalty by substituting the words "who has been convicted of" in place of "who knowingly and intentionally, does" and changing "conspires" to "conspiracy."

SECTION 4

> **Oath of Office.** All eligible public officers, before entering upon the duties of their respective offices, shall take and subscribe to the following oath or affirmation: "I do solemnly swear (or affirm) that I will support and defend the Constitution of the United States, and the Constitution of the State of Hawaii, and that I will faithfully discharge my duties as . . . to the best of my ability. " As used in this section, "eligible public officers" means the governor, the lieutenant governor, the members of both houses of the legislature, the members of the board of education, the members of the

---

[106] *Constitutional Convention, 1978 Proceedings* (Honolulu: State of Hawaii, 1980), vol. II, *Committee of the Whole Debates* (hereinafter cited as *1978 Proceedings II*), 94.

national guard, State or county employees who possess police powers, district court judges, and all those whose appointment requires the consent of the senate.

This loyalty oath provision originated in the Statehood Constitution and was not changed until November 1992 when voters ratified a legislatively proposed amendment inserting more specific language.

In its original form, the first sentence stated that "All public officers" had to take the oath or affirmation. By statute, the phrase "public officers" applies to all persons elected, appointed, or employed by the state of the local governments (see for example, Haw. Rev. Stat. § 85–32), including faculty hired by the University of Hawaii. As stated by the state senate judiciary committee, a major impetus for proposing the amendment to Section 4 was the recent refusal of a noteworthy scholar to join the University of Hawaii faculty particularly because of the requirement to sign a loyalty oath. In addition, the committee noted that the university "brings together scholars from many different nations and cultures" and that the section caused conflicts for faculty members who were not U.S. citizens.[107]

The ratified amendment inserted the word "eligible" into the opening clause and added the second sentence specifying those who are eligible public officers. Legislative action to amend or repeal conflicting statutory provisions is likely in the near future.

The 1992 amendment also deleted a sentence that gave the legislature power to provide further oaths, a provision included by the 1950 convention as part of the effort to allay congressional fears of communist influence.

Since the provision does not indicate any penalties for refusing to take the oath, it is not clear whether someone who refuses, forfeits the opportunity to serve or is subject to some other punishment.

SECTION 5

Intergovernmental Relations. The legislative may provide for cooperation on the part of this State and its political subdivisions with the United States, or other states and territories, or their political subdivisions, in matters affecting the public health, safety and general welfare. Funds may be appropriated to effect such cooperation.

It is unusual to find a state constitutional provision covering intergovernmental cooperation between the state and county governments and the national government, other states (and their cities and counties), and territories of the United States. A legislature's power to act in this area does not need to be spelled out formally in a constitution. However, the 1950 convention apparently included it in order to assure that the legislature's power to appropriate funds extends to effecting the goal of cooperation. This section has not been changed substantively since then.

---

[107] Hawaii Senate, Judiciary Committee, *Standing Committee Report no. 2050*, 28 February 1992.

SECTION 6

Federal Lands. The United States shall be vested with or retain title to or an interest in or shall hold the property in the Territory of Hawaii set aside for the use of the United States and remaining so set aside immediately prior to the admission of this State, in all respects as and to the extent set forth in the act or resolution providing for the admission of this State to the Union.

See the commentary following Section 11.

SECTION 7

Compliance with Trust. Any trust provisions which the Congress shall impose, upon the admission of this State, in respect of the lands patented to the State by the United States or the proceeds and income therefrom, shall be complied with by appropriate legislation. Such legislation shall not diminish or limit the benefits of native Hawaiians under Section 4 of Article XII.

See the commentary following Section 11.

SECTION 8

Administration of Undisposed Lands. All provisions of the Act of Congress approved March 18, 1959 reserving rights or powers to the United States, as well as those prescribing the terms or conditions of the grants of lands or other property therein made to the State of Hawaii are consented to fully by the State and its people.

See the commentary following Section 11.

SECTION 9

Tax Exemption of Federal Property. No taxes shall be imposed by the State upon any lands or other property now owned or hereafter acquired by the United States, except as the same shall become taxable by reason of disposition thereof by the United States or by reason of the consent of the United States to such taxation.

See the commentary following Section 11.

SECTION 10

Hawaii National Park. All provisions of the act or resolution admitting this State to the Union, or providing for such admission, which reserve to the United States jurisdiction of Hawaii National Park, or the ownership or control of lands within Hawaii National Park, are consented to fully by the State and its people.

See the commentary following Section 11.

SECTION 11

Judicial Rights. All those provisions of the act or resolution admitting this State to the Union, or providing for such admission, which reserve to the United States judicial rights or powers are consented to fully by the State and its people; and those provisions of such act or resolution which preserve judicial rights and powers for the State are hereby accepted and adopted, and such rights and powers are hereby assumed, to be exercised and discharged pursuant to this constitution and the laws of the State.

Sections 6 through 11 were placed in the Statehood Constitution in order to comply with requirements set by Congress for Hawaii's admission to statehood and to demonstrate Hawaii's understanding of the relationship between states and the national government. Changes made to these sections since statehood have not modified their basic nature.

Section 6, "Federal Lands," stipulates that the U.S. government retains title to property it held, or was given authority over, immediately prior to Hawaii's admission to the Union.

Section 7, "Compliance with Trust," guarantees that the state will comply with congressional trust provisions regarding lands granted by the United States to the state through appropriate legislation. This section was only changed once. In order to avoid conflict with the newly added Section 4 of Article XII (Hawaiian Affairs), the 1978 convention added a final sentence clarifying that such compliance legislation could not diminish or limit the benefits of native Hawaiians provided under the section.

The language of the current Section 8, "Administration of Undisposed Lands," is different from that drafted by the 1950 convention. At the time of the statehood election, June 1959, the language was amended pursuant to congressional admission requirements. It consents to the United States reserving the right and power to administer undisposed lands.

Section 9, "Tax Exemption of Federal Property," grants a tax-exempt status to federal lands in Hawaii unless they become taxable by reason of disposition or consent by the United States. The words "or by reason of the consent of the United States" were added in 1978.

Section 10, "Hawaii National Park," grants the United States jurisdiction over the Hawaii National Park, on the island of Hawaii, which is now called the Hawaii Volcanoes National Park. The state's power of eminent domain (see Article I, Section 20) includes the power to acquire land for a national park under federal jurisdiction (*State v. W. Tin Yan*, 1960).

In Section 11, "Judicial Rights," the state consents to the judicial powers and rights reserved to the United States government and assumes those judicial powers and rights that the act of admission has preserved for the state.

SECTION 12

Quieting Title. No person shall be deprived of title to an estate or interest in real property by another person claiming actual, continuous, hostile, exclusive, open and notorious possession of such lands, except to real property of five acres or less. Such claim may be asserted in good faith by any person not more than once in twenty years.

The title of this section refers to the legal proceeding called a quiet title action; in order to establish the plaintiff's title to land, an adverse claimant is brought into court and compelled to either establish a claim or be forever barred from asserting it.

Added to the constitution in 1978, this section prohibits adverse possession—a legal action for acquiring, through continuous use or other means, title to land that is owned by someone else, whether or not the latter has documents demonstrating ownership. During debate, delegates emotionally relayed stories of how adverse possession was used to deprive ethnic Hawaiians of their land, land often handed down from generation to generation even though there was no paper title to pass on with it. They referred to adverse possession as a "legal means of thievery" that "had long been used by land barons against the small landowner, particularly the Hawaiians."[108] Though there were statutory provisions covering adverse possession, delegates were convinced the time had come to give constitutional status to this issue in order to remedy past wrongs suffered by those of Hawaiian ancestry.[109]

As originally proposed, and adopted by the convention sitting as committee of the whole, this section placed a total ban on adverse possession. However, at a plenary session the language was modified. The delegates added the phrase "exempting property of five acres or less from the prohibition" so that small landowners, particularly those Hawaiian families holding land for generations (but without official ownership documentation), could use the legal process to acquire official title to that land. At the same time, the sentence limiting exercise of a claim of title through adverse possession to not more than once in twenty years was adopted to ensure that whoever uses the process uses it only in good faith.

[108] *1978 Proceedings I*, Committee of the Whole Report no. 12, 1017.

[109] See Naomi Hirayasu, "Adverse Possession and Quiet Title Actions in Hawaii—Recent Constitutional Developments," *Hawaii Bar Journal* 19 (1985): 59.

SECTION 13

Plain Language. Insofar as practicable, all governmental writing meant for the public, in whatever language, should be plainly worded, avoiding the use of technical terms.

The requirement for plain language was proposed from the floor of the 1978 convention and produced considerable debate. The supporters' position is best summarized by the telling, but humorous, remark by one delegate: "I abjure obfuscation but approve delineation of terms."[110] Opponents generally argued that this detail had no place in a constitution and voiced concern that the action would prohibit the use of Hawaiian terms for expressing traditional rights. It was incorporated into the document on a very narrow vote of forty-four to forty-one.

The sponsors of the section acknowledged that agreement on a definition of plain language would be extraordinarily difficult to obtain. They deliberately used the word "should" instead of "shall" so that the section would encourage, rather than mandate, use of plain language.

SECTION 14

Titles, Subtitles; Construction. Titles and subtitles shall not be used for purposes of construing this constitution.

Titles and subtitles of articles and sections are not to be used for interpreting the constitution. Since titles and subtitles are short phrases, they do not encompass all the detail within a particular article or section; basing interpretation on them might be highly misleading. Though not addressing this specific provision, the Hawaii Supreme Court has commented on the issue of construing constitutional provisions. "In the construction of a constitutional provision, the rule is well established that the words of the constitution are presumed to be used in their natural sense" (*Employees' Retirement System v. Budget Director Ho*, 1960). Some years later the court added that if the words used in a constitutional provision are clear and unambiguous, they are to be applied as written (*Spears v. Honda*, 1968).

Prior to 1978, this section consisted of two parts. In addition to the existing sentence, a second sentence stated: "Whenever any personal pronoun appears in this constitution, it shall be construed to mean either sex." It was deleted as unnecessary since the convention of that year substituted gender-neutral language for all masculine personal pronouns in the document.

---

[110] *1978 Proceedings II*, 103.

SECTION 15

General Power. The enumeration in this constitution of specified powers shall not be construed as limitations upon the power of the State to provide for the general welfare of the people.

Unaltered since statehood, this section declares that the ability of the state to provide for the general welfare of the people is not limited to those powers listed in the constitution.

Like the savings clause in Article I (Section 22), this section seeks to avoid an interpretation of the constitution leading to the conclusion that the explicit inclusion of some powers implies the exclusion of other powers not so stated. Section 22 in the Bill of Rights article guarantees to the people rights not specifically listed in the constitution, while Section 15 does the same with respect to the powers of state government. It must be noted that the provision in Section 15 is qualified by the phrase "to provide for the general welfare of the people."

Without such qualifying words, the section might suggest extraordinary powers for the state government.

SECTION 16

Provisions Are Self-Executing. The provisions of this constitution shall be self-executing to the fullest extent that their respective natures permit.

Since written into the Statehood Constitution, this section has not been changed substantively. In 1979, Hawaii's high court offered the following definition: "The self-executing clause only means that the rights therein established or recognized do not depend upon further legislative action in order to become operative" (*Figueroa v. State*, 1979).

Two years later, in *State v. Rodrigues* (1981), this was amplified when the court stated:

> [A] constitutional provision is self-executing if it meets the following test adopted by the United States Supreme Court: "A constitutional provision may be said to be self-executing if it supplies a sufficient rule by means of which the right given may be enjoyed and protected, or the duty imposed may be enforced; and it is not self-executing when it merely indicates principles, without laying down rules by means of which those principles may be given the force of law."

The court also added that when the phrase "as provided by law" is used in the constitution, it is a direction to the legislature to enact implementing legislation (*State v. Rodrigues*, 1981).

Article XVII

Revision and Amendment

The processes spelled out in the national and state constitutions for their revision and amendment are based on the assumption that changing such a basic document ought to be neither impossible nor too easy. Accordingly, this article in Hawaii's constitution specifies that proposals to amend or revise will succeed only after surviving a series of hurdles, the last of which is ratification by the voters, and even this is made more complex than in regular elections. In 1978, the article was renumbered from Article XV to Article XVII.

SECTION 1

Methods of Proposal. Revisions of or amendments to this constitution may be proposed by constitutional convention or by the legislature.

Unchanged since statehood, this section allows only two methods for proposing revisions or amendments: by constitutional convention and by the legislature. They are detailed in Sections 2 and 3 below.

Whichever method of proposal is used, actually changing the constitution rests in the hands of the voters since the process always culminates in an election. And, as the state supreme court has explained, every "'reasonable presumption is to be indulged in favor of a constitutional amendment which the people have adopted at a general election"' for they "'are presumed to know what they want, to have understood the proposition submitted to them in all of its implications, and by their approval vote to have determined that [the] amendment is for the public good and expresses the free opinion of a sovereign people'" (*Kahalekai v. Doi*, 1979).

It is important to note that while this section allows a type of referendum, it does not provide for modifying Hawaii's constitution by initiative; eighteen states do, however, permit initiatives to be used for constitutional change. Though initiative was debated at the constitutional conventions, it has never commanded support from enough delegates to be incorporated into the constitution.

SECTION 2

Constitutional Convention. The legislature may submit to the electorate at any general or special election the question, "Shall there be a convention to propose a revision of or amendments to the Constitution?" If any nine-year period shall elapse during which the question shall not have been submitted, the lieutenant governor shall certify the question, to be voted on at the first general election following the expiration of such period.

—**Election of Delegates.** If a majority of the ballots cast upon such a question be in the affirmative, delegates to the convention shall be chosen at the next regular election unless the legislature shall provide for the election of delegates at a special election.

Notwithstanding any provision in this constitution to the contrary, other than Section 3 of Article XVI, any qualified voter of the district concerned shall be eligible to membership in the convention.

The legislature shall provide for the number of delegates to the convention, the areas from which they shall be elected and the manner in which the convention shall convene. The legislature shall also provide for the necessary facilities and equipment for the convention. The convention shall have the same powers and privileges, as nearly as practicable, as provided for the convention of 1978.

—**Meeting.** The constitutional convention shall convene not less than five months prior to the next regularly scheduled general election.

—**Organization; Procedure.** The convention shall determine its own organization and rules of procedure. It shall be the sole judge of the elections, returns and qualifications of its members and, by a two-thirds vote, may suspend or remove any member for cause. The governor shall fill any vacancy by appointment of a qualified voter from the district concerned.

—**Ratification; Appropriations.** The convention shall provide for the time and manner in which the proposed constitutional revision or amendments shall be submitted to a vote of the electorate; provided that each amendment shall be submitted in the form of a question embracing but one subject; and provided further, that each question shall have designated spaces to mark YES or NO on the amendment.

At least thirty days prior to the submission of any proposed revision or amendments, the convention shall make available for public inspection, a full text of the proposed amendments. Every public library, office of the clerk of each county, and the chief election officer shall be provided such texts and shall make them available for public inspection. The full text of any proposed revision or amendments shall also be made available for inspection at every polling place on the day of the election at which such revision or amendments are submitted.

The convention shall, as provided by law, be responsible for a program of voter education concerning each proposed revision or amendment to be submitted to the electorate.

The revision or amendments shall be effective only if approved at a general election by a majority of all the votes tallied upon the question, this majority constituting at least fifty per cent of the total vote cast at the election, or at a special election by a majority of all the votes tallied upon the question, this majority constituting at least thirty per cent of the total number of registered voters.

The provisions of this section shall be self-executing, but the legislature shall make the necessary appropriations and may enact legislation to facilitate their operation.

Because of significant changes made over the years, this section reads quite differently from how it did originally.

The legislature may place the question of whether there will be a constitutional convention before the voters at a general or a special election. There is no limit to the number of times the legislature may do this, but if nine years elapse without the question appearing on the ballot, the lieutenant governor must place the question on the ballot for the following general election. This provision ensures that the voters periodically have an opportunity to call a convention.

Originally, the section read "ten-year period". However, prior to the 1978 convention, as noted in Part I, conflict surfaced over whether this required the lieutenant governor to place the question on the ballot at the tenth or the twelfth year when the legislature has not acted. The legislature finally did place the question on the 1976 ballot, and in *League of Women Voters v. Doi* (1976), the Hawaii Supreme Court, finding the issue moot, declined to make a ruling applicable for the future.

In order to avoid further uncertainty, the 1978 convention specified a nine-year, rather than a ten-year, period, thus making clear that absent legislative action, the lieutenant governor must put the convention question on the ballot at the election held in the tenth year after the voters had last voted on it.

However the question is placed on the ballot, whether or not a convention is to be called always rests in the hands of the citizens since an affirmative majority of those voting on the issue is required. Only if the calling of a convention is approved do the subsections that follow come into play.

Delegates are elected at the next regular election or at a special election stipulated by the legislature. All qualified voters, except those who fail the "loyalty" provisions in Article XVI, Section 3, are eligible to run and serve.

In 1978, the subsection on delegate elections was amended to require that the legislature determine the number of delegates and designate the districts from which they are elected. The original language allowed the legislature to avoid this task by stating that if the legislature did not specify the number of delegates and districts, they would be the same as used for the previous convention.

The 1978 convention also added the subsection titled "Meeting." In order to clarify and make certain that delegates have enough time for deliberations, future conventions must be convened not less than five months before the next regularly scheduled general election.

The subsection on "Organization; Procedure" grants the convention powers over its own organization and procedures and the power to both seat and remove delegates.

The final subsection, outlining the method of ratification, has undergone considerable alteration. Originally, one clause therein declared that "no constitutional amendment altering this proviso [relating to the ratification requirements] or the representation from any senatorial district in the senate shall become effective unless it shall also be approved by a majority of the votes tallied upon the question in each of a majority of the counties." This clause had the effect of establishing two different ratification formulas: one formula for amending the ratification requirements themselves and/or senate districting and another for modifying other provisions in the document (see below). In 1965, the U.S. District Court for the District of Hawaii ruled that clause unconstitutional (*Holt v. Richardson*, 1965 (*Holt I*)), and with this in mind, the 1968 convention deleted it.

With respect to the form in which the amendments will be placed before the voters, the language applicable at the time of the 1968 and the 1978 conventions simply stated that "[T]he convention shall provide for the time and manner in which the proposed constitutional revision or amendments shall be submitted to a vote of the electorate." Shortly after the election ratifying the work of the 1978 convention, two cases arose involving both the form of the ballot that the convention, under this authority, had decided to use and the manner in which the convention educated the public on proposed changes.

As discussed in Part I, the Hawaii Supreme Court found no inherent bias in the ballot format allowing voters three possibilities: voting "yes" or "no" to all the proposed changes or opposing specific proposals by using the "yes-but" option (*Kahalekai v. Doi*, 1979). Nevertheless, it invalidated the ratification vote on seven proposed amendments—actually a small fraction of the total number voted on—because they were not explicitly detailed in the public education materials produced by the convention. These amendments involved Article III, Sections 2 and 3; Article IV, Sections 5 and 6; Article XI, Section 10; Article XII, Section 7; and Article XVII, Section 1. (See those articles for descriptions of the invalidated amendments; see also Part I.)

In the other case, the U.S. district court did not address alleged inadequacies of ballot format and public education, but did hold that a challenge in federal court will be dismissed if plaintiffs do not seek pre-election relief when they are aware of the alleged inadequacies before the election. Post-election relief will be considered "only where the plaintiffs were not aware of a major problem prior to the election or where by the nature of the case they had no opportunity to seek pre-election relief" (*Hart v. King*, 1979).

In order to avoid format problems, evident not only from the legal challenges, but also from disagreement within the 1978 convention body itself, the legislature subsequently proposed, and in 1980 voters approved an amendment for new constitutional language. The section now requires that each amendment be submitted in the form of a question embracing one subject and that each question have designated spaces for voting "yes" or "no." Added by the same amendment were the two paragraphs specifying the responsibilities for educating the public. There must be wide dissemination of the text of all proposals and a program of voter information. As no convention has been held since these changes were ratified, they have not been put into practice.

Ratification of proposed amendments depends on a cumbersome formula based not just on a majority of affirmative votes, but also on the type of election. An amendment is ratified at a general election if a majority of those voting on the particular amendment vote affirmatively and if the number of voters making up that majority constitutes at least 50 percent of the total votes cast at the general election. At a special election, an amendment is ratified if the number of voters making up the affirmative majority equals at least 30 percent of the total number of registered voters.

This formula has changed over time. Originally the number of affirmative votes had to equal at least 35 percent of the total votes cast in a general election or 35 percent of the number of registered voters at a special election. The 1968 convention reduced the requirement to 30 percent, but only with respect to special elections. The 1978 convention did not make any revisions, but, in 1980, voters approved a legislatively proposed amendment increasing the required percentage of the total votes cast at a general election from 35 to 50 percent.

Although general practice in Hawaii has established the date of the ratification vote by the people as the date an amendment becomes effective, the constitution is silent on this matter. It has been argued that, as a result, problems may arise, particularly when an amendment specifically calls for implementation legislation, for it is unclear whether such an amendment is effective on the date of ratification or only when such legislation is enacted.[111]

The final paragraph of the section has not been changed. Even though the provisions are self-executing, the legislature has the power to appropriate funds and pass implementation legislation.

In 1986, when the question of whether to hold another convention appeared on the general election ballot, the voters responded by rejecting the idea. As a result, the 1978 and 1980 changes to the above subsections have yet to be applied to a convention.

SECTION 3

Amendments Proposed by Legislature. The legislature may propose amendments to the constitution by adopting the same, in the manner required for legislation, by a two-thirds vote of each house on final reading at any session, after either or both houses shall have given the governor at least ten days' written notice of the final form of the proposed amendment, or, with or without such notice, by a majority vote of each house on final reading at each of two successive sessions.

Upon such adoption, the proposed amendments shall be entered upon the journals, with the ayes and noes, and published once in each of four successive weeks in at least one newspaper of general circulation in each senatorial district wherein such a newspaper is published, within the two months' period immediately preceding the next general election.

At such general election the proposed amendments shall be submitted to the electorate for approval or rejection upon a separate ballot.

The conditions of and requirements for ratification of such proposed amendments shall be the same as provided in section 2 of this article for ratification at a general election.

This section remains as originally written in the Statehood Constitution, and it sets forth the process by which the legislature proposes constitutional amendments. Such proposals make their way through the legislature just as bills do, until the last stage where two alternative methods are allowed for final passage. However, both incorporate hurdles that do not apply to other legislative actions. For an amendment proposal to pass, the final reading cannot take place until after the governor receives at least ten days' notice, and the amendment must obtain a two-thirds vote on final reading in each chamber. Alternatively, the proposal passes, with or without notice to the governor, if it receives a majority vote in both houses at two successive sessions.

Including the governor in the process adds a limited check. While not able to exercise a veto (see Section 4 below), the executive is given the opportunity to

[111] Bettencourt and Zwald, "The Prosecutor's Duty," 162–63.

use the power of persuasion for objecting to or supporting proposals. Failure to meet the notification requirement has, in fact, caused some proposed amendments to die. However, once properly passed by the legislature, proposals do not need the signature of the governor in order to be placed on the ballot.

The second paragraph covers the subjects of public accountability and the need to inform voters about proposed amendments. Each legislator's vote must be recorded upon adoption, and the proposals must be published in newspapers. This latter provision is much less demanding than the expanded requirements for public education on convention proposals now found in Section 2, as a result of the legislatively proposed changes approved by voters in 1980. The legislature has yet to put before the voters any proposals for modifying the constitution to make its responsibilities for dissemination and voter education on its proposed amendments the same as are now required of a convention.

Nor has the legislature asked the voters to decide whether legislatively proposed amendments must be submitted in the form of a question embracing just one subject (as was done for convention proposals in Section 2); there is no statutory requirement that they do so. Presently, the fourth paragraph specifies only that legislatively proposed amendments must be placed on a ballot separate from that used for other items voted on at an election. At the time of the *Kahalekai v. Doi* (1979) decision, the constitution did not include any language requiring that proposed constitutional amendments, when placed on the ballot, satisfy a one-subject rule. In that decision, the court found that while Article III, Section 14 includes a one-subject prescription, it applies only to legislation. It concluded that unless otherwise provided for in the constitution, there is no limitation on the number of subjects that a proposed constitutional amendment may include. Since only the section on convention-proposed amendments has been revised in this respect, the *Kahalekai* interpretation appears to apply now just to legislatively proposed changes: They do not have to satisfy a one-subject rule.

While Section 2 allows convention proposals to be voted on at a special or a general election, Section 3 limits voting on legislatively proposed amendments to general elections. Whether Section 3 permits the legislature to place at least two alternative amendments on the primary election ballot, with the one receiving the most favorable votes then appearing on the general election ballot for the voters' approval or rejection as a constitutional amendment, was at issue in *Blair v. Cayetano* (1992). This unprecedented two-step process was called for by the 1992 legislature in putting forth two alternative amendments concerning school governance (see also Article X, Section 2). In declaring the process invalid, the Hawaii Supreme Court pointed out that it would have given the electorate-at-large a role in initiating constitutional amendment proposals even though such a role was rejected by the 1950 constitutional convention and is expressly disallowed by the language of Section 3.

Ratification of legislatively proposed amendments is determined by the same formula detailed for convention-proposed amendments in Section 2.

SECTION 4

Veto. No proposal for amendment of the constitution adopted in either manner provided by this article shall be subject to veto by the governor.

Unchanged since statehood, this section prohibits the governor from vetoing amendments proposed either by convention or by the legislature. Does this prohibition also deny the governor power to veto legislation passed pursuant to specific language in an amendment calling for implementation legislation? In raising this intriguing question, two commentators suggest that if denying the executive veto power over proposed amendments is to have any meaning, then it must also include a denial of veto power over implementation legislation because the practical effect of such a veto is "to nullify the amendment."[112] The issue is unresolved.

SECTION 5

Conflicting Revisions or Amendments. If a revision or amendment proposed by a constitutional convention is in conflict with a revision or amendment proposed by the legislature and both are submitted to the electorate at the same election and both are approved, then the revision or amendment proposed by the convention shall prevail. If conflicting revisions or amendments are proposed by the same body and are submitted to the electorate at the same election and both are approved, then the revision or amendment receiving the highest number of votes shall prevail.

Added by the 1968 convention, this section establishes a mechanism for precluding the incorporation into the constitution of simultaneously approved, but conflicting, revisions or amendments.

---

[112] Ibid., 161.

Article XVIII

Schedule

The sections in this article, called Schedule, are intended to ensure an orderly transition when new constitutional provisions are adopted. Hawaii's constitution has always included a Schedule. The Statehood Constitution's Schedule dealt with the transition from territorial status to statehood, while the Schedule in the 1968 and the 1978 constitutions covered changes made to the immediately preceding document. In 1978, this article was renumbered from Article XVI to Article XVIII. The Schedule is followed by an unnumbered paragraph entitled "Effective Date," placed at the end of the constitution drafted in 1950.

Because of the temporary nature of some Schedule provisions, both the 1968 and the 1978 conventions deleted those earlier parts that were obsolete and altered language to bring others into conformity with new provisions in the constitution. Each convention also added new sections where necessary. For example, consistent with changes made elsewhere in the document, the 1978 convention included provisions for starting staggered terms for senators, beginning a two-term limit for governor and lieutenant governor, initiating the use of a judicial selection commission, establishing county control over real property tax, drawing new districts for board of education members, and implementing the Office of Hawaiian Affairs. Both conventions, however, left the original language in "Debts" (Section 10) and in "Residence, Other Qualifications" (Section 11) untouched.

Except for clarifying remarks following Section 1, the Schedule is reproduced below without comment.

SECTION 1. Districting and Apportionment

In the Statehood Constitution, the representative districts applicable until the next reapportionment were described, while the 1968 Constitution described both representative and senate districts. The text of this section is now omitted as obsolete in official publications of Hawaii's constitution.

Descriptions are no longer needed in the constitution since a reapportionment commission is responsible for defining legislative districts. The 1978 Convention proposed substituting the following transition language:

> Until the next reapportionment the senatorial districts and the number of senators to be elected from each shall be as set forth in the 1973 reapportionment plan. Until the next reapportionment the representative districts and the number of representatives to be elected from each shall be as set forth in the 1973 reapportionment plan.

However, in *Kahalekai v. Doi* (1979), the state supreme court held that this amendment was not validly ratified by the voters; thus, the section number and title are printed without any accompanying text.

It should be noted, for historical purposes only, that, in 1962, the voters ratified a legislatively proposed constitutional amendment to this section; it adjusted the boundary between two state house districts.

SECTION 2

1978 Senatorial Elections. Article III, Section 4, to the contrary notwithstanding, the terms of office of the members of the senate elected in the 1978 general election shall be as follows: members of the senate shall be divided into two classes. The first class shall consist of the following number elected with the highest number of votes from their respective senatorial districts: first district, one; second district, one; third district, one; fourth district, two; fifth district, two; sixth district, two; seventh district, two; eighth district, one. Members of the first class shall hold office for a term of four years beginning with their election and ending on the day of the second general election held thereafter. The remaining members elected shall constitute the second class and shall hold office for a term of two years beginning with their election and ending on the day of the next general election held thereafter.

SECTION 3

Salaries of Legislators. Until otherwise provided by law in accordance with Section 9 of Article III, the salary of each member of the legislature shall be twelve thousand dollars a year.

SECTION 4

Effective Date for Term Limitations for Governor and Lieutenant Governor. The amendments to Sections 1 and 2 of Article V shall limit the term of any person elected to the office of governor or lieutenant governor in the 1978 general election to two consecutive full terms commencing from noon on the first Monday in December, 1978.

SECTION 5

Judiciary: Transition; Effective Date. The three members initially appointed to the judicial selection commission by the governor shall serve for terms of two, four and six years respectively. The members initially appointed to the commission by the president of the senate and the speaker of the house of representatives shall serve for two years. The two members initially appointed to the commission by the chief justice of the supreme court shall serve terms of four and six years respectively. The two members initially elected to the commission by the members of the bar of the State shall serve for terms of four and six years respectively. The current terms of justices and judges in office shall terminate as heretofore provided by law, subject to earlier termination and removal as provided in Article VI. The amendments to Article VI shall take effect upon ratification. The judicial selection commission shall be created no later than April 1, 1979.

SECTION 6

Effective Date and Application of Real Property Tax Transfer. The amendment to Section 3 of Article VIII shall take effect on the first day of July after two full calendar years have elapsed following the ratification of such amendment [November 7, 1978]; provided that for a period of eleven years following such ratification, the policies and methods of assessing real property taxes shall be uniform throughout the State and shall be established by agreement of a majority of the political subdivisions. Each political subdivision shall enact such uniform policies and methods of assessment by ordinance before the effective date of this amendment [July 1, 1981], and in the event the political subdivisions fail to enact such ordinances, the uniform policies and methods of assessment shall be established by general law. Any amendments to the uniform policies and methods of assessment established by the political subdivisions may only be made by agreement of a majority of the political subdivisions and enactment thereof by ordinance in each political subdivision.

Real property tax exemptions and dedications of land for specific use for assessment at its value in such use as provided by law and in effect upon ratification of the amendment to Section 3 of Article VIII [November 7, 1978] shall be enacted by ordinance and shall not be eliminated or diminished for a period of eleven years following such ratification; provided that increases in such exemptions, or the additions of new and further exemptions or dedications of lands, may be established or granted only by agreement of a majority of the political subdivisions, and such increases or additions shall be enacted by ordinance in each political subdivision.

SECTION 7

1978 Board of Education Elections. Members elected to the board of education in the 1978 general election shall serve for two-year terms.

SECTION 8

Effective Date for Office of Hawaiian Affairs. The legislature shall provide for the implementation of the amendments to Article XII in Sections 5 and 6 on or before the first general election following ratification of the amendments to Article XII in Sections 5 and 6.

SECTION 9

Continuity of Laws. All laws in force at the time amendments to this constitution take effect that are not inconsistent with the constitution as amended shall remain in force, mutatis mutandis, until they expire by their own limitations or are amended or repealed by the legislature.

Except as otherwise provided by amendments to this constitution, all existing writs, actions, suits, proceedings, civil or criminal liabilities, prosecutions, judgments, sentences, orders, decrees, appeals, causes of action, contracts, claims, demands, titles and rights shall continue unaffected notwithstanding the taking effect of the amendments and may be maintained, enforced or prosecuted, as the case may be, before the appropriate or corresponding tribunals or agencies of or under the State or of the United States, in all respects as fully as could have been done prior to the taking effect of the amendments.

SECTION 10

Debts. The debts and liabilities of the Territory shall be assumed and paid by the State, and all debts owed to the Territory shall be collected by the State.

SECTION 11

Residence, Other Qualifications. Requirements as to residence, citizenship or other status or qualifications in or under the State prescribed by this constitution shall be satisfied pro tanto by corresponding residence, citizenship or other status or qualifications in or under the Territory.

EFFECTIVE DATE

This constitution shall take effect and be in full force immediately upon the admission of Hawaii into the Union as a State. Done in Convention, at Iolani Palace, Honolulu, Hawaii, on the twenty-second day of July, in the year one thousand nine hundred fifty and of the Independence of the United States of America the one hundred and seventy-fifth.

BIBLIOGRAPHICAL ESSAY

This essay highlights major sources on Hawaii's constitutional history and development and interpretations of specific constitutional provisions.

I. CONSTITUTIONAL HISTORY AND DEVELOPMENT

The literature on Hawaii's constitutional history and development can be divided into two major groupings: (1) the specific constitutional conventions and the resulting constitutions and (2) broad historical, political, and social factors of significance to the document's evolution.

Ralph S. Kuykendall's *Constitutions of the Hawaiian Kingdom, A Brief History and Analysis*, Papers of the Hawaiian Historical Society no. 21 (Honolulu: Hawaiian Historical Society, 1940) presents a clear account of the events leading up to the constitutions of 1840, 1852, 1864, and 1887 and outlines the major elements of each document. Although Henry E. Chambers, *Constitutional History of Hawaii* (Baltimore: The Johns Hopkins Press, 1896; New York: Johnson Reprint Corp., 1973) reviews those documents, as well as the constitution of the republic, this little pamphlet is somewhat disconcerting to read today because of the condescending attitude displayed toward ethnic Hawaiians. For example, when referring to Kamehameha I, he states, "It must be said that for a savage this first king of the Hawaiian Islands was a person of marked ability. . . ."

Prior to the 1950, 1968, and 1978 Constitutional Conventions, the Hawaii Legislative Reference Bureau prepared resource manuals for delegates and the public. All are available through Hawaii libraries. One volume was prepared for the 1950 convention: *Manual on State Constitutional Provisions Prepared for the Constitutional Convention, Territory of Hawaii, 1950* (Honolulu: Legislative Reference Bureau, 1950). It presents detailed comparative information on provisions found in constitutions around the country in order to illustrate various options available to those drafting a statehood constitution. *Hawaii Constitutional Convention Studies* (Honolulu: Legislative Reference Bureau, 1968), prepared for the 1968 convention, consists of seventeen volumes. *Hawaii Constitutional Convention Studies 1978* (Honolulu: Legislative Reference Bureau, 1978), prepared for the 1978 convention, consists of sixteen volumes. Because these manuals centered on an already existing state constitution, they are of greater value. In general, each volume covers a separate article, providing background information as well as arguments pro and con possible revisions or amendments.

Materials published by other organizations give insight into issues facing convention delegates. For example, prior to the 1968 convention a seminar on constitutional issues for prospective delegates was held at the University of Hawaii. The papers presented there, and the follow-up questions and answers, were then published in Benjamin C. Sigal and Joyce M. Najita, eds., *Convention Issues, The Changing Constitution* (Honolulu: Labor-Management Education Program, University of Hawaii, 1968). Participants presented their expert, but personal, evaluations about such topics as reapportionment; the bill of rights; the legislative, executive, and judicial branches; and state-local government relations. *Issues 1978* (Honolulu: 'O Ka Po'e Ke Kumu O Ke Kanawai, a Project of the League of Women Voters of Hawaii Education Fund, Inc., 1978) is based on a series of community meetings held throughout the state in order to obtain citizen input on what the convention should address. Some of the issues discussed include citizens' access to government, government services, water rights, land use, and native Hawaiian land concerns.

The proceedings of the three conventions have been published and are necessary reading for any research into Hawaii's constitutional development. Each consists of two volumes; for each, the first volume summarizes debate and actions taken in plenary session and includes such documents as committee proposals and committee reports, while the second volume presents a verbatim account of delegate debate during committee-of-the-whole sessions: (1) *Constitutional Convention, 1950 Proceedings* (Honolulu: State of Hawaii, 1960), vol. I, *Journal and Documents;* vol. II, *Committee of the Whole Debates;* (2) *Constitutional Convention, 1968 Proceedings* (Honolulu: State of Hawaii, 1973), vol. I, *Journal and Documents;* vol. II, *Committee of the Whole Debates;* (3) *Constitutional Convention, 1978 Proceedings* (Honolulu: State of Hawaii, 1980), vol. I, *Journal and Documents;* vol. II, *Committee of the Whole Debates;* Volume I of each of the *Proceedings* also includes a useful preface presenting highlights of that convention.

More has been written about the convention called to draft a statehood constitution and the resulting document than about the two subsequent conventions and the changes they brought. In addition to the sources cited in the footnotes to Part I, see also W. Brooke Graves, *Major Problems in State Constitutional Revision* (Chicago: Public Administration Service, 1960), especially the chapter comparing constitutional conventions in Hawaii, Puerto Rico, and Alaska; Harold S. Roberts, "Making Hawaii's Constitution," *State Government* 23 (1950): 276–80; and Norman Meller, "A New Constitution for Hawaii," *State Government* 21 (1948): 129–32.

Focusing on the 1968 convention, Normal Meller, *With an Understanding Heart: Constitution Making in Hawaii* (New York: National Municipal League, 1971), constitutes the most extensive look at a constitutional convention in Hawaii. Unfortunately no longer in print, this excellent work closely examines and evaluates the events leading up to the convention, the delegates, the convention at work, the finished product, and the ratification election. Since comparative data about the 1950 convention are woven throughout, the work also contributes to an understanding of that convention as well.

Elmer E. Cornwall, Jr.; Jay S. Goodman; and Wayne R. Swanson, *State Constitutional Conventions, The Politics of the Revision Process in Seven States* (New York: Praeger Publishers, 1975), covers the 1968 convention, along with conventions held during the same decade in six other states.

Election results and delegate characteristics for all three conventions can be found in Richard H. Kosaki, "Constitutions and Constitutional Conventions of Hawaii," *The Hawaiian Journal of History* 12 (1978): 120–38, published shortly before the 1978 convention convened. The article also contains a brief review of constitutional development prior to the 1978 convention and an interesting discussion of public opinion on various issues just prior to the convention. A short, but valuable, account of the 1978 convention and the resulting document is Norman Meller and Richard H. Kosaki, "Hawaii's Constitutional Convention—1978," *National Civic Review* 69 (May 1980): 248–57, 271. Although focusing on the legal question of whether the intentions conveyed in constitutional convention committee reports must be followed by the legislature when passing enabling or implementation legislation, additional insight into the 1978 convention can be found in Comment, "Enabling and Implementing Legislation and State Constitutional Convention Committee Reports," *University of Hawaii Law Review* 6 (1984): 523–60.

There was extensive coverage by the state's two major newspapers before, during, and after each convention. The many articles found in the *Honolulu Advertiser* and the *Honolulu Star-Bulletin* are an excellent source of information on controversial issues, the personalities involved, the climate in which each convention operated, the changes proposed, and the outcome of the ratification elections.

The classic work covering Hawaii's history up until becoming a territory, including its early constitutional history, is Ralph S. Kuykendall's detailed three volumes, still available from the University of Hawaii Press: *The Hawaiian Kingdom*, vol. I, *1778–1854, Foundation and Transformation* (1938); *The Hawaiian Kingdom*, vol. II, *1854–1874, Twenty Critical Years* (1953); and *The Hawaiian Kingdom*, vol. III, *1874–1893, The Kalakaua Dynasty* (1967). Also available is a shorter condensed volume, including the period until statehood, by Ralph S. Kuykendall and A. Grove Day, *Hawaii, A History from Polynesian Kingdom to American Statehood* (Englewood Cliffs, N.J.: Prentice-Hall, 1961).

Three other historical accounts useful for obtaining glimpses into constitutional development up until the time of statehood are Edward Joesting, *Hawaii, An Uncommon History* (New York: W. W. Norton & Co., 1972); Gavan Daws, *Shoal of Time, A History of the Hawaiian Islands* (Honolulu: University of Hawaii Press, 1968); and Lawrence H. Fuchs, *Hawaii Pono: A Social History* (New York: Harcourt, Brace & World, 1961). A different perspective of Hawaii's history, utilizing the theory of economic dependency, is found in Noel J. Kent, *Hawaii, Islands Under the Influence* (New York: Monthly Review Press, 1983).

Considerable literature exists regarding specific governmental, political, and social issues important to Hawaii's constitutional development. A most recent collection of essays is Zachary A. Smith and Richard C. Pratt, eds., *Politics and Public Policy in Hawaii* (Albany: State University of New York Press, 1992); several of the chapters are cited in the footnotes to Part II. To gain insight into Hawaii's long tradition of centralization, see the seminal work by Norman Meller, "Centralization in Hawaii: A Retrospect and Prospect," *American Political Science Review* 52 (1958): 98–107; see also his chapter "Policy Control: Institutionalized Centralization in the Fiftieth State," in Smith and Pratt's *Politics and Public Policy in Hawaii.*

Although covering the period prior to the 1970s, the best works giving an account of Hawaii's political culture and heritage are Norman Meller and Daniel W. Tuttle, Jr., "Hawaii: The Aloha State," in *Politics in the American West,* edited by Frank H. Jonas (Salt Lake City: University of Utah Press, 1969), 152–79; and, by the same authors, "Hawaii: The Aloha State," in *Western Politics,* edited by Frank H. Jonas (Salt Lake City: University of Utah Press, 1961), 137–60. James C. F. Wang, *Hawaii State and Local Politics* (Hilo: University of Hawaii at Hilo, 1982), includes a great deal of basic information about government and politics in Hawaii.

Regarding the important role labor unions have played in Hawaii's politics, see Sanford Zalburg, *A Spark Is Struck! Jack Hall and the ILWU in Hawaii* (Honolulu: The University Press of Hawaii, 1979); a more recent overview can be found in Anne F. Lee, "Hawaii: Planters, Public Employees, and the Public Interest," in *Interest Group Politics in the American West,* edited by Ronald J. Hrebenar and Clive S. Thomas (Salt Lake City: University of Utah Press, 1987), 59–66. See also Ronald Takaki, *Pau Hana, Plantation Life and Labor in Hawaii, 1835–1920* (Honolulu: University of Hawaii Press, 1983).

A very popular book in Hawaii, clearly laying out the emergence and significance of the Democratic party, is Tom Coffman, *Catch a Wave, A Case Study of Hawaii's New Politics* (Honolulu: The University Press of Hawaii, 1972); see also Paul C. Phillips, *Hawaii's Democrats, Chasing the American Dream* (Lanham, Md.: University Press of America, 1982).

Land and native Hawaiian issues have been of particular importance in Hawaii, both legally and politically. In addition to the important works cited in the footnotes to Part II, see George Cooper and Gavan Daws, *Land and Power in Hawaii, The Democratic Years* (Honolulu: Benchmark Books, 1985); Jon J. Chinen, "The Hawaiian Land Revolution," *Hawaii Bar Journal* 5 (1967): 11–16; Robert H. Horwitz and Norman Meller, *Land and Politics in Hawaii,* 3d ed. (Honolulu: The University of Hawaii Press, 1966); and Jon J. Chinen, *The Great Mahele; Hawaii's Land Division of 1848* (Honolulu: University of Hawaii Press, 1958).

Hawaii's reapportionment controversies have been covered quite extensively; the major works are cited in the footnote accompanying Article IV in Part II. Of the three branches of government, only Hawaii's judiciary has received scholarly attention. See James E. T. Koshiba, "Judicial Selection and Retention in the State of Hawaii: Hawaii's Judicial Selection Commission—The First Six Years," *Hawaii Bar Journal* 20 (1986): 1–10; Roy Kodani, "The Selection of Judges: A Critical Factor in the Administration of Justice," *Hawaii Bar Journal* 18 (1983): 53–59; M. Goodbody and Ruth Hood, "An Introduction to Hawaii's New Appellate System," *Hawaii Bar Journal* 15 (1980): 47–68; Peter J. Levinson, "Appellate Caseload in Hawaii," *Hawaii Bar Journal* 13 (1977): 3–7; J. Russell Cades, "Judicial Legislation in the Supreme Court of Hawaii: A Brief Introduction of 'Knowne Uncertaintie' of the Law," *Hawaii Bar Journal 1* (1970): 58–67; C. Niles Tavares, "The Administration of Justice in Hawaii Today," *Hawaii Bar Journal* 5 (1967): 18–27; and H.Y.C. Choy, "Hawaii's Legal System: A Brief Survey," *Hawaii Bar Journal* 1 (1963): 1, 5–6. See also two articles by then Chief Justice William S. Richardson: "Judicial Independence: The Hawaii Experience," *University of Hawaii Law Review* 2 (1981): 1–66; and "Remarks on Alternative Proposals to Remedy Appellate Court Congestion in Hawaii," *Hawaii Bar Journal* 14 (1978): 55–66.

Chief Justice William S. Richardson and the court under his leadership are the focus of a very good book, Carol S. Dodd, *The Richardson Years:* 1966–1982 (Honolulu: University of Hawaii Foundation, 1985). See also Dodd's earlier article, "The Richardson Court: Ho'Oponopono," *University of Hawaii Law Review* 6 (1984): 9–31. The entire issue of *University of Hawaii Law Review* 14 (1992): 1–443, is devoted to evaluations of the supreme court under Richardson's successor, Chief Justice Herman Lum. Most of the individual contributions to this symposium issue are cited in footnotes accompanying appropriate constitutional commentary in Part II.

II. CONSTITUTIONAL INTERPRETATION

The Organic Act of 1900, Hawaii's "constitution" while a territory, is reproduced in volume I of *Hawaii Revised Statutes,* published by the state of Hawaii. Explanatory comments and case annotations are provided by the Revisor of Statutes for the State of Hawaii. The Organic Act can also be found in volume 15 of *Hawaii Revised Statutes Annotated,* published by the Michie Corporation.

Both the 1950 and the 1968 constitutions can be found in booklet form in Hawaii libraries. The *Convention Studies* prepared for the 1968 and the 1978 conventions (cited above) contain the language of the earlier document then under review.

Hawaii's current constitution, with case notes and annotations provided by the Revisor of Statutes for the State of Hawaii, can be found in volume I of *Hawaii Revised Statutes,* published by the state of Hawaii, and in volume 15 of

Hawaii Revised Statutes Annotated, published by the Michie Corporation. The case notes and annotations in both publications summarize relevant court decisions and other documents and/or publications; these notes are updated periodically in supplements found at the back of each volume. The supplements also include language of constitutional sections amended since publication of the hardbound volume. A student of the constitution is advised to refer to both publications because of instances where case notes differ for the same constitutional section. However, for a thorough understanding of all the cases cited, the actual court opinions must be consulted.

Initiated in 1979, the *University of Hawaii Law Review* has published considerable legal analysis concerning specific state court decisions and legal issues of importance in Hawaii. Another important source of legal commentary is the *Hawaii Bar Journal.* Articles from these sources, dealing with particular parts of the constitution, are cited in the footnotes to Part II.

■ TABLE OF CASES

D

E

F

G

H

I

J

K

L

M

McCloskey v. Honolulu Police Department, 71 H. 568, 799 P.2d 953 (1990), **52, 53**
McMahon v. Office of City and County of Honolulu, 51 H. 589, 465 P.2d 549 (1970), **134**
Maeda v. Amemiya, 60 H. 662, 594 P.2d 136 (1979), **46, 48**
Mahiai v. Suwa, 69 H. 349, 742 P.2d 359 (1987), **47, 48**
Marsland v. First Hawaiian Bank, 70 H. 126, 764 P.2d 1228 (1988), **155**
Medeiros v. Hawaii County Planning Commission, 8 H. App. 183, 797 P.2d 59 (1990), **46**
Medeiros v. Kiyosaki, 52 H. 436, 478 P.2d 314 (1970), **42, 52, 171**
Mehau v. Gannett Pacific Corp., 66 H. 133, 658 P.2d 312 (1983), **93**
Midkiff v. Tom, 483 F. Supp. 62 (D. Haw. 1979), **74**
Midkiff v. Tom, 702 F.2d 788 (9th Cir. 1983), **74**
Mink v. Pua, 68 H. 263, 711 P.2d 723 (1985), appeal dismissed, 476 U.S. 1101 (1986), **58**
Miranda v. Arizona, 384 U.S. 436 (1966), **61–62**

N

Nachtwey v. Doi, 59 H. 430, 583 P.2d 955 (1978), **48, 102**
Nagle v. Board of Education, 63 H. 389, 629 P.2d 109 (1981), **47, 48**
Nakano v. Matayoshi, 68 H. 140, 706 P.2d 814 (1985), **52–53, 204**
Naliielua v. Hawaii, 795 F. Supp. 1015 (D. Haw. 1991), aff'd without opinion, 940 F.2d 1535 (9th Cir. 1991), **191**

P

Patterson v. Burns, 327 F. Supp. 745 (D. Haw. 1971), **91**
Pele Defense Fund v. Paty, 73 H., 837 P.2d 1247 (1992), **198**
Price v. Akaka, 928 F.2d 824 (9th Cir. 1990), **197**
Price v. Hawaii, 764 F.2d 623 (9th Cir. 1985), cert, denied, 474 U.S. 1055, reh'g denied, 475 U.S. 1091 (1986), **192**
Price v. Hawaii, 921 F.2d 950 (9th Cir. 1990), **197**

R

Reppun v. Board of Water Supply, 65 H. 531, 656 P.2d 57 (1982), cert, denied, 471 U.S. 1014 (1985), **183**
Reynolds v. Sims, 377 U.S. 533 (1964), **15, 106**
Richardson v. Koshiba, 693 F.2d 911 (9th Cir. 1982), **132**
Robinson v. Ariyoshi, 753 F.2d 1468 (9th Cir. 1985); 796 F.2d 339 (9th Cir. 1986), **183**
Robinson v. Ariyoshi, 441 F. Supp. 559 (D. Haw. 1977); 676 F. Supp. 1002 (D. Haw. 1987), **182, 183**
Robinson v. Ariyoshi, 65 H. 641, 658 P.2d 287 (1982), reconsideration denied, 66 H. 528, 726P.2d 1133 (1983), **183**
Roe v. Akamine, Civ. No. 91-00252 DAE, September 26, 1991 (D. Haw. 1991), **44, 204**
Roe v. Wade, 410 U.S. 113 (1973), **50**
Runyon v. Fasi, 762 F. Supp. 280 (D. Haw. 1991), **43, 164**

S

Safeway v. Board of Agriculture, 590 F. Supp. 778 (D. Haw. 1984), **178**
Sandy Beach Defense Fund v. City Council of City and County of Honolulu, 70 H. 361, 773 P.2d 250 (1989), **46, 47**

T

U

V

Y

INDEX

About the Author

ANNE FEDER LEE has taught political science at universities in Ohio and Hawaii and has authored articles on governmental, political, and legal issues. Active in community affairs, she served as president of the League of Women Voters of Hawaii, as a member of the Hawaii Bicentennial Commission on the U.S. Constitution, and was recently reappointed by the governor to serve a second term on the State of Hawaii Pesticides Advisory Committee. She earned a doctorate in political science from Miami University.

www.ingramcontent.com/pod-product-compliance
Ingram Content Group UK Ltd.
Pitfield, Milton Keynes, MK11 3LW, UK
UKHW020848150926
475595UK00003B/61

9 780199 779055